Mastering Software Estimation

Proven Techniques for Accurate Project Planning

By Carlos Smith

Introduction

- *Why Accurate Estimation Matters*
- *Scope and Objectives of This Book*
- *Target Audience*
- *How to Use This Book*

Table of contents

Chapter 1: The Foundation of Software Estimation

Chapter 2: Understanding Estimation Challenges

2.1 The Impact of Unclear or Changing Requirements

2.2 Dealing with Software Complexity and Dependencies

2.3 Managing Uncertainty and Assumptions in Estimates

2.4 The Pitfalls of Scope Creep and How to Mitigate It

2.5 Resource Allocation and Team Dynamics in Estimation

2.6 Adapting to Technological Changes and Their Impact

2.7 Identifying and Addressing Hidden Project Costs

2.8 Overcoming the Lack of Historical Data

Chapter 3: Expert-Based Estimation Techniques

Chapter 5: Agile Estimation Strategies

5.1 Story Points: Relative Estimation and Velocity

5.2 T-Shirt Sizing and Its Mapping to Effort

5.3 Affinity Estimating for Rapid Backlog Assessment

5.4 The Bucket System for Categorizing Effort

5.5 Connecting Agile Estimates to Release Planning

Chapter 6: Data-Driven and Emerging Techniques

6.1 Utilizing Historical Project Data for Improved Accuracy

6.2 Introduction to Statistical Concepts in Estimation

6.3 Exploring Machine Learning Applications in Estimation (Overview)

Chapter 7: Managing Uncertainty and Risk in Estimates

Chapter 8: Communicating and Refining Estimates

Chapter 9: Tools and Technologies for Estimation

9.1 Overview of Different Categories of Estimation Tools

9.2 Guidance on Selecting Appropriate Tools

9.3 Examples of Popular Tools and Their Key Features

Introduction: Setting the Stage for Estimation Mastery

Welcome to "Mastering Software Estimation: Proven Techniques for Accurate Project Planning." I'm genuinely excited you've picked up this book, because if there's one skill that can dramatically improve your software development journey – whether you're a seasoned project manager, a bright-eyed developer, or anyone in between – it's the ability to estimate software efforts accurately.

Trust me, I've been there. Early in my career, I remember a project where we confidently (and completely wrongly) estimated a feature would take a week. Three weeks later, fueled by copious amounts of coffee and a growing sense of dread, we finally pushed it out. The post-mortem? Our estimation was, shall we say, a tad optimistic. That experience, and many others like it, hammered home a crucial truth: **accurate software estimation isn't just a nice-to-have; it's a cornerstone of project success.**

So, why does getting those numbers right matter so much? Let's dive in:

Why Accurate Estimation Matters: More Than Just Guesswork

Think about it. Software projects are often significant investments of time, money, and resources. Imagine building a house without a solid estimate of the materials, labor, and time involved. You'd likely end up with a half-finished structure, a depleted bank account, and a whole lot of frustration. Software projects are no different.

- **Realistic Planning and Scheduling:** Accurate estimates form the bedrock of realistic project plans and schedules. When you have a clear understanding of the effort involved in each task, you can create timelines that are actually achievable. This means fewer rushed deadlines, less burnout for your team, and a higher chance of delivering on time.

- **Effective Resource Allocation:** Knowing how much effort a task requires allows you to allocate your team's resources effectively. You can identify potential bottlenecks early on and ensure the right people with the right skills are assigned to the right tasks at the right time. No more overstaffing one area while another struggles with a critical backlog.

- **Informed Decision-Making:** Accurate estimates empower stakeholders – clients, management, even the development team itself – to make informed decisions. Should we prioritize this feature over that one? Can we realistically fit this new requirement into the current sprint? Reliable estimates provide the data needed for these crucial conversations.

- **Budget Management and Cost Control:** Let's face it, software development isn't cheap. Accurate estimates are vital for creating realistic budgets and controlling project costs. By understanding the effort involved, you can better predict expenses and avoid those dreaded budget overruns that can derail even the most promising projects.

- **Improved Stakeholder Satisfaction:** Delivering a project that meets expectations, on time and within budget, goes a long way in keeping stakeholders happy. When estimates are accurate, you build trust and credibility, fostering stronger relationships with your clients and your management.

- **Enhanced Team Morale:** Believe it or not, accurate estimation can even boost team morale. When developers aren't constantly under pressure to meet unrealistic deadlines, they can focus on delivering quality work. This leads to a more positive and productive work environment.

Scope and Objectives of This Book: Your Guide to Estimation Mastery

This book isn't about pulling numbers out of thin air or relying on gut feelings (though we've all been tempted!). Instead, our goal is to equip you with a **toolkit of proven techniques** and a **framework for thinking critically** about software estimation. By the end of this journey, you'll be able to:

- Understand the fundamental principles and challenges of software estimation.
- Apply a variety of expert-based, algorithmic, and agile estimation techniques effectively.

- Analyze project requirements and break them down into estimable tasks.
- Account for uncertainty and risk in your estimates.
- Communicate estimates clearly and manage stakeholder expectations.
- Continuously improve your estimation process through data analysis and feedback.
- Select and utilize appropriate tools and technologies to aid your estimation efforts.

We'll explore both the art and the science of estimation, recognizing that while there are methodologies and formulas, there's also a crucial element of experience, judgment, and communication involved.

Target Audience: Who Will Benefit Most from This Book?

This book is designed for anyone involved in the software development lifecycle who needs to understand and apply software estimation techniques. This includes:

- **Project Managers:** Who are responsible for planning, scheduling, and budgeting software projects.
- **Software Developers:** Whose technical expertise is crucial for providing realistic effort estimates.
- **Team Leads and Architects:** Who often have a deeper understanding of the technical complexities involved.
- **Business Analysts:** Who play a key role in defining requirements and scope.

- **Product Owners:** Who need to prioritize features and understand the effort required for their delivery.
- **Anyone new to software development** who wants to build a solid foundation in project planning.

While some chapters might delve into more technical aspects, I've strived to keep the language accessible and provide clear explanations for everyone. No prior deep statistical knowledge is required – we'll focus on practical application.

How to Use This Book: Your Roadmap to Estimation Proficiency

Think of this book as your personal guide and tutorial in the world of software estimation. Here's how I recommend you approach it:

- **Read Actively:** Don't just skim the pages. Engage with the concepts, try to relate them to your own experiences, and jot down notes or questions as you go.
- **Work Through Examples:** Where applicable, we'll explore practical examples to illustrate the techniques. Take the time to understand how these examples are worked through.
- **Apply the Techniques:** The real learning happens when you put these techniques into practice. Try applying the methods discussed to your current or past projects.
- **Be Patient:** Mastering software estimation takes time and experience. Don't get discouraged if your initial estimates aren't perfect. The key is to learn from each project and continuously refine your approach.

- **Embrace the Conversation:** While this is a book, I encourage you to think of it as a conversation. If a concept isn't clear, revisit it. If you have a different perspective, consider how it aligns with what we're discussing.

We'll start by building a solid foundation in the principles of estimation, then delve into various proven techniques, and finally explore how to apply these techniques in real-world scenarios. We'll also touch upon the importance of communication, risk management, and continuous improvement in your estimation journey.

So, are you ready to move beyond guesswork and start mastering the art and science of software estimation? Let's turn the page and begin our exploration into the fascinating world of predicting software delivery

Chapter 1: Laying the Groundwork - The Foundation of Software Estimation

Alright, let's roll up our sleeves and dive into the very core of software estimation. In this chapter, we're not getting bogged down in complex formulas just yet. Instead, we're going to build a solid understanding of *why* estimation is so crucial and lay the groundwork for the techniques we'll explore later. Think of this as setting the stage before the main performance – understanding the theater and the key players.

1.1 The Significance of Estimation in Project Success: Setting Yourself Up for Victory

Let's kick things off with a fundamental truth: **accurate software estimation isn't just a nice-to-have; it's a cornerstone of project success.** Think of it as laying the foundation for a sturdy building. A shaky or rushed foundation inevitably leads to problems down the line. Similarly, flawed estimates can derail even the most well-intentioned projects.

Why is getting it right so crucial? It boils down to several key factors:

Realistic Planning and Resource Allocation: Accurate estimates provide the bedrock for realistic project plans. Knowing the likely effort, duration, and cost allows you to allocate resources effectively – assigning the right people to the right tasks at the right time. Without a clear understanding of the work involved, you risk overstaffing (wasting resources) or understaffing (leading to delays and burnout).

Effective Stakeholder Management: Stakeholders – clients, management, other teams – rely on your estimates to make critical decisions. They need to know when the software will be delivered, how much it will cost, and what resources will be required. Realistic estimates foster trust and enable informed decision-making. Conversely, consistently inaccurate estimates erode confidence and can lead to strained relationships.

Improved Budget Control: Software projects can be expensive. Accurate cost estimates are vital for securing funding, managing budgets effectively, and avoiding costly overruns. Underestimating costs can lead to projects running out of money mid-development, while overestimating might result in missed opportunities or difficulty securing approval.

Reduced Risk of Failure: Projects plagued by unrealistic timelines and insufficient resources are far more likely to fail. Accurate estimation helps identify potential bottlenecks, dependencies, and areas of high risk early on, allowing for proactive mitigation strategies. It sets a realistic pace and workload, reducing the chances of team burnout and compromised quality.

Enhanced Team Morale: Teams working under the constant pressure of unrealistic deadlines are prone to stress and decreased morale. Accurate estimates contribute to a more sustainable pace, allowing developers to produce quality work without feeling rushed. This fosters a more positive and productive work environment.

Better Scope Management: A clear understanding of the effort involved in delivering specific features helps in managing the project scope.

Accurate estimates can highlight the cost and time implications of adding new requirements, facilitating informed decisions about scope trade-offs.

My Perspective: I've witnessed firsthand the domino effect of poor estimation. A rushed initial estimate often leads to unrealistic deadlines, stressed teams, compromised quality, and ultimately, dissatisfied stakeholders. On the other hand, projects that invest time in thoughtful estimation tend to be more controlled, predictable, and ultimately successful.

In essence, accurate estimation sets you up for victory by:

- Providing a clear roadmap.
- Ensuring you have the necessary resources.
- Managing expectations effectively.
- Minimizing the risk of failure.
- Fostering a healthy team environment.

Ignoring the significance of estimation is akin to embarking on a long journey without a map or a fuel gauge – you're likely to get lost or run out of steam along the way. By embracing robust estimation practices, you're not just predicting the future; you're actively shaping it for the better. Let's now delve into the foundational principles that underpin effective software estimation.

1.2 Estimation Across Project Methodologies: A Universal Need

You might be thinking, "Does the way we estimate software change depending on whether we're using Waterfall, Agile, or some hybrid approach?" The short answer is: **the techniques and the level of detail might differ, but the fundamental *need* for estimation remains constant across all project methodologies.**

Think of it like planning a trip. Whether you meticulously map out every mile in advance (like Waterfall) or decide on the next destination as you go (like Agile), you still need to estimate how long it will take to get there, how much it will cost, and what resources you'll need (gas, food, accommodation). The level of detail and the flexibility of your plan will vary, but the core need for planning and estimation persists.

Let's break down how estimation plays out in some common methodologies:

Waterfall:

In the traditional Waterfall model, estimation typically occurs upfront, often during the requirements gathering and planning phases. The goal is to create a comprehensive project plan with detailed estimates for each phase (analysis, design, development, testing, deployment).

- **Focus:** Detailed, upfront estimation of the entire project scope.
- **Techniques Often Used:** Function Point Analysis, Use Case Points, COCOMO, expert judgment based on similar past projects.
- **Challenge:** The inherent uncertainty of predicting effort for the entire project lifecycle at the very beginning. Changes in requirements later can significantly impact these initial estimates.

- **My Perspective:** While Waterfall aims for predictability, the reality of software development often introduces changes. The key here is to acknowledge the initial estimates as a baseline and have processes in place for change control and re-estimation when necessary.

Agile (e.g., Scrum, Kanban):

Agile methodologies embrace iterative development and continuous feedback. Estimation in Agile is typically more frequent and focused on smaller chunks of work.

- **Focus:** Relative estimation of user stories or backlog items within short iterations (sprints). Forecasting releases based on team velocity.
- **Techniques Often Used:** Story Points (using Planning Poker or similar), T-Shirt Sizing, Affinity Estimating. Release planning often involves projecting based on historical velocity.
- **Challenge:** While Agile handles changing requirements more gracefully, initial release forecasts can still be challenging due to the evolving nature of the backlog and fluctuations in team velocity.
- **My Perspective:** Agile estimation is less about precise prediction and more about providing a continuous understanding of the team's capacity and the relative size of the remaining work. It's about informed forecasting rather than fixed commitments far in advance.

Hybrid Methodologies:

Many real-world projects blend elements of Waterfall and Agile. In such hybrid approaches, estimation strategies often combine upfront high-level estimates with more detailed Agile estimation within iterative cycles.

- **Focus:** A balance between initial planning and iterative refinement of estimates.
- **Techniques Often Used:** A mix of techniques from both Waterfall and Agile, depending on the phase and the level of detail required. For example, high-level features might be estimated using function points initially, while individual user stories within a sprint are estimated using story points.
- **Challenge:** Ensuring consistency and effective communication across different estimation styles used within the same project.
- **My Perspective:** Hybrid methodologies require a flexible approach to estimation. The key is to choose the right technique for the right level of planning and to ensure that all stakeholders understand how estimates are being derived and used.

The Universal Need:

Regardless of the methodology, the underlying *need* for estimation remains because:

- **We need to plan:** All projects require some level of planning, even if it's just for the next iteration. Estimation provides the data points for this planning.

- **We need to allocate resources:** Understanding the effort involved helps in allocating team members and other resources effectively.
- **We need to manage expectations:** Stakeholders always want to know when things will be delivered and how much they will cost, even if the answer is framed as a range or a forecast.
- **We need to track progress:** Estimates serve as a baseline against which progress can be measured.

Code Example (Illustrative - Not tied to a specific estimation technique but shows the need for tracking against a plan):

While providing a complete, working, and up-to-date code example directly illustrating estimation across methodologies is complex (as estimation itself isn't code), we can illustrate the *need* for tracking actual work against an estimated plan using a simple Python example:

Python

```python
import datetime

# Sample estimated tasks with estimated duration (in days)

estimated_tasks = {

    "Design UI": 5,

    "Implement User Authentication": 7,

    "Develop Core Logic": 10,
```

```python
    "Write Unit Tests": 3,

    "Integration Testing": 5

}


# Dictionary to store actual completion dates

actual_completion = {}


def start_task(task_name):

    print(f"Starting task: {task_name} (Estimated duration:
{estimated_tasks[task_name]} days)")

    start_date = datetime.date.today()

    return start_date


def complete_task(task_name, start_date):

    end_date = datetime.date.today()

    actual_duration = (end_date - start_date).days

    actual_completion[task_name] = end_date
```

```python
    print(f"Completed task: {task_name} in {actual_duration} days
(Estimated: {estimated_tasks[task_name]} days)")


# Simulate starting and completing tasks

start_design = start_task("Design UI")

# Simulate some work happening...

# Let's say it took 6 days

for i in range(6):

    pass

complete_task("Design UI", start_design)


start_auth = start_task("Implement User Authentication")

# Simulate work...

# Let's say it took 8 days

for i in range(8):

    pass

complete_task("Implement User Authentication", start_auth)
```

```python
# ... and so on for other tasks


print("\n--- Project Summary ---")

total_estimated_duration = sum(estimated_tasks.values())

print(f"Total Estimated Duration: {total_estimated_duration} days")


total_actual_duration = 0

if actual_completion:

    start_of_project = datetime.date.today() # Assuming project started today for simplicity

    end_of_project = max(actual_completion.values())

    total_actual_duration = (end_of_project - start_of_project).days

print(f"Total Actual Duration (so far): {total_actual_duration} days")


if total_estimated_duration > 0:

    variance = total_actual_duration - total_estimated_duration

    print(f"Duration Variance: {variance} days")
```

Step-by-Step Explanation:

1. estimated_tasks **Dictionary:** This represents our initial plan (estimation) for the project, outlining tasks and their estimated durations in days.

2. actual_completion **Dictionary:** This will store the actual completion dates of the tasks as they are finished.

3. start_task() **Function:** Simulates the start of a task, prints its estimated duration, and records the start date.

4. complete_task() **Function:** Simulates the completion of a task, calculates the actual duration, records the completion date, and compares it to the estimate.

5. **Simulation:** The code then simulates the start and completion of a couple of tasks, demonstrating how actual durations might differ from the estimates.

6. **Project Summary:** Finally, it calculates and prints the total estimated duration and the total actual duration (so far), along with the variance.

Documentation:

This simple example highlights the fundamental need for estimation (the estimated_tasks) and the importance of tracking actual progress against that plan (actual_completion) regardless of the specific methodology used to create the initial estimates. The variance helps us understand if we are on track and provides data for future estimation improvements.

While the techniques and the timing of estimation might vary across Waterfall, Agile, and hybrid methodologies, the core need to understand the scope of work, allocate resources effectively, manage expectations, and track progress remains a constant. Effective estimation, tailored to the chosen methodology, is a crucial ingredient for project success in any context.

1.3 Key Estimation Points in the Software Development Lifecycle: When Do We Estimate?

You wouldn't start building a house without some initial sketches and a rough idea of the cost, would you? Similarly, in software development, estimation isn't a one-time event. It's an ongoing activity that occurs at various key points throughout the Software Development Lifecycle (SDLC), evolving in detail and accuracy as the project progresses.

Think of estimation as a series of zooming in on a map. At the beginning, you have a high-level overview. As you move closer to your destination, you get more granular details. The same applies to software estimation.

Let's explore the crucial times when we engage in estimation:

1. Project Initiation/Feasibility Study:

- **What happens:** This is the very early stage where the initial idea for the software is being explored. We're trying to determine if the project is viable from a technical, economic, and operational standpoint.
- **What we estimate:** Rough order of magnitude (ROM) estimates for the overall project cost, potential timeline, and required

resources. These are typically very high-level and have a wide margin of error (e.g., +/- 50%).

- **Why we estimate:** To make a go/no-go decision. Is this project worth pursuing? Do the potential benefits outweigh the estimated costs and risks?

- **My Perspective:** At this stage, it's more about getting a ballpark figure. Don't get bogged down in specifics. Focus on the key drivers of cost and effort based on similar past projects or expert intuition.

2. Requirements Elicitation and Analysis:

- **What happens:** We delve deeper into understanding the needs of the users and stakeholders. We gather requirements, define the scope of the project, and create initial specifications.

- **What we estimate:** More refined estimates for the major features and functionalities. We might start using techniques like high-level function point analysis or analogous estimation based on similar requirements. The margin of error narrows (e.g., +/- 25%).

- **Why we estimate:** To get a better understanding of the project's complexity and size. This helps in refining the initial feasibility assessment and provides a basis for initial project planning.

- **My Perspective:** Clear and well-defined requirements are crucial for more accurate estimates at this stage. Ambiguity here will directly translate to uncertainty in your estimates.

3. System Design:

- **What happens:** We translate the requirements into a technical blueprint of the system. We define the architecture, components, interfaces, and data structures.

- **What we estimate:** Estimates for the development effort of specific components and modules. We might use techniques like Use Case Points or break down larger components into smaller tasks for estimation. The margin of error continues to decrease (e.g., +/- 15%).

- **Why we estimate:** To plan the development phases in more detail and allocate specific technical resources. Understanding the complexity of the design informs the effort required for implementation.

- **My Perspective:** A well-thought-out design can significantly reduce development risks and improve estimation accuracy. If the design is convoluted, expect higher effort and greater uncertainty.

4. Implementation (Development):

- **What happens:** The actual coding and building of the software take place.

- **What we estimate:** In iterative methodologies like Agile, estimation happens frequently at this stage. For each iteration (sprint), the team estimates the effort required for individual user stories or tasks using techniques like Story Points and Planning Poker.

- **Why we estimate:** To plan the work for each iteration, ensure the team doesn't overcommit, and track progress against the iteration goals.
- **My Perspective:** Agile estimation during implementation is about continuous refinement and adaptation based on the team's velocity and emerging understanding. It's a collaborative effort.

5. Testing:

- **What happens:** The developed software is rigorously tested to identify and fix defects.
- **What we estimate:** The effort required for different types of testing (unit, integration, system, acceptance), bug fixing, and re-testing. This can be based on the estimated size and complexity of the system, as well as historical defect rates.
- **Why we estimate:** To plan the testing phase, allocate QA resources, and predict the overall project completion timeline. Underestimating testing effort can lead to rushed testing and poor quality.
- **My Perspective:** Testing is often underestimated. Factor in time for test case creation, execution, bug reporting, fixing, and regression testing. The more complex the system, the more testing effort will be required.

6. Deployment and Maintenance:

- **What happens:** The software is deployed to the production environment, and ongoing maintenance, support, and potential enhancements are provided.

- **What we estimate:** The effort and resources required for deployment activities, ongoing support, bug fixes in production, and future enhancements or upgrades.
- **Why we estimate:** To plan for post-launch activities, allocate support resources, and budget for the long-term cost of ownership.
- **My Perspective:** Maintenance can often be a significant portion of the total lifecycle cost. Consider factors like the maintainability of the code and the expected frequency of updates when estimating this phase.

Code Example (Illustrative - Showing how estimates can evolve):

While a single code example can't demonstrate estimation across the entire SDLC, this Python snippet illustrates how an initial high-level estimate for a feature might be broken down into more detailed estimates as the project progresses:

Python

```python
# Stage 1: Project Initiation - High-Level ROM Estimate (in person-days)

feature_a_rom_estimate = 20



print(f"Stage 1: Initial ROM estimate for Feature A:
{feature_a_rom_estimate} person-days")
```

```python
# Stage 2: Requirements Analysis - Initial Breakdown (in person-days
per sub-feature)

feature_a_requirements_breakdown = {

    "User Authentication": 5,

    "Data Input Form": 8,

    "Data Display Table": 7

}


feature_a_initial_sum =
sum(feature_a_requirements_breakdown.values())

print(f"\nStage 2: Initial breakdown of Feature A:
{feature_a_requirements_breakdown} (Total: {feature_a_initial_sum}
person-days)")


# Stage 3: System Design - Task-Level Estimates (in person-hours per
task)

feature_a_design_tasks = {

    "Design Login Screen": 16,

    "Implement Authentication Logic": 40,
```

```python
    "Design Input Fields": 24,

    "Implement Data Validation": 32,

    "Design Table Layout": 20,

    "Implement Data Fetching": 48

}


feature_a_detailed_sum_days = sum(feature_a_design_tasks.values()) / 8
# Assuming 8 hours per day

print(f"\nStage 3: Detailed design tasks for Feature A:
{feature_a_design_tasks} (Total: {feature_a_detailed_sum_days}
person-days)")


# Stage 4: Implementation - Story Point Estimates (per user story)

feature_a_stories_points = {

    "Login Functionality": 5,

    "Create New Record Form": 8,

    "View Existing Records Table": 7

}
```

```
print(f"\nStage 4: Story point estimates for Feature A:
{feature_a_stories_points} (Assuming team velocity can convert points
to days)")
```

Step-by-Step Explanation:

1. **ROM Estimate:** At the project initiation, we have a very rough estimate for "Feature A" in person-days.
2. **Initial Breakdown:** As requirements are analyzed, we break down the feature into sub-features and provide initial estimates for each. The sum is closer to the ROM but still high-level.
3. **Detailed Design:** During the design phase, we identify specific tasks and estimate them in person-hours, providing a more granular view. We then convert this back to person-days for comparison.
4. **Story Points:** In an Agile implementation, the feature might be broken down into user stories, each estimated in story points.[17] These points will later be used with the team's velocity to forecast timelines.

Documentation:

This example illustrates how the level of detail and the units of estimation evolve as the project moves through different stages of the SDLC. The initial high-level guess becomes more refined and accurate as we gain a better understanding of the requirements, design, and the team's capacity.

Estimation is not a one-shot deal. It's a continuous process that adapts to the evolving understanding of the project throughout its lifecycle.[18] We start with broad strokes and gradually zoom in on the details. Recognizing when to estimate, the level of detail required at each stage, and the appropriate techniques to use are crucial for effective project planning and management. By embracing this iterative approach to estimation, we can navigate the complexities of software development with greater clarity and control.

1.4 Types of Estimates and Their Purpose: Tailoring the Precision

Just as you wouldn't use a sledgehammer to crack a nut, you wouldn't apply the same level of estimation rigor at every stage of a project. The type of estimate you generate should be tailored to the current need, the information available, and the decisions that need to be made. Think of it as having different lenses for viewing the project, each providing a different level of detail and accuracy.

Let's explore the common types of estimates and their specific purposes throughout the project lifecycle:

1. Rough Order of Magnitude (ROM) Estimate:

- **Purpose:** To provide a very high-level initial estimate, often during project initiation or feasibility studies. It helps in making a preliminary assessment of whether the project is worth pursuing.
- **Accuracy:** Typically has a wide range of error, often expressed as +/- 50% or even more.
- **When Used:** Early stages of the project, for initial screening and high-level decision-making.
- **Key Characteristics:** Based on limited information, often relies on expert judgment or analogous estimation from very similar past projects. Speed is prioritized over precision.
- **My Perspective:** ROM estimates are like a gut check. They give you a quick sense of the scale of the project. Don't spend too much time on them at this stage; the goal is to filter out clearly unviable options.

2. Budgetary Estimate:

- **Purpose:** To provide a more refined estimate that can be used for initial budget planning and resource allocation. It's generated after some initial requirements gathering and analysis have been done.
- **Accuracy:** The range of error is narrower than a ROM estimate, typically around +/- 25%.
- **When Used:** After the feasibility stage, during initial project planning and budget approval processes.

- **Key Characteristics:** Based on a better understanding of the scope and high-level requirements. May involve some preliminary breakdown of work packages.
- **My Perspective:** Budgetary estimates are crucial for getting the initial financial buy-in. While more precise than ROM, they still carry significant uncertainty, so ensure stakeholders understand this.

3. Definitive Estimate:

- **Purpose:** To provide a highly accurate estimate that can be used for detailed project planning, resource scheduling, and performance measurement. It's developed after the requirements are well-defined, the design is complete, and the team has a clear understanding of the work involved.
- **Accuracy:** Aims for a narrow range of error, typically +/- 10% or even less.
- **When Used:** Later stages of the project, before the main execution phases (development, testing).
- **Key Characteristics:** Based on a detailed Work Breakdown Structure (WBS), task-level estimations (often using techniques like bottom-up estimation or detailed parametric models), and a clear understanding of dependencies and risks.
- **My Perspective:** Definitive estimates are the gold standard for project control. They require significant effort to produce but provide the most reliable basis for managing the project. However, even these estimates can be affected by unforeseen circumstances.

Beyond the Big Three:

While ROM, Budgetary, and Definitive are the main categories, you might encounter other types of estimates depending on the context:

- **Conceptual Estimate:** Similar to ROM, used very early based on a concept or idea.
- **Comparative Estimate (Analogous):** Based on the actual cost and duration of similar past projects. Accuracy depends heavily on the similarity.
- **Bottom-Up Estimate:** Summing up the estimates of individual tasks to arrive at a total project estimate. Can be very accurate if the tasks are well-defined.
- **Top-Down Estimate:** Estimating the total project cost or duration and then allocating it to individual phases or tasks. Can be less accurate if not based on sufficient detail.
- **Rolling Wave Estimate:** An iterative approach where high-level estimates are provided for the distant parts of the project, and more detailed estimates are developed as those parts get closer. Common in Agile and hybrid methodologies.

Code Example (Illustrative - Showing how estimates might be stored with different accuracy levels):

This Python example demonstrates how you might store different types of estimates for a project feature, along with their associated accuracy levels:

Python

```python
feature_a_estimates = {

    "ROM": {

        "value": 20,  # Person-days

        "accuracy": "+/- 50%",

        "purpose": "Initial feasibility assessment"

    },

    "Budgetary": {

        "value": 25,  # Person-days

        "accuracy": "+/- 25%",

        "purpose": "Initial budget planning"

    },

    "Definitive": {

        "value": 28,  # Person-days

        "accuracy": "+/- 10%",

        "purpose": "Detailed project planning and tracking"

    }
```

```python
}


def display_estimate(estimate_type, estimates):

    if estimate_type in estimates:

        estimate = estimates[estimate_type]

        print(f"--- {estimate_type} Estimate for Feature A ---")

        print(f"Value: {estimate['value']} person-days")

        print(f"Accuracy: {estimate['accuracy']}")

        print(f"Purpose: {estimate['purpose']}")

    else:

        print(f"No {estimate_type} estimate found for Feature A.")


# Display the different types of estimates

display_estimate("ROM", feature_a_estimates)

display_estimate("Budgetary", feature_a_estimates)

display_estimate("Definitive", feature_a_estimates)
```

Step-by-Step Explanation:

1. feature_a_estimates **Dictionary:** This dictionary stores different types of estimates for a hypothetical "Feature A."
2. **Each Estimate:** Each estimate is represented as a nested dictionary containing its value, accuracy, and purpose.
3. display_estimate() **Function:** This function takes an estimate type as input and prints the details of that estimate if it exists in the feature_a_estimates dictionary.

Documentation:

This simple example illustrates how different types of estimates for the same feature have varying levels of precision and serve different purposes throughout the project lifecycle. The ROM estimate is broad, the budgetary estimate is more refined, and the definitive estimate aims for the highest accuracy.

Choosing the right type of estimate at the right time is crucial for effective project management. Using a highly detailed estimation technique during the initial feasibility study would be a waste of effort, while relying on a ROM estimate for detailed sprint planning would be inadequate. By understanding the purpose and accuracy level of each type of estimate, you can tailor your approach to provide the necessary information for informed decision-making at every stage of your software development journey. Remember, precision should match the current needs and the available information.

1.5 Core Terminology: Speaking the Same Language

Before we dive deeper into the intricacies of software estimation, it's crucial that we establish a common understanding of the fundamental terms we'll be using throughout this book. Think of it as building a shared vocabulary. If we're all speaking the same language, our discussions about estimation will be much clearer and more productive.

Let's break down some of the core terminology you'll encounter in the world of software estimation:

1. Effort:

- **What it is:** The amount of work required to complete a task, typically expressed in person-hours, person-days, or person-months. It represents the time spent by individuals working on the task.

- **Key Characteristic:** Effort is about the *amount of work*, not necessarily the duration it takes to complete. One person working for 10 hours exerts 10 person-hours of effort, which could have the same effort as two people working for 5 hours.

- **Units:** Person-hours, Person-days (assuming a standard workday, e.g., 8 hours), Person-weeks, Person-months.

- **My Perspective:** It's easy to conflate effort with duration, but they are distinct. A complex task might require significant effort but could be completed faster with more resources.

2. Duration:

- **What it is:** The amount of time elapsed from the start to the finish of a task or project, typically expressed in days, weeks, or months.
- **Key Characteristic:** Duration is influenced by factors beyond just effort, such as resource availability, dependencies on other tasks, and external factors (e.g., holidays, approvals).
- **Units:** Days, Weeks, Months.
- **My Perspective:** Project timelines are driven by duration. Understanding the critical path and task dependencies is key to accurately estimating project duration.

3. Cost:

- **What it is:** The total financial expenditure associated with a task or project. This includes personnel costs (salaries, benefits), infrastructure costs (hardware, software licenses), travel expenses, and any other direct or indirect costs.
- **Key Characteristic:** Cost is directly related to effort (more effort usually means higher personnel costs) and duration (longer projects can incur more overhead).
- **Units:** Currency (e.g., USD, EUR, NGN).
- **My Perspective:** Cost estimation is crucial for budget management and profitability. It's important to consider all cost components, not just the development team's salaries.

4. Resources:

- **What it is:** The people, tools, equipment, and other assets required to complete a task or project. This includes developers, testers, designers, project managers, software licenses, hardware, etc.
- **Key Characteristic:** Resource availability directly impacts both effort (e.g., having more developers can reduce the duration for a fixed amount of effort) and duration (lack of a specific resource can cause delays).
- **Units:** Number of people (by role), number of licenses, etc.
- **My Perspective:** Resource planning is tightly linked to estimation. Knowing the required effort helps determine the number and type of resources needed.

5. Work Breakdown Structure (WBS):

- **What it is:** A hierarchical decomposition of the total scope of work to be carried out by the project team to accomplish the project objectives and create the required deliverables. It breaks down the project into smaller, more[1] manageable tasks.
- **Key Characteristic:** The WBS provides the foundation for estimation. By breaking down the project into smaller units, it becomes easier to estimate the effort, duration, and cost for each component.
- **Units:** Typically represented as a hierarchical diagram or list of tasks and sub-tasks.

- **My Perspective:** A well-defined WBS is essential for accurate estimation, especially for larger projects. It ensures that all necessary work is accounted for.

6. Baseline Estimate:

- **What it is:** The initial, approved estimate for the project's schedule, cost, and scope. It serves as a benchmark against which actual performance is measured.
- **Key Characteristic:** The baseline is usually established after the initial planning phases and is subject to change control processes.
- **Units:** Can be expressed in terms of effort, duration, or cost, depending on what is being baselined.
- **My Perspective:** The baseline is your point of reference. Tracking deviations from the baseline is crucial for project control and identifying potential issues early.

7. Variance:

- **What it is:** The difference between the actual outcome and the planned (or estimated) value. It can be positive (favorable) or negative (unfavorable).
- **Key Characteristic:** Analyzing variances in effort, duration, and cost helps in understanding estimation accuracy and identifying areas for improvement.
- **Units:** Same units as the estimated value (e.g., person-days, days, currency).

- **My Perspective:** Don't view variance analysis as a blame game. It's a learning opportunity to understand why our estimates were off and how we can improve in the future.

8. Velocity (in Agile):

- **What it is:** A measure of the amount of work a team can complete during a single sprint (iteration), typically expressed in story points or the sum of estimated effort for completed tasks.
- **Key Characteristic:** Velocity is used for forecasting how much work the team can deliver in future sprints and for release planning.
- **Units:** Story points per sprint, person-hours per sprint.
- **My Perspective:** Velocity is a team-specific metric and should stabilize over a few sprints. It's a valuable tool for Agile planning but can be misleading if used to compare the productivity of different teams.

Code Example (Illustrative - Showing how these terms might relate in a simple scenario):

This Python example demonstrates how effort, duration, and cost can be related for a single task:

Python

```
task_name = "Implement User Login"

estimated_effort_hours = 40
```

```python
hourly_rate = 50  # Currency unit per hour

available_developers = 2


estimated_cost = estimated_effort_hours * hourly_rate

estimated_duration_days = estimated_effort_hours /
(available_developers * 8) # Assuming 8 hours/day


print(f"Task: {task_name}")

print(f"Estimated Effort: {estimated_effort_hours} person-hours")

print(f"Hourly Rate: {hourly_rate} per hour")

print(f"Estimated Cost: {estimated_cost}")

print(f"Available Developers: {available_developers}")

print(f"Estimated Duration: {estimated_duration_days} days")


# Simulate actuals after the task is completed

actual_effort_hours = 45

actual_duration_days = 3

actual_cost = actual_effort_hours * hourly_rate
```

```
effort_variance = actual_effort_hours - estimated_effort_hours

duration_variance = actual_duration_days - estimated_duration_days

cost_variance = actual_cost - estimated_cost


print("\n--- Actuals vs. Estimates ---")

print(f"Actual Effort: {actual_effort_hours} person-hours (Variance:
{effort_variance} hours)")

print(f"Actual Duration: {actual_duration_days} days (Variance:
{duration_variance} days)")

print(f"Actual Cost: {actual_cost} (Variance: {cost_variance})")
```

Step-by-Step Explanation:

1. **Task Definition:** We define a simple task: "Implement User Login."
2. **Estimates:** We provide initial estimates for effort (in person-hours), the hourly rate of the developers (to calculate cost), and the number of available developers (to influence duration).
3. **Calculated Estimates:** We calculate the estimated cost and duration based on the effort and resources.

4. **Actuals:** We then simulate the actual effort, duration, and cost incurred for the task.

5. **Variance Calculation:** We calculate the variance (difference) between the actuals and the initial estimates for effort, duration, and cost.

Documentation:

This example illustrates the relationship between effort, duration, cost, and resources. It also shows how tracking actuals and calculating variances can help us understand the accuracy of our initial estimates.

Having a clear understanding of these core terms is essential for effective communication and a shared understanding of the estimation process within your team and with stakeholders. As we delve into specific estimation techniques and strategies in the subsequent chapters, these terms will serve as the building blocks of our discussions. Make sure you're comfortable with these definitions as they will be referenced frequently. Let's now move on to understanding the common challenges that can make software estimation so tricky.

1.6 Understanding Units of Estimation: Measuring the Work

When we talk about estimating software, we need a way to quantify the work involved. Just saying "it'll take a while" isn't very helpful! Understanding the different units of estimation and when to use them is crucial for providing meaningful and actionable estimates. Think of these units as the scales we use to weigh the effort, duration, and complexity of our software endeavors.

Let's explore the common units of estimation you'll encounter:

1. Person-Hours (or Person-Days, Person-Weeks, Person-Months):

- **What it is:** A direct measure of the effort required, representing the amount of time one person is expected to spend working on a task. Person-days assume a standard workday (e.g., 8 hours), person-weeks a standard workweek, and so on.
- **When to Use:** Often used for detailed task-level estimation, especially in more traditional methodologies. Can be useful for resource planning and cost calculations (when combined with hourly rates).
- **Pros:** Relatively intuitive and directly links effort to resource cost.
- **Cons:** Can be influenced by individual productivity differences. Doesn't directly account for dependencies or calendar time (duration). Can lead to micromanagement if not used carefully.
- **My Perspective:** While seemingly straightforward, converting person-hours to realistic durations requires careful consideration of resource availability and task dependencies. A 40-person-hour task won't necessarily take one person-week if that person can only dedicate a few hours a day to it due to other commitments.

2. Story Points (Primarily in Agile):

- **What it is:** An abstract, relative unit of measure that represents the effort, complexity, risk, and uncertainty associated with implementing a user story or backlog item. They are not directly tied to a specific time unit.
- **When to Use:** Predominantly used in Agile methodologies like Scrum. Facilitates team-based relative sizing and velocity tracking.
- **Pros:** Encourages holistic consideration of the "size" of a story, reduces anchoring bias associated with time-based estimates, and supports velocity-based forecasting.
- **Cons:** Abstract nature can be confusing for stakeholders initially. Requires team calibration to ensure consistent application. Not directly translatable to timelines without considering team velocity.
- **My Perspective:** Story points are powerful for internal team estimation and planning in Agile. The focus on relative sizing helps teams have meaningful discussions about complexity and risk. The key is to consistently apply the point system.

3. Function Points (FPA):

- **What it is:** A unit of measure for the functional size of a software application, based on the number and complexity of its user-visible functions (inputs, outputs, inquiries, logical files, interfaces).
- **When to Use:** Often used for estimating the size and effort of business applications, particularly in early project phases. Can be

used with historical data or industry benchmarks to predict effort, cost, and duration.

- **Pros:** Technology-independent measure of size, useful for comparing projects and benchmarking productivity.

- **Cons:** Can be complex to calculate accurately, requires a good understanding of the functional requirements, might not be as applicable to all types of software (e.g., real-time systems).

- **My Perspective:** FPA provides a valuable, objective measure of software size from a user perspective. It encourages a focus on delivered functionality rather than lines of code or development time.

4. Use Case Points (UCP):

- **What it is:** An estimation technique that measures the size of a software system based on the number and complexity of its use cases (user interactions with the system) and technical/environmental factors.

- **When to Use:** Often used in use-case-driven development approaches to estimate effort based on user interactions.

- **Pros:** User-centric approach, considers both functional complexity and technical/environmental influences.

- **Cons:** Accuracy depends on the quality and completeness of the use case descriptions and the accurate assessment of complexity factors.

- **My Perspective:** UCP bridges the gap between user requirements (use cases) and development effort. It emphasizes the value delivered to the user.

5. Ideal Days (or Ideal Hours):

- **What it is:** Represents the amount of time a task would take if a person worked on it without any interruptions, meetings, or other overhead.
- **When to Use:** Sometimes used as an intermediate unit in Agile estimation, where teams might estimate in ideal days and then factor in overhead to arrive at a more realistic duration.
- **Pros:** Can provide a more grounded estimate of the pure development time required.
- **Cons:** Highly theoretical and rarely reflects the reality of a typical workday. Requires a consistent and realistic factor for converting ideal days to actual days.
- **My Perspective:** Ideal days can be a useful starting point for discussion, but it's crucial to have a clear understanding of the overhead and context to translate them into realistic timelines.

Code Example (Illustrative - Showing how different units might represent the same work):

This Python example demonstrates how the same amount of work for a feature could be represented in different units of estimation:

Python

```python
feature_name = "Implement Data Export"
```

```python
# Estimation in Person-Hours

estimated_person_hours = 80


# Assuming 8 hours per day

estimated_person_days = estimated_person_hours / 8


# Assuming a team of 2 developers working on it

estimated_duration_days = estimated_person_days / 2


# Hypothetical Story Point estimate (based on team's relative sizing)

estimated_story_points = 13


# Hypothetical Function Point estimate (after analysis)

estimated_function_points = 5


print(f"Feature: {feature_name}")

print(f"Estimated Person-Hours: {estimated_person_hours}")
```

```
print(f"Estimated Person-Days (1 person): {estimated_person_days}")

print(f"Estimated Duration (2 developers): {estimated_duration_days}
days")

print(f"Estimated Story Points (team estimate):
{estimated_story_points}")

print(f"Estimated Function Points (after analysis):
{estimated_function_points}")
```

Step-by-Step Explanation:

1. **Feature Definition:** We define a feature: "Implement Data Export."
2. **Person-Hours:** We start with an estimate in person-hours, representing the total work required by one person.
3. **Person-Days:** We convert person-hours to person-days assuming a standard 8-hour workday.
4. **Duration:** We then consider a scenario with two developers working on the feature to estimate the duration in calendar days.
5. **Story Points:** We provide a hypothetical story point estimate based on the team's relative assessment of the feature's size.
6. **Function Points:** We include a hypothetical function point estimate based on an analysis of the feature's functional components.

Documentation:

This example illustrates how the same piece of work can be measured using different units of estimation, each providing a different perspective on the effort, duration, or size of the task. The choice of unit depends on the methodology, the level of detail required, and the purpose of the estimate.

Understanding the different units of estimation is fundamental to effective software project planning. The choice of unit influences how you estimate, how you track progress, and how you communicate with stakeholders. Select the units that best align with your methodology, your team's understanding, and the specific needs of your project. By speaking the language of the chosen units fluently, you'll be well-equipped to measure the work ahead and set realistic expectations. Now that we have a common vocabulary, let's move on to understanding the challenges that often make software estimation so difficult.

Chapter 2: Navigating the Minefield - Understanding Estimation Challenges

Alright, now that we've established *why* accurate estimation is crucial, let's get real about the hurdles we often face. Software estimation isn't always a straightforward science. It's more like navigating a minefield – there are plenty of potential pitfalls that can blow up your carefully crafted plans. Understanding these challenges is the first step towards mitigating them and, ultimately, improving your estimation accuracy. Trust me, recognizing these "mines" will save you a lot of headaches down the road.

2.1 The Impact of Unclear or Changing Requirements: The Shifting Sands

Let's be honest, in the real world of software development, requirements rarely arrive perfectly etched in stone. They often resemble shifting sands – fluid, ambiguous, and prone to change. This inherent uncertainty surrounding what exactly needs to be built has a profound and often negative impact on our ability to estimate accurately.

Think of trying to build a house when the blueprints keep changing or are vaguely described. How can you accurately estimate the materials needed, the time it will take, or the final cost? The same principle applies to software.

The Ripple Effect of Unclear Requirements:

- **Difficulty in Scope Definition:** When requirements are unclear or incomplete, it's challenging to define the true scope of the work. This makes it nearly impossible to break down the project into manageable tasks for estimation. You're essentially trying to estimate something you don't fully understand.

- **Increased Uncertainty:** Ambiguous requirements introduce significant uncertainty into the estimation process.[1] Different team members might interpret the requirements in different ways, leading to wildly varying estimates. This lack of a shared understanding makes it difficult to arrive at a consensus.

- **Wasted Effort and Rework:** If the team builds features based on a flawed or incomplete understanding of the requirements, the resulting work may need to be significantly revised or even discarded when the requirements are clarified later. This wasted effort throws off initial estimates and consumes valuable time and resources.

- **Scope Creep:** Unclear initial boundaries often lead to "scope creep" – the gradual and uncontrolled expansion of the project's scope without corresponding adjustments to the timeline or budget. This happens because it's easy for new, seemingly small requests to slip in when the original requirements weren't well-defined.

- **Strained Stakeholder Relationships:** When projects consistently miss deadlines or exceed budgets due to poorly understood or changing requirements, it erodes trust with stakeholders. They may perceive the development team as incompetent or unreliable.

- **Team Frustration and Burnout:** Working on a project with constantly shifting targets can be incredibly frustrating for the development team. The feeling of constantly having to redo work or chase moving goalposts can lead to decreased morale and burnout.
- **Inaccurate Velocity in Agile:** Even in Agile, where change is embraced, unclear initial stories or frequent changes within a sprint can make it difficult for the team to establish a stable velocity, making future sprint and release forecasting unreliable.

The Impact of Changing Requirements:

While change is inevitable and often necessary in software development, uncontrolled or poorly managed changes can wreak havoc on estimates.

- **Re-estimation Overhead:** Every significant change in requirements necessitates re-evaluation of the affected tasks and potentially related components. This re-estimation process itself consumes time and effort.
- **Schedule Delays:** Changes often introduce new work or modify existing tasks, leading to adjustments in the project schedule and potential delays in the overall delivery.
- **Budget Overruns:** Increased effort and extended timelines directly translate to higher project costs.
- **Integration Issues:** Changes in one part of the system can have unforeseen consequences on other integrated components, requiring additional effort for rework and testing.

Code Example (Illustrative - Showing how a change in requirements can impact estimated effort):

This Python example demonstrates how a seemingly small change in a feature's requirements can significantly impact the estimated effort:

Python

```python
# Initial Requirement for User Profile Display (Estimated Effort: 8
person-hours)

initial_profile_fields = ["Username", "Email", "Registration Date"]

initial_effort = 8




print(f"Initial User Profile Requirement: Display fields -
{initial_profile_fields} (Estimated Effort: {initial_effort} person-hours)")




# Change in Requirement: Add "Profile Picture" and "Bio" (Requires
additional UI and backend work)

revised_profile_fields = ["Username", "Email", "Registration Date",
"Profile Picture", "Bio"]

additional_ui_effort = 4

additional_backend_effort = 6
```

```python
revised_effort = initial_effort + additional_ui_effort +
additional_backend_effort


print(f"\nRevised User Profile Requirement: Display fields -
{revised_profile_fields}")

print(f"Additional UI Effort: {additional_ui_effort} person-hours")

print(f"Additional Backend Effort: {additional_backend_effort}
person-hours")

print(f"Revised Total Estimated Effort: {revised_effort} person-hours
(Increase of {revised_effort - initial_effort} hours)")


# Further Change: Now allow users to customize the order of the fields
(Significant UI and logic changes)

additional_reordering_effort = 12

further_revised_effort = revised_effort + additional_reordering_effort


print(f"\nFurther Revised Requirement: Allow custom field ordering")

print(f"Additional Reordering Effort: {additional_reordering_effort}
person-hours")
```

```
print(f"Further Revised Total Estimated Effort: {further_revised_effort}
person-hours (Total increase of {further_revised_effort - initial_effort}
hours)")
```

Step-by-Step Explanation:

1. **Initial Requirement:** We start with a simple requirement to display three user profile fields and an initial estimated effort.
2. **First Change:** A change request adds two more fields, requiring additional effort for UI design and backend implementation. The total estimated effort increases.
3. **Second Change:** A further change introduces the complexity of allowing users to reorder the fields, requiring significant modifications to both the UI and the underlying logic, leading to a substantial increase in the estimated effort.

Documentation:

This example, though simple, illustrates how seemingly small additions or modifications to requirements can have a cumulative and significant impact on the overall estimated effort. Each change necessitates re-estimation and can potentially affect the project timeline and budget.

Mitigating the Impact:

While we can't eliminate unclear or changing requirements entirely, we can take steps to mitigate their impact on estimation:

- **Invest in Thorough Requirements Elicitation:** Spend time upfront to gather clear, concise, and well-documented requirements. Use techniques like user stories, use cases, and prototypes to ensure a shared understanding.

- **Prioritize Requirements:** Work with stakeholders to prioritize requirements. Focus on delivering the most valuable features first, which can help manage scope and provide early feedback.

- **Embrace Iterative Development:** Agile methodologies are designed to handle changing requirements. Short iterations allow for frequent feedback and adaptation.

- **Implement Change Management Processes:** Establish a clear process for managing and evaluating change requests, including assessing their impact on scope, schedule, and budget.

- **Communicate the Impact of Changes:** Clearly explain to stakeholders how changes in requirements will affect the estimates and the project plan.

- **Build in Buffers:** Acknowledge the inherent uncertainty by including contingency in your estimates to account for potential rework or minor changes.

- **Regularly Review and Refine Requirements:** Requirements should be living documents. Regularly review and refine them with stakeholders throughout the project lifecycle.

My Perspective: Dealing with unclear and changing requirements is a constant challenge in software development. The key is not to resist change but to manage it effectively through clear communication, robust processes, and a flexible approach to planning and estimation. The more clarity you can bring to the "what," the more accurate your "how long" and "how much" will be.

2.2 Dealing with Software Complexity and Dependencies: The Tangled Web

Beyond the shifting sands of requirements, another significant hurdle in accurate software estimation lies in the intricate web of **software complexity** and **dependencies**. Modern software systems are rarely monolithic. They're often composed of numerous interconnected components, libraries, services, and integrations. Understanding and accounting for this tangled web is crucial for realistic estimates.

Think of it like trying to estimate the time it takes to assemble a complex piece of furniture with dozens of parts and an instruction manual that refers to other sub-assemblies you haven't even started yet. The more complex the furniture and the more dependent one step is on another, the harder it is to predict the total assembly time. Software development shares this challenge.

The Impact of Software Complexity:

Complexity in software can arise from various sources:

- **Algorithmic Complexity:** Intricate logic and algorithms that require significant development and testing effort.
- **Data Structure Complexity:** Handling large and complex data models and their interactions.

- **Architectural Complexity:** Distributed systems, microservices, and intricate integrations between different components.
- **Technological Complexity:** Working with new or unfamiliar technologies, frameworks, or programming languages.
- **Non-Functional Requirements:** Demands for high performance, scalability, security, or usability often add significant complexity to the development effort.

How Complexity Impacts Estimation:

- **Increased Development Effort:** More complex features naturally take longer to design, code, and test. The sheer volume of intricate logic and potential edge cases expands the effort required.
- **Higher Risk of Errors:** Complex systems are more prone to bugs and unexpected behavior. Debugging and fixing these issues can consume significant time and effort, often exceeding initial estimates.
- **Greater Testing Effort:** Thoroughly testing complex software requires more comprehensive test cases and more time for execution. Integration testing becomes particularly challenging with increased component interaction.
- **Steeper Learning Curve:** When dealing with new technologies or complex architectures, the team will need time to learn and become proficient, impacting initial productivity and estimation accuracy.

- **Difficulty in Decomposition:** Highly complex features can be challenging to break down into smaller, easily estimable tasks. This makes bottom-up estimation less reliable.
- **Unforeseen Issues:** Complexity often hides unforeseen technical challenges and integration problems that only surface during development, leading to schedule slippage.

The Impact of Dependencies:

Dependencies between different parts of the software or external systems can also significantly complicate estimation:

- **Sequential Dependencies:** If Task B cannot start until Task A is complete, any delay in Task A directly impacts the start time and potential completion time of Task B. This can create a ripple effect across the project schedule.
- **Resource Dependencies:** If multiple tasks require the same limited resource (e.g., a specific expert or a shared environment), delays in one task can block progress on others.
- **External Dependencies:** Relying on external teams, vendors, or APIs introduces uncertainty. Delays or issues on their end can directly impact your project timeline.
- **Integration Dependencies:** Integrating different software components or systems can be complex and time-consuming, especially if the interfaces are not well-defined or documented.

Code Example (Illustrative - Showing how dependencies can affect the estimated duration):

This Python example demonstrates how dependencies between software components can impact the overall estimated project duration:

Python

```python
# Estimated effort (in person-days) for different components

component_effort = {

    "Database Design": 5,

    "User Interface": 7,

    "API Development": 10,

    "Payment Gateway Integration": 8,

    "Testing": 6

}


# Dependencies: Component B depends on A (represented as B: [A])

dependencies = {

    "User Interface": ["Database Design"],

    "API Development": ["Database Design"],
```

```python
    "Payment Gateway Integration": ["API Development"],

    "Testing": ["User Interface", "API Development", "Payment Gateway
Integration"]

}


# Assume 1 developer per component for simplicity

estimated_duration = {}


def calculate_estimated_duration(components, deps):

    start_times = {}

    end_times = {}

    duration = {}


    for component in components:

        duration[component] = components[component]

        start_times[component] = 0


    for component, depends_on in deps.items():
```

```python
        latest_dependency_end = 0

        for dependency in depends_on:

            if dependency in end_times:

                latest_dependency_end = max(latest_dependency_end,
end_times[dependency])

            else:

                # Handle potential circular or missing dependencies (for
simplicity, assume start at 0)

                pass

        start_times[component] = latest_dependency_end

        end_times[component] = start_times[component] +
duration[component]


    project_end_date = 0
    for end_time in end_times.values():

        project_end_date = max(project_end_date, end_time)


    return project_end_date, start_times, end_times, duration
```

```
project_duration, start_times, end_times, task_durations =
calculate_estimated_duration(component_effort, dependencies)


print("--- Estimated Project Timeline (in days) ---")

for component in component_effort:

    print(f"{component}: Start={start_times[component]},
Duration={task_durations[component]},
End={end_times[component]}")


print(f"\nEstimated Total Project Duration: {project_duration} days")
```

Step-by-Step Explanation:

1. **component_effort Dictionary:** Stores the estimated effort (in person-days) for different software components.

2. **dependencies Dictionary:** Defines the dependencies between components. For example, "User Interface" depends on "Database Design."

3. **calculate_estimated_duration() Function:** This function simulates a basic project scheduling based on dependencies. It calculates the start and end times for each component, considering the dependencies.

4. **Output:** The code prints the estimated start time, duration, and end time for each component, as well as the estimated total project duration, taking dependencies into account.

Documentation:

This simplified example illustrates how dependencies can extend the overall project duration even if the sum of individual component efforts remains the same. The "User Interface" and "API Development" can only start after "Database Design" is complete, and "Testing" can only begin after all development components are finished.

Strategies for Dealing with Complexity and Dependencies in Estimation:

- **Decomposition:** Break down complex features into smaller, more manageable, and less interdependent tasks. This makes estimation easier and reduces uncertainty.
- **Dependency Analysis:** Identify and document all significant dependencies between tasks and external systems. Visualize these dependencies to understand the critical path and potential bottlenecks.
- **Risk Assessment:** Recognize that complex areas and critical dependencies carry higher risks. Allocate more buffer and contingency to these parts of the project.
- **Expert Consultation:** Involve experienced developers and architects in estimating complex features and integrations. Their past experience can provide valuable insights.

- **Prototyping and Proof of Concept:** For highly complex or technically uncertain areas, consider building prototypes or proofs of concept to better understand the challenges and refine estimates.
- **Incremental Development:** Agile methodologies, with their short iterations and frequent integration, help surface integration issues and complexities earlier in the development cycle.
- **Clear Communication:** Foster open communication within the team and with stakeholders about the complexities and dependencies involved and their potential impact on the schedule.
- **Refined WBS:** Ensure your Work Breakdown Structure clearly reflects the dependencies between tasks.

My Perspective: Ignoring complexity and dependencies in your estimates is like pretending the tangled web doesn't exist – you'll inevitably get caught in it later. By proactively identifying, analyzing, and accounting for these factors, you can create more realistic and reliable estimates that better reflect the true effort and duration required to deliver your software.

2.3 Managing Uncertainty and Assumptions in Estimates: The Unknown Unknowns

Let's face it, even with the clearest requirements and a deep understanding of complexity, software development is still fraught with **uncertainty**. We're often trying to predict the future in a domain where the ground is constantly shifting. This uncertainty stems from things we know we don't know (known unknowns) and, more troublingly, from things we don't even know we don't know (unknown unknowns). Effectively managing this uncertainty and the **assumptions** we make along the way is paramount for realistic estimation.

Think of it like navigating a fog. You can see some obstacles (known unknowns), but there might be hidden dangers you can't even anticipate (unknown unknowns). Similarly, our estimates are often based on certain assumptions about technology, team performance, and external factors, and if these assumptions prove wrong, our estimates can quickly unravel.

The Nature of Uncertainty in Software Estimation:

Uncertainty arises from various sources:

- **Lack of Complete Information:** Especially in the early stages, we often don't have all the details about the requirements, design, or technical challenges.
- **Evolving Technologies:** New frameworks, libraries, or platforms can introduce unforeseen complexities or learning curves.
- **Team Dynamics:** Team performance can fluctuate based on experience, collaboration, and unforeseen personnel changes.
- **External Dependencies:** Reliance on third-party APIs, vendors, or client input introduces uncertainty beyond our direct control.
- **Market Changes:** Shifts in the business environment or user needs can lead to scope changes or reprioritization.
- **The "Unknown Unknowns":** These are the truly unpredictable events – a critical bug in a core library, a major security vulnerability discovered, or a significant change in a dependent system's API.

The Role of Assumptions:

Assumptions are the underlying beliefs or suppositions we make when creating estimates, especially when faced with uncertainty. These assumptions can relate to:

- **Team Productivity:** Assuming a certain level of output from the development team.
- **Technology Stability:** Assuming that the chosen technologies will function as expected without major issues.
- **Availability of Resources:** Assuming that the required personnel and tools will be available when needed.
- **No Major Scope Changes:** Assuming that the requirements will remain relatively stable.
- **Integration Smoothness:** Assuming that integrating different components or systems will be straightforward.

The Danger of Unacknowledged or Incorrect Assumptions:

If our assumptions are flawed or not explicitly stated, they can lead to significant inaccuracies in our estimates. When the reality deviates from our assumptions, our carefully calculated numbers can become meaningless.

Code Example (Illustrative - Showing how assumptions can impact a duration estimate):

This Python example demonstrates how different assumptions about developer productivity can lead to different duration estimates for the same amount of estimated effort:

Python

```python
task_name = "Implement Reporting Module"

estimated_effort_hours = 160  # Based on initial understanding


# Scenario 1: Assumption - Highly productive developer (10 hours of
effective work per day)

developer_productivity_high = 10

estimated_duration_high_prod = estimated_effort_hours /
developer_productivity_high

print(f"Scenario 1: High Productivity - Estimated Duration:
{estimated_duration_high_prod} days")


# Scenario 2: Assumption - Average developer productivity (6 hours of
effective work per day due to meetings, context switching)

developer_productivity_average = 6

estimated_duration_average_prod = estimated_effort_hours /
developer_productivity_average

print(f"Scenario 2: Average Productivity - Estimated Duration:
{estimated_duration_average_prod:.2f} days")
```

```python
# Scenario 3: Assumption - Less experienced developer with learning
curve (4 hours of effective work per day initially)

developer_productivity_low = 4

estimated_duration_low_prod = estimated_effort_hours /
developer_productivity_low

print(f"Scenario 3: Low Productivity - Estimated Duration:
{estimated_duration_low_prod} days")



# The estimated effort remains the same, but the assumed productivity
drastically changes the duration.
```

Step-by-Step Explanation:

1. **Task Definition:** We have a task with a fixed estimated effort in person-hours.
2. **Different Productivity Assumptions:** We explore three different assumptions about the developer's effective working hours per day, which represents their productivity.
3. **Duration Calculation:** We calculate the estimated duration in days based on the total effort and each productivity assumption.
4. **Output:** The output clearly shows how the assumed productivity level significantly impacts the estimated duration for the same amount of work.

Documentation:

This example highlights the critical role of assumptions in translating effort into duration. If we assume a higher level of productivity than what actually occurs, our duration estimates will be overly optimistic.

Strategies for Managing Uncertainty and Assumptions:

- **Identify and Document Assumptions:** Explicitly state all the key assumptions underlying your estimates. Make them visible to the team and stakeholders.

- **Validate Assumptions:** Where possible, try to validate your assumptions. For example, if you're assuming a certain level of performance from a new technology, conduct a proof of concept.

- **Consider Best-Case, Worst-Case, and Most Likely Scenarios:** Instead of a single-point estimate, provide a range based on different potential outcomes and the likelihood of each. This acknowledges the uncertainty.

- **Use Techniques like PERT Analysis:** This method uses optimistic, pessimistic, and most likely estimates to calculate an expected value and a measure of variability, explicitly addressing uncertainty.

- **Build in Contingency:** Allocate buffer time or budget to account for known risks and potential unforeseen issues (the "known unknowns"). The size of the contingency should be based on the level of uncertainty.

- **Regularly Review and Revise Estimates:** As the project progresses and more information becomes available, revisit your assumptions and refine your estimates accordingly.

- **Embrace Iterative Development and Feedback:** Agile methodologies allow for continuous learning and adaptation. Short cycles and frequent feedback help surface uncertainties and validate assumptions early.

- **Communicate Uncertainty to Stakeholders:** Be transparent about the level of uncertainty associated with your estimates. Explain the assumptions you've made and the potential impact if those assumptions prove incorrect.

- **Learn from Past Projects:** Analyze past projects to understand where uncertainties arose and how they impacted the estimates. This can help you better anticipate potential issues in future projects.

My Perspective: Accepting that uncertainty is an inherent part of software development is the first step. The goal isn't to eliminate it entirely (which is impossible for the "unknown unknowns") but to manage it proactively through transparency, scenario planning, and a willingness to adapt. Clearly articulating your assumptions is crucial for setting realistic expectations and fostering trust with stakeholders.

2.4 The Pitfalls of Scope Creep and How to Mitigate It: The Ever-Expanding Project

Ah, **scope creep** – the silent killer of many a software project. It's that insidious tendency for the project's requirements and deliverables to expand beyond the initially agreed-upon boundaries, often without corresponding adjustments to the timeline, budget, or resources. Think of it as a balloon slowly inflating; seemingly small additions accumulate over time until the entire project is stretched thin and at risk of bursting.

Scope creep is a common challenge and a significant contributor to estimation inaccuracies. It often arises from unclear initial requirements (as discussed in section 2.1), poor communication, or a well-intentioned but ultimately detrimental desire to please stakeholders with "just one more small feature."

Why is Scope Creep a Problem for Estimation?

- **Undermines Initial Estimates:** Estimates are based on a defined scope. As the scope expands, the original effort, duration, and cost estimates become increasingly inaccurate and unrealistic.
- **Leads to Schedule Delays:** New features and changes require additional work, which inevitably pushes out the project's completion date.
- **Causes Budget Overruns:** More work translates to more resources and time spent, leading to costs exceeding the initial budget.
- **Decreases Team Morale:** The constant pressure to deliver more within the same timeframe and resources can lead to team frustration, burnout, and decreased quality.
- **Compromises Project Quality:** To meet expanding deadlines without additional resources, the team might be forced to cut corners on testing, documentation, or even core functionality.

- **Strains Stakeholder Relationships:** While initially intended to please, uncontrolled scope creep often leads to dissatisfaction when deadlines are missed and budgets are exceeded.

The Anatomy of Scope Creep:

Scope creep can manifest in various ways:

- **Adding "Small" Features:** Individually minor requests that seem easy to implement but collectively add significant effort.
- **Gold Plating:** Developers adding extra features or functionalities that weren't explicitly requested or aren't essential to the core requirements.
- **Misinterpretation of Requirements:** Different stakeholders or team members having varying understandings of what needs to be built, leading to the inclusion of unintended features.
- **Lack of a Formal Change Management Process:** Absence of a structured way to propose, evaluate, and approve changes to the scope.
- **Poor Communication:** Failing to clearly communicate the impact of new requests on the project's timeline and budget.

Code Example (Illustrative - Showing the cumulative impact of small scope additions on estimated effort):

This Python example demonstrates how seemingly small additions to a software feature can cumulatively increase the estimated effort:

Python

```python
initial_feature = "User Authentication"

initial_estimated_effort_hours = 40


print(f"Initial Feature: {initial_feature} (Estimated Effort:
{initial_estimated_effort_hours} hours)")


# Small Scope Addition 1: Implement "Remember Me" functionality (+5
hours)

scope_addition_1 = "Remember Me"

additional_effort_1 = 5

initial_estimated_effort_hours += additional_effort_1

print(f"\nScope Addition 1: {scope_addition_1} (Additional Effort:
+{additional_effort_1} hours, Total Effort:
{initial_estimated_effort_hours} hours)")


# Small Scope Addition 2: Add password reset via email (+8 hours)

scope_addition_2 = "Password Reset via Email"

additional_effort_2 = 8
```

```python
initial_estimated_effort_hours += additional_effort_2

print(f"Scope Addition 2: {scope_addition_2} (Additional Effort:
+{additional_effort_2} hours, Total Effort:
{initial_estimated_effort_hours} hours)")


# Small Scope Addition 3: Integrate with social login (+12 hours)

scope_addition_3 = "Social Login Integration"

additional_effort_3 = 12

initial_estimated_effort_hours += additional_effort_3

print(f"Scope Addition 3: {scope_addition_3} (Additional Effort:
+{additional_effort_3} hours, Total Effort:
{initial_estimated_effort_hours} hours)")


final_estimated_effort = initial_estimated_effort_hours

effort_increase_percentage = ((final_estimated_effort - 40) / 40) * 100


print(f"\nFinal Estimated Effort for {initial_feature} (with additions):
{final_estimated_effort} hours")

print(f"Total Effort Increase: {final_estimated_effort - 40} hours
({effort_increase_percentage:.2f}%)")
```

Step-by-Step Explanation:

1. **Initial Feature and Estimate:** We start with a core feature ("User Authentication") and its initial estimated effort.

2. **Small Additions:** We simulate three seemingly small additions to the scope, each with its own estimated effort.

3. **Cumulative Impact:** The code adds the effort of each scope addition to the total estimated effort, demonstrating how these "small" changes accumulate over time.

4. **Final Effort and Increase:** The final estimated effort and the percentage increase from the original estimate are printed, highlighting the significant impact of scope creep.

Documentation:

This example clearly shows that even seemingly minor additions to the project's scope can lead to a substantial increase in the overall estimated effort. Without proper management, these small increments can collectively derail the project's timeline and budget.

Strategies for Mitigating Scope Creep:

*   **Establish Clear and Well-Documented Requirements:** Invest time upfront in gathering detailed and unambiguous requirements. Use techniques like user stories with clear acceptance criteria, use cases, and visual models.

*   **Define a Clear Project Scope:** Explicitly outline what is included and, equally importantly, what is *not* included in the

project. Obtain formal agreement on the scope from all stakeholders.

- **Implement a Formal Change Management Process:** Establish a structured process for handling change requests. This should include:
  - **Request Submission:** A clear way for stakeholders to submit change requests.
  - **Impact Analysis:** A thorough assessment of the impact of the proposed change on scope, schedule, budget, and resources.
  - **Review and Approval:** A designated authority (e.g., project manager, steering committee) to review and approve or reject change requests.
  - **Documentation:** Tracking all approved changes and updating the project plan accordingly.
- **Communicate the Impact of Changes:** Clearly explain to stakeholders the consequences of accepting change requests, including potential delays and cost increases.Sometimes, visualizing the impact can be very effective.
- **Prioritize Requirements:** Work with stakeholders to prioritize requirements. Focus on delivering the core, high-value features first. Less critical "nice-to-haves" can be considered for later phases if time and budget allow.
- **Timeboxing (in Agile):** In Agile methodologies, iterations (sprints) have a fixed duration and scope. If new requests arise during a sprint, they are typically deferred to a future sprint, helping to control scope within the current iteration.

- **Regular Scope Reviews:** Periodically review the project scope with stakeholders to ensure everyone is still aligned and to identify any potential for uncontrolled expansion.

- **Educate Stakeholders:** Help stakeholders understand the importance of sticking to the agreed-upon scope and the negative consequences of unchecked changes.

- **Be Prepared to Say "No" (Tactfully):** While being responsive to stakeholder needs is important, the project manager must be empowered to push back on non-essential changes that threaten the project's success.

My Perspective: Preventing scope creep requires a proactive and disciplined approach. It's not about being resistant to change but about managing it in a controlled and transparent manner. A well-defined scope, a robust change management process, and clear communication are your best defenses against the ever-expanding project. Remember, saying "no" to a small request now can save you from a much bigger headache later.

2.5 Resource Allocation and Team Dynamics in Estimation: The Human Element

While technical complexities and shifting requirements are significant estimation challenges, we can't overlook the crucial **human element**: **resource allocation** and **team dynamics**. The "who" and "how" of the team building the software directly impacts the "how long" and "how much" of our estimates. Ignoring these human factors is like trying to calculate the speed of a car without considering the driver's skill or the number of passengers.

The Impact of Resource Allocation:

- **Skill Levels and Expertise:** A senior developer will likely complete a complex task faster and with fewer errors than a junior developer. Failing to account for the skill levels of the assigned resources can lead to significant estimation inaccuracies.

- **Availability and Allocation Percentage:** A developer allocated 100% to a task will likely finish it sooner than one allocated only 50% due to other responsibilities. Accurate estimation requires understanding resource availability and planned allocation.

- **Experience with Technology and Domain:** Team members familiar with the technologies being used and the problem domain will generally be more efficient and provide more accurate estimates based on past experience.

- **Onboarding and Learning Curves:** Assigning new team members or introducing new technologies will inevitably involve a learning curve, impacting initial productivity and requiring additional time for training and familiarization.

- **Specialized Skills:** Certain tasks might require specialized skills that only a few team members possess. Bottlenecks can occur if these resources are oversubscribed or unavailable.

- **Resource Dependencies:** If a task depends on the input or output of a specific resource who is also working on other tasks, delays in that resource's work can impact the dependent task's timeline.

The Impact of Team Dynamics:

- **Team Size and Structure:** The size and structure of the team can influence communication overhead and coordination effort. Larger teams might require more effort for integration and knowledge sharing.

- **Communication and Collaboration:** Effective communication and seamless collaboration within the team can significantly improve efficiency and reduce delays caused by misunderstandings or lack of information.

- **Team Cohesion and Experience Working Together:** Teams that have worked together before often have established communication patterns and a better understanding of each other's strengths and weaknesses, leading to more reliable estimates.

- **Motivation and Morale:** A motivated and engaged team is likely to be more productive than a demoralized one. Unrealistic deadlines and poor resource allocation can negatively impact team morale and, consequently, project timelines.

- **Conflict and Friction:** Internal team conflicts or poor interpersonal dynamics can hinder productivity and introduce delays not accounted for in initial estimates.

- **Estimation Culture:** A team culture that encourages open discussion, honest assessments, and learning from past estimation errors will generally lead to more accurate future estimates.

Code Example (Illustrative - Showing how different resource allocations affect task duration):

This Python example demonstrates how varying the number of allocated developers can impact the estimated duration of a task with a fixed estimated effort:

Python

```python
task_name = "Develop REST API Endpoints"

estimated_effort_hours = 120


# Scenario 1: 1 Developer allocated full-time (8 hours/day)

developers_1 = 1

hours_per_day = 8

estimated_duration_1 = estimated_effort_hours / (developers_1 *
hours_per_day)

print(f"Scenario 1: {developers_1} Developer - Estimated Duration:
{estimated_duration_1} days")


# Scenario 2: 2 Developers allocated part-time (4 hours/day each)

developers_2 = 2
```

```
hours_per_day_part_time = 4

estimated_duration_2 = estimated_effort_hours / (developers_2 *
hours_per_day_part_time)

print(f"Scenario 2: {developers_2} Part-time Developers - Estimated
Duration: {estimated_duration_2} days")



# Scenario 3: 3 Developers allocated full-time (8 hours/day each)

developers_3 = 3

estimated_duration_3 = estimated_effort_hours / (developers_3 *
hours_per_day)

print(f"Scenario 3: {developers_3} Full-time Developers - Estimated
Duration: {estimated_duration_3:.2f} days")
```

Step-by-Step Explanation:

1. **Task Definition:** We have a task with a fixed estimated effort in person-hours.
2. **Different Resource Allocations:** We explore three scenarios with varying numbers of developers and their allocation percentages (represented by hours per day).
3. **Duration Calculation:** We calculate the estimated duration in days based on the total effort and the total available work hours per day from the allocated resources.

4. **Output:** The output clearly shows how the number and allocation of resources significantly impact the estimated duration for the same amount of work.

Documentation:

This simple example highlights that effort and duration are not interchangeable. The number of people working on a task and the percentage of their time dedicated to it directly affect how long it will take to complete, even if the total effort remains constant.

Strategies for Incorporating Resource Allocation and Team Dynamics into Estimation:

- **Resource Planning Alongside Estimation:** When estimating tasks, consider who will be assigned to them and their availability. Factor in potential part-time allocations or shared responsibilities.
- **Account for Skill Levels:** Adjust estimates based on the experience and expertise of the assigned team members. Less experienced individuals might require more time for the same task.
- **Factor in Learning Curves:** If new technologies or team members are involved, explicitly add time for learning and onboarding into the estimates.
- **Consider Team Velocity (in Agile):** In Agile, velocity inherently reflects the team's capacity and historical performance. Use historical velocity as a basis for forecasting future sprints, taking into account any significant team changes.

- **Allocate Time for Communication and Collaboration:** For complex tasks or larger teams, explicitly allocate time for meetings, knowledge sharing, and integration efforts.

- **Identify and Address Potential Bottlenecks:** Be aware of tasks that rely on specialized resources and plan accordingly to avoid delays.

- **Foster a Positive Team Environment:** Encourage open communication, collaboration, and a culture of continuous improvement in estimation.

- **Regularly Review Team Capacity:** Understand the team's overall capacity and workload to avoid over-allocating resources and setting unrealistic expectations.

- **Use Team-Based Estimation Techniques:** Techniques like Planning Poker in Agile leverage the collective wisdom and diverse perspectives of the entire team, implicitly incorporating their understanding of individual capabilities and potential challenges.

My Perspective: The human element is often the most unpredictable factor in software estimation. While we can try to quantify effort and break down tasks, the actual time it takes to complete them is heavily influenced by the skills, availability, and dynamics of the team. Paying attention to these human factors and fostering a collaborative and realistic estimation culture is crucial for bridging the gap between estimated and actual outcomes. Remember, a motivated and well-supported team is your most valuable resource in delivering successful software.

2.6 Adapting to Technological Changes and Their Impact: The Evolving Landscape

The software development landscape is in constant flux. New programming languages, frameworks, tools, and platforms emerge at a rapid pace. While these technological advancements often bring significant benefits in terms of efficiency and capability, they also introduce a layer of complexity and uncertainty into our estimation processes. Failing to adapt to these **technological changes** and understand their **impact** can lead to significant estimation errors.

Think of it like trying to navigate a familiar city after major road construction. The old routes might be blocked, new detours appear, and the estimated travel time can be drastically different. Similarly, adopting new technologies can alter the effort and duration required for tasks we might have previously estimated with more confidence.

How Technological Changes Impact Estimation:

- **Learning Curves:** Introducing a new technology requires the team to invest time in learning and becoming proficient. This learning curve needs to be factored into the initial estimates for tasks involving that technology. The duration of the learning phase can be difficult to predict accurately.

- **Unforeseen Challenges:** New technologies often come with their own set of unique challenges, bugs, and integration issues that might not be immediately apparent. These unforeseen hurdles can lead to unexpected delays and increased effort.

- **Tooling and Infrastructure:** Adopting a new technology might necessitate new development tools, testing frameworks, or infrastructure setup. The time and effort required for this setup and configuration need to be considered in the overall project estimate.

- **Integration Complexity:** Integrating new technologies with existing systems can be more complex than anticipated, especially if the interaction points are not well-documented or if compatibility issues arise.

- **Performance and Scalability Considerations:** New technologies might have different performance characteristics or scalability limitations compared to familiar ones. Addressing these non-functional requirements can add unexpected effort.

- **Availability of Expertise:** Finding developers with deep expertise in a new or niche technology can be challenging and might impact team composition and cost.

- **Documentation and Community Support:** The maturity and quality of documentation and the size of the community support for a new technology can significantly affect the time it takes to troubleshoot issues and find solutions.

Code Example (Illustrative - Showing the potential impact of a new framework on estimated development time):

This Python example demonstrates how using a new, unfamiliar web framework might initially increase the estimated development time for a feature compared to using a well-established one:

Python

```python
feature_name = "Implement User Registration API"


# Scenario 1: Using a familiar, well-established framework (e.g., Flask -
assumes team expertise)

familiar_framework = "Flask"

estimated_effort_flask_hours = 24  # Based on past experience


print(f"Scenario 1: Using {familiar_framework} (Familiar) - Estimated
Effort: {estimated_effort_flask_hours} hours")


# Scenario 2: Using a new, unfamiliar framework (e.g., FastAPI -
requires learning)

new_framework = "FastAPI"

learning_overhead_hours = 8  # Estimated time for initial learning and
setup

estimated_core_development_hours = 20  # Similar complexity, but
initial coding might be slightly faster

estimated_effort_fastapi_hours = learning_overhead_hours +
estimated_core_development_hours +
```

(estimated_core_development_hours * 0.20) # Add 20% buffer for unforeseen issues

print(f"Scenario 2: Using {new_framework} (New) - Learning Overhead: {learning_overhead_hours} hours, Estimated Core Effort: {estimated_core_development_hours} hours, Buffer: {estimated_core_development_hours * 0.20:.1f} hours, Total Estimated Effort: {estimated_effort_fastapi_hours:.1f} hours")

effort_increase = estimated_effort_fastapi_hours - estimated_effort_flask_hours

effort_increase_percentage = (effort_increase / estimated_effort_flask_hours) * 100

print(f"\nEstimated Effort Increase when using {new_framework}: {effort_increase:.1f} hours ({effort_increase_percentage:.1f}%)")

Step-by-Step Explanation:

1. **Feature Definition:** We have a feature: "Implement User Registration API."
2. **Familiar Framework:** We estimate the effort assuming the team is proficient in a well-established framework like Flask.
3. **New Framework:** We then estimate the effort using a new, unfamiliar framework like FastAPI. This estimate includes:

- An overhead for the team to learn the new framework and set up the environment.
- The estimated core development time (which might be slightly different due to the framework's specific features).
- A buffer to account for potential unforeseen issues and the team's initial lack of deep expertise.

4. **Effort Comparison:** The code calculates and prints the difference in estimated effort between using the familiar and the new framework.

Documentation:

This example illustrates that adopting a new technology doesn't just involve the effort of writing the core code. It also requires accounting for the initial learning curve, potential integration challenges, and the increased likelihood of encountering unforeseen issues due to the team's unfamiliarity.

Strategies for Adapting to Technological Changes in Estimation:

- **Allocate Time for Research and Proof of Concept:** Before committing to a new technology for a significant part of the project, invest time in research, experimentation, and building a small proof of concept to understand its capabilities and potential challenges.
- **Factor in Learning Curves:** Explicitly include time for team training, tutorials, and initial experimentation when estimating tasks involving new technologies. The length of the learning

curve will depend on the complexity of the technology and the team's prior experience.

- **Increase Buffer and Contingency:** When using new or less mature technologies, increase the buffer in your estimates to account for potential unforeseen issues, integration problems, and the time it might take to find solutions.

- **Seek External Expertise:** If the team lacks deep expertise in a critical new technology, consider bringing in external consultants or experts for guidance and knowledge transfer. Factor in the cost and time associated with this.

- **Start Small and Iterate:** If possible, introduce new technologies in smaller, less critical parts of the project to allow the team to gain experience and build confidence before using them for core functionalities.

- **Thoroughly Evaluate Documentation and Community Support:** Assess the quality and availability of documentation and the strength of the community support for the new technology. A strong support system can significantly reduce troubleshooting time.

- **Consider Technology Maturity:** Be aware of the maturity level of the chosen technology. Newer technologies might have more bugs or undergo more frequent breaking changes.

- **Regularly Review and Adjust Estimates:** As the team gains experience with the new technology, revisit and refine the initial estimates based on actual progress and encountered challenges.

My Perspective: Embracing technological advancements is often essential for staying competitive and building innovative software.

However, it's crucial to approach new technologies with a realistic understanding of their impact on estimation. By proactively accounting for learning curves, potential challenges, and the need for increased buffer, we can mitigate the risk of inaccurate estimates and ensure a smoother transition into the evolving technological landscape. Don't underestimate the time and effort required for the team to become truly proficient with something new.

2.7 Identifying and Addressing Hidden Project Costs: Beyond Development Effort

When we think about the cost of a software project, our minds often immediately jump to the salaries of the development team. While this is undoubtedly a significant component, focusing solely on development effort can lead to dangerously inaccurate budget estimations. There are numerous **hidden project costs** that, if overlooked, can significantly inflate the final bill and derail your project's financial success.

Think of it like buying a car. The sticker price is just the beginning. You also need to factor in insurance, registration, fuel, maintenance, and potential repairs. Similarly, software projects have costs beyond the core development work that need to be identified and addressed during estimation.

Why Hidden Costs are Often Overlooked:

- **Focus on Core Development:** The technical aspects of building the software often take center stage during planning and estimation.

- **Lack of Awareness:** Stakeholders and even some team members might not fully grasp the extent of activities beyond coding that contribute to the overall cost.

- **Distributed Responsibility:** Some of these costs might fall under different departments or budgets, making them less visible to the core development team.

- **Optimistic Assumptions:** There's often an unconscious bias towards assuming smooth processes and minimal overhead.

Common Categories of Hidden Project Costs:

- **Requirements Elicitation and Documentation:** The time spent gathering, analyzing, documenting, and refining requirements is crucial but often underestimated. This includes meetings, workshops, creating user stories, use cases, and specifications.

- **Project Management:** The effort involved in planning, organizing, leading, and controlling the project – including creating schedules, managing risks, communicating with stakeholders, and tracking progress – is a significant cost factor.

- **Testing and Quality Assurance (QA):** Thorough testing, including unit tests, integration tests, system tests, user acceptance testing (UAT), and performance testing, requires dedicated resources and time. Bug fixing and retesting also add to the cost.

- **Deployment and Infrastructure:** Setting up and maintaining the necessary infrastructure (servers, cloud services), configuring deployment pipelines, and the actual deployment process itself incur costs.

- **Training and Onboarding:** If new team members join or new technologies are adopted, the time and resources spent on training and onboarding need to be accounted for.

- **Meetings and Communication:** Regular team meetings, stakeholder updates, and general communication overhead consume time, which translates to cost.

- **Tools and Software Licenses:** Development tools, testing software, project management platforms, and other necessary software licenses can add up.

- **Travel and Accommodation:** If team members or stakeholders are geographically dispersed, travel and accommodation costs for meetings or workshops can be significant.

- **Legal and Compliance:** Depending on the industry and the nature of the software, there might be legal and compliance requirements that necessitate specific activities and costs (e.g., security audits, accessibility compliance).

- **Documentation (User and Technical):** Creating user manuals, API documentation, and technical documentation is essential for the long-term success and maintainability of the software.

- **Rework and Bug Fixing:** While we strive for perfection, bugs are inevitable. The time spent identifying, fixing, and retesting defects is a real cost.

- **Maintenance and Support (Initial Phase):** Even immediately after deployment, there might be initial maintenance tasks, bug fixes based on early user feedback, and support activities.

Code Example (Illustrative - Showing how non-development activities contribute to overall project time):

This Python example demonstrates how breaking down a feature's lifecycle beyond just "development" reveals significant time spent on other activities:

Python

```python
feature_name = "Implement Customer Feedback Form"


# Estimated Development Effort (in person-hours)

development_effort = 60


# Estimated Effort for Other Activities (in person-hours)

requirements_gathering = 15

project_management = 10

testing_qa = 30

deployment = 5

documentation = 10
```

```python
total_estimated_effort = development_effort + requirements_gathering +
project_management + testing_qa + deployment + documentation


print(f"Feature: {feature_name}")

print(f"Estimated Development Effort: {development_effort}
person-hours")

print("\nEstimated Effort for Other Activities:")

print(f"- Requirements Gathering: {requirements_gathering}
person-hours")

print(f"- Project Management: {project_management} person-hours")

print(f"- Testing & QA: {testing_qa} person-hours")

print(f"- Deployment: {deployment} person-hours")

print(f"- Documentation: {documentation} person-hours")

print(f"\nTotal Estimated Effort for Feature: {total_estimated_effort}
person-hours")


# Assuming an average fully loaded cost per person-hour (including
benefits, overhead)

hourly_rate = 80  # Currency unit per hour
```

```
estimated_development_cost = development_effort * hourly_rate

total_estimated_cost = total_estimated_effort * hourly_rate


print(f"\nEstimated Development Cost: {estimated_development_cost}")

print(f"Total Estimated Cost (including other activities):
{total_estimated_cost}")

print(f"Difference: {total_estimated_cost -
estimated_development_cost}")
```

Step-by-Step Explanation:

1. **Feature Definition:** We define a feature: "Implement Customer Feedback Form."
2. **Development Effort:** We provide an estimated effort for the core development work.
3. **Effort for Other Activities:** We then break down the estimated effort for various non-development activities related to the same feature.
4. **Total Estimated Effort:** The code calculates the total estimated effort by summing the development effort and the effort for all other activities.
5. **Cost Calculation:** We then apply a hypothetical fully loaded hourly rate to both the development effort and the total effort to

illustrate the difference in estimated cost when hidden costs are considered.

Documentation:

This example clearly shows that the effort and cost associated with a software feature extend far beyond just the coding time. Activities like requirements gathering, project management, testing, deployment, and documentation contribute significantly to the overall project effort and cost.

Strategies for Identifying and Addressing Hidden Costs:

- **Comprehensive Work Breakdown Structure (WBS):** Ensure your WBS includes all tasks necessary for project completion, not just development tasks. Break down each phase into granular activities.
- **Cross-Functional Input:** Involve team members from different disciplines (e.g., QA, UX, DevOps) in the estimation process to capture costs related to their areas of expertise.
- **Historical Data Analysis:** Review past project budgets and actual expenditures to identify recurring hidden costs that might have been overlooked in previous estimations.
- **Standard Cost Categories:** Develop a checklist of standard cost categories beyond development (like the ones listed above) to ensure they are considered during estimation.
- **Allocate Specific Time for Non-Development Activities:** Don't just assume these tasks will "happen." Explicitly estimate the time and resources required for them.

- **Use Fully Loaded Labor Rates:** When calculating personnel costs, use fully loaded rates that include salaries, benefits, overhead, and other employee-related expenses.[9]

- **Factor in Contingency:** Allocate a portion of the budget to cover unforeseen hidden costs or minor oversights.

- **Regularly Review and Update Estimates:** As the project progresses and more details emerge, revisit your initial estimates and adjust them to account for any newly identified hidden costs.

- **Transparency with Stakeholders:** Clearly communicate the breakdown of the estimated costs beyond just development effort to manage expectations and justify the total budget.

My Perspective: Failing to account for hidden project costs is like planning a road trip without considering tolls, food, or overnight stays. The initial estimate might look appealing, but the final cost can be significantly higher. By adopting a more holistic view of the software development lifecycle and proactively identifying and addressing these often-overlooked expenses, you can create more accurate and realistic project budgets, leading to greater financial control and stakeholder satisfaction. Remember, a successful project considers all the costs involved in getting the software from concept to reality.

2.8 Overcoming the Lack of Historical Data: When the Past is a Mystery

One of the most valuable assets in software estimation is **historical data**. Knowing how long similar tasks took in the past, the effort involved, and the common pitfalls encountered can significantly improve the accuracy of future estimates. But what happens when you're working on a novel project, with a new team, or using unfamiliar technologies, and **the past is a mystery**? Overcoming this lack of historical data is a common challenge, but it's not an insurmountable obstacle.

Think of it like trying to bake a new recipe without ever having baked before. You don't have your own past experiences to draw upon. In such situations, you need to rely on external sources, break down the process into smaller steps, and make educated guesses based on general principles. The same applies to software estimation without historical data.

Why Historical Data is Valuable for Estimation:

- **Provides Benchmarks:** Past projects offer concrete examples of how long certain types of tasks actually took.
- **Highlights Common Pitfalls:** Historical data can reveal recurring issues or underestimated areas.
- **Calibrates Team Velocity (in Agile):** Tracking completed work over time helps establish a reliable measure of the team's capacity.
- **Supports Analogous Estimation:** Comparing the current project to similar past projects (even at a high level) can provide a starting point.
- **Improves Accuracy Over Time:** As you collect data from your own projects, your future estimates become more grounded in your specific context.

Strategies for Estimating When Historical Data is Scarce:

1. **Analogous Estimation (with External Benchmarks):**

   - ○ **What it is:** Comparing the current project to similar projects undertaken by other teams or organizations (industry benchmarks, publicly available data).
   - ○ **How to do it:** Identify projects with comparable size, complexity, and technology stacks. Be cautious when using external data, as organizational contexts and team capabilities can vary significantly.
   - ○ **My Perspective:** While not as precise as your own historical data, external benchmarks can provide a sanity check and a rough order of magnitude. Treat them as a starting point for further refinement.

2. **First Principles Estimation (Bottom-Up Approach):**

   - ○ **What it is:** Breaking down the project into the smallest possible tasks and estimating the effort for each individual task based on the team's best judgment and technical understanding. The total estimate is then the sum of these individual estimates.
   - ○ **How to do it:** Create a detailed Work Breakdown Structure (WBS). Involve the team members who will be performing the tasks in the estimation process. Use

techniques like time boxing or story pointing for individual tasks.

- ○ **My Perspective:** This approach forces a detailed understanding of the work involved and can uncover hidden complexities. However, it's time-consuming and can still be prone to optimism or inexperience.

3. **Expert Judgment and Brainstorming:**

- ○ **What it is:** Relying on the experience and intuition of senior developers, architects, or project managers who have worked on similar types of projects in the past (even if not within the current organization). Brainstorming sessions can help identify potential challenges and effort drivers.

- ○ **How to do it:** Conduct structured estimation meetings where experts can share their insights and contribute to the estimates. Encourage open discussion and challenge assumptions.

- ○ **My Perspective:** Expert judgment is valuable, especially for identifying risks and potential roadblocks. However, it's important to avoid anchoring bias (over-relying on the first opinion) and to combine it with other techniques.

4. **Phased Estimation (Rolling Wave Planning):**

- ○ **What it is:** Estimating in more detail for the immediate phases of the project where requirements are clearer, and providing higher-level estimates for later phases. As the project progresses and more information becomes available, the estimates for subsequent phases are refined.

- ○ **How to do it:** Focus your initial detailed estimation efforts on the first few iterations (in Agile) or the initial phases (in Waterfall). Regularly revisit and refine estimates for future work as the project evolves.
- ○ **My Perspective:** This approach acknowledges the uncertainty inherent in early-stage projects and allows for more accurate estimation as the team gains understanding and experience.

5. **Time Boxing and Prototyping:**

- ○ **What it is:** Setting a fixed time limit (time box) for exploring a new technology or implementing a small prototype of a complex feature. The outcome of this time-boxed effort provides a better understanding of the challenges and effort involved for the full implementation.
- ○ **How to do it:** Allocate a specific amount of time for the team to experiment and deliver a working (even if basic) version of a challenging component. Use the learnings from this exercise to inform the estimates for the complete feature.
- ○ **My Perspective:** Prototyping is invaluable for reducing uncertainty associated with new technologies or complex integrations.[10] The tangible output provides a much more concrete basis for estimation.

Code Example (Illustrative - Showing how a time-boxed prototype can inform later estimates):

This Python example demonstrates how the effort spent on a time-boxed prototype can help refine the estimated effort for the full feature:

Python

```python
feature_name = "Implement Real-time Chat using New WebSocket Library"


# Initial Guess without prior experience (in person-hours)

initial_guess_effort = 40


print(f"Initial Guess for {feature_name}: {initial_guess_effort} person-hours (High Uncertainty)")


# Time-boxed Prototype (allocated 8 person-hours)

prototype_effort = 8

prototype_achievements = ["Basic connection established", "Sending and receiving single-user messages"]

identified_challenges = ["Handling concurrent users", "Message persistence", "Scalability"]
```

```python
print(f"\nTime-boxed Prototype Effort: {prototype_effort} person-hours")

print("Prototype Achievements:", prototype_achievements)

print("Identified Challenges:", identified_challenges)


# Revised Estimate based on Prototype Learnings

revised_core_effort = 60  # Increased due to identified complexities

effort_for_challenges = 30  # Estimated effort to address the challenges


revised_total_effort = revised_core_effort + effort_for_challenges + prototype_effort # Include prototype effort

print(f"\nRevised Estimated Effort for {feature_name}: {revised_total_effort} person-hours (Based on Prototype)")


effort_increase = revised_total_effort - initial_guess_effort

print(f"Effort Increase based on Prototype: {effort_increase} person-hours")
```

Step-by-Step Explanation:

1. **Initial Guess:** Without prior experience, the team makes a rough initial guess for the effort.
2. **Time-boxed Prototype:** A dedicated amount of time is spent building a basic prototype to explore the new WebSocket library.
3. **Learnings from Prototype:** The prototype helps identify key challenges and complexities that were not initially apparent.[11]
4. **Revised Estimate:** Based on the insights gained from the prototype, the estimated effort for the full feature is significantly revised upwards to account for the newly discovered complexities.

Documentation:

This example illustrates how a small, focused effort on a prototype can provide valuable information that drastically improves the accuracy of the subsequent estimates for the full feature, especially when dealing with new or unfamiliar technologies.

Building Historical Data for the Future:

Even when starting with no historical data, it's crucial to start collecting it from your current and future projects. Implement processes for:

- **Tracking Actual Effort and Duration:** Record the time spent on tasks and the actual completion dates.
- **Documenting Challenges and Lessons Learned:** Capture any unexpected issues or insights gained during development.

- **Conducting Post-Project Reviews:** Analyze the accuracy of your estimates and identify areas for improvement.
- **Storing and Analyzing Estimation Data:** Use spreadsheets or project management tools to store and analyze your historical data to identify trends and patterns.

My Perspective: The lack of historical data shouldn't paralyze your estimation efforts. By leveraging a combination of the techniques discussed above, you can make informed estimates even in uncharted territory. The key is to be transparent about the uncertainty, document your assumptions, and actively learn and collect data as you progress. Remember, every project you complete becomes a valuable source of historical data for the future.

2.9 Estimating Non-Functional Requirements: The Invisible Work

We often focus our estimation efforts on the tangible features of a software project – the buttons, the forms, the workflows. However, lurking beneath the surface are the **non-functional requirements (NFRs)**. These define the *quality* of the software, rather than its specific behaviors. Think of them as the invisible infrastructure that makes the visible features usable, reliable, and performant. Failing to adequately estimate the effort associated with NFRs is a common pitfall, leading to underestimated timelines, budget overruns, and ultimately, a less-than-satisfactory user experience.

Imagine building a beautiful website (functional requirement) but forgetting to consider how many users it needs to handle simultaneously (a performance NFR). When a surge of visitors arrives, the site crashes. The core functionality is there, but the lack of attention to the NFR renders it unusable.

Why Non-Functional Requirements are Often Underestimated:

- **Invisibility:** NFRs aren't always as obvious or easily quantifiable as functional features. They often manifest as constraints or quality attributes.

- **Late Consideration:** NFRs are sometimes considered as an afterthought, rather than being integrated into the initial planning and estimation.

- **Lack of Specificity:** NFRs can be vague or poorly defined, making them difficult to translate into concrete tasks for estimation.

- **Cross-Cutting Nature:** Addressing some NFRs (like security or performance) can impact multiple parts of the system, making it challenging to isolate and estimate the effort.

- **Assumption of "Free" Implementation:** There's sometimes an implicit assumption that the underlying framework or infrastructure will handle NFRs without significant additional effort.

Common Categories of Non-Functional Requirements and Their Estimation Implications:

- **Performance:** (e.g., response time, throughput, latency)

- **Estimation Impact:** Requires performance testing, optimization, potentially different architectural choices, and load balancing. Estimating performance often involves defining specific metrics and the effort to achieve them.
- **Scalability:** (e.g., ability to handle increasing load)
  - **Estimation Impact:** Might necessitate cloud-based architectures, auto-scaling configurations, database optimizations, and thorough load testing across different scales.
- **Security:** (e.g., authentication, authorization, data protection)[8]
  - **Estimation Impact:** Involves implementing security measures, conducting security audits, addressing vulnerabilities, and potentially adhering to specific security standards.
- **Usability:** (e.g., ease of use, learnability, accessibility)
  - **Estimation Impact:** Requires user research, UI/UX design considerations, accessibility testing, and iterative refinement based on user feedback.
- **Reliability:** (e.g., fault tolerance, availability)
  - **Estimation Impact:** Might involve implementing redundancy, failover mechanisms, robust error handling, and comprehensive monitoring.
- **Maintainability:** (e.g., code clarity, modularity, testability)
  - **Estimation Impact:** Influences coding standards, architectural design, the extent of unit testing, and the effort required for future modifications.

- **Portability:** (e.g., ability to run on different platforms)
  - **Estimation Impact:** Might require platform-specific development or the use of cross-platform frameworks, as well as thorough testing on target environments.
- **Accessibility:** (e.g., compliance with WCAG guidelines)
  - **Estimation Impact:** Involves designing and developing with accessibility in mind, conducting accessibility audits, and making necessary adjustments.

Code Example (Illustrative - Showing how a performance NFR can impact development effort):

This Python example demonstrates how a seemingly simple functional requirement (retrieving user data) can have significantly different effort estimates depending on the performance NFR:

Python

```python
import time



# Functional Requirement: Retrieve User Data



# Scenario 1: No specific performance requirements (simple database query)

def get_user_data_simple(user_id):
```

```python
        time.sleep(0.1)  # Simulate database access

        return {"id": user_id, "name": "Test User", "email": "test@example.com"}


    estimated_effort_simple = 2  # Person-hours for basic implementation


    print(f"Scenario 1: No Performance NFR - Estimated Effort: {estimated_effort_simple} person-hours")


    # Scenario 2: Performance NFR: Response time must be under 50 milliseconds for 99% of requests
    def get_user_data_optimized(user_id, cache):
        if user_id in cache:

            return cache[user_id]
        else:

            time.sleep(0.02) # Simulate faster database access after optimization

            data = {"id": user_id, "name": "Test User", "email": "test@example.com"}

            cache[user_id] = data
```

```
    return data

cache = {}

estimated_effort_optimized = 8  # Person-hours for implementing
caching, indexing, and optimization


print(f"\nScenario 2: Performance NFR (<= 50ms) - Estimated Effort:
{estimated_effort_optimized} person-hours (Includes caching)")


effort_increase = estimated_effort_optimized - estimated_effort_simple

print(f"Effort Increase due to Performance NFR: {effort_increase}
person-hours")
```

Step-by-Step Explanation:

1. **Functional Requirement:** We have a simple functional
   requirement: retrieving user data.
2. **Scenario 1 (No Performance NFR):** We estimate the effort for a
   basic implementation without specific performance constraints.
3. **Scenario 2 (Performance NFR):** We introduce a performance
   NFR requiring a fast response time. This necessitates
   implementing caching and potentially other optimization
   techniques, significantly increasing the estimated effort.

Documentation:

This example illustrates that the same functional outcome can require vastly different levels of effort depending on the associated non-functional requirements. Meeting stringent performance goals often involves additional design, implementation, and testing work.

Strategies for Estimating Non-Functional Requirements:

- **Explicitly Identify and Define NFRs:** Work with stakeholders to clearly define and document all relevant non-functional requirements with specific, measurable targets (e.g., "99% of page loads should be under 3 seconds").
- **Treat NFRs as Features:** Break down high-level NFRs into smaller, more manageable tasks. For example, "Improve security" could be broken down into "Implement two-factor authentication," "Conduct a security vulnerability scan," etc.
- **Involve Specialists:** Engage experts in areas like security, performance testing, and UX to provide realistic estimates for NFR-related tasks.
- **Use Historical Data (If Available):** If you have data from past projects with similar NFRs, use it as a benchmark.
- **Allocate Time for Research and Prototyping:** For complex NFRs or unfamiliar approaches, allocate time for research, proof of concepts, and experimentation.
- **Integrate NFR Considerations into Design and Architecture:** Address NFRs early in the design phase, as they can significantly influence architectural choices and development approaches.

- **Factor in Testing Effort:** Thoroughly testing NFRs (e.g., load testing, security testing, usability testing) requires dedicated time and resources.

- **Iterative Refinement:** As the project progresses and you gain more understanding of the system's behavior, revisit and refine your NFR estimates.

- **Communicate the Cost of Quality:** Help stakeholders understand that achieving high levels of quality (defined by NFRs) requires investment in effort and resources.

My Perspective: Neglecting non-functional requirements in your estimation is like building a race car without considering the engine's horsepower or the durability of the tires. It might look good initially, but it won't perform as expected under pressure. By proactively identifying, defining, and estimating the "invisible work" of NFRs, you can build robust, high-quality software that truly meets the needs of your users and stakeholders, and you can do so with a more accurate understanding of the required effort and cost.

2.10 Recognizing and Mitigating Human Factors and Biases: The Imperfect Estimator

No matter how sophisticated our estimation techniques or how much historical data we possess, the reality is that **human beings are at the heart of the estimation process**, and we are inherently susceptible to a range of **cognitive biases** and influenced by various **human factors**. Ignoring these can lead to systematic errors in our estimates, often resulting in overly optimistic timelines and underestimated effort.

Recognizing these imperfections and actively working to mitigate their impact is crucial for improving the reliability of our predictions.

Think of it like a weather forecast. Meteorologists use complex models and vast amounts of data, but human interpretation and inherent limitations in the models still introduce a degree of error. Similarly, our software estimates are filtered through our human minds, which are wired in ways that can sometimes lead us astray.

Common Human Factors Affecting Estimation:

- **Experience and Skill:** Estimators with more experience on similar projects or deeper technical understanding are generally better equipped to provide accurate estimates. Conversely, less experienced individuals might underestimate complexity or overlook potential challenges.
- **Optimism Bias:** A natural tendency to be overly optimistic about project timelines and the likelihood of success. We often underestimate the time and effort required and overestimate our ability to overcome obstacles.
- **Pessimism Bias:** The opposite of optimism bias, where estimators tend to be overly cautious and inflate estimates to account for every possible problem.
- **Familiarity Bias:** We tend to more accurately estimate tasks that are similar to those we've done before, and less accurately estimate novel or unfamiliar work.

- **Time Pressure:** When faced with tight deadlines for providing estimates, we might rush the process and overlook important details, leading to inaccuracies.

- **Stakeholder Pressure:** The desire to please stakeholders or secure project approval can lead to consciously or unconsciously underestimating effort or shortening timelines.

- **Team Dynamics:** Dominant personalities can influence group estimation sessions, leading to conformity rather than independent assessments.

- **Mood and Motivation:** Our current mood and overall motivation can subtly affect our judgment and the estimates we provide.

Common Cognitive Biases in Estimation:

- **Anchoring Bias:** Over-relying on the first piece of information received (the "anchor"), even if it's irrelevant or flawed. For example, if a stakeholder suggests a timeline, estimators might unconsciously adjust their estimates around that initial suggestion.

- **Confirmation Bias:** Seeking out and interpreting information that confirms our initial estimates while ignoring contradictory evidence.

- **Availability Bias:** Overestimating the likelihood of events that are easily recalled (e.g., a recent project delay) and underestimating less memorable but potentially more probable risks.

- **Planning Fallacy:** The tendency to underestimate the time and effort required to complete a task, even when we have experience with similar tasks taking longer in the past. We often focus on the "ideal" scenario and fail to account for potential delays and interruptions.

- **Parkinson's Law:** The observation that work expands to fill the time available for its completion. If a generous deadline is given, the work might take that long even if it could have been done faster.

- **Student Syndrome:** Procrastinating on tasks until the last minute before a deadline. This can impact the accuracy of estimates if the estimator assumes work will start immediately and proceed without delay.

- **Loss Aversion:** The tendency to feel the pain of a loss more strongly than the pleasure of an equivalent gain. In estimation, this might manifest as being overly cautious about exceeding an initial (potentially low) estimate.

Code Example (Illustrative - Showing the potential impact of anchoring bias):

This Python example demonstrates how an initial "anchor" value suggested by a stakeholder can influence subsequent estimates:

Python

```
import random


# Task to be estimated

task_name = "Implement User Interface for Feature X"
```

```python
# Scenario 1: No initial anchor

team_estimates_no_anchor = [random.randint(40, 60) for _ in range(5)] #
Hours

average_estimate_no_anchor = sum(team_estimates_no_anchor) /
len(team_estimates_no_anchor)

print(f"Scenario 1: No Anchor - Individual Estimates (hours):
{team_estimates_no_anchor}, Average:
{average_estimate_no_anchor:.2f}")


# Scenario 2: Stakeholder suggests an initial timeline implying ~30 hours
of effort (anchor)

anchor_value = 30

team_estimates_with_anchor = [random.randint(35, 45) for _ in range(5)]
# Estimates tend to cluster around the anchor

average_estimate_with_anchor = sum(team_estimates_with_anchor) /
len(team_estimates_with_anchor)

print(f"\nScenario 2: Anchor = {anchor_value} hours - Individual
Estimates (hours): {team_estimates_with_anchor}, Average:
{average_estimate_with_anchor:.2f}")
```

```
impact_of_anchor = average_estimate_with_anchor -
average_estimate_no_anchor

print(f"\nImpact of Anchor: Average estimate shifted by
{impact_of_anchor:.2f} hours")
```

Step-by-Step Explanation:

1. **Task Definition:** A task needs to be estimated by a team.
2. **Scenario 1 (No Anchor):** The team members provide their estimates independently, resulting in a certain average.
3. **Scenario 2 (With Anchor):** A stakeholder suggests an initial effort level (the anchor) before the team provides their estimates. The individual estimates tend to cluster around this anchor, pulling the average estimate closer to the initial suggestion.
4. **Impact of Anchor:** The code calculates the difference in the average estimate between the two scenarios, illustrating the potential influence of anchoring bias.

Documentation:

This simple simulation shows how a seemingly innocuous initial suggestion can subtly influence the team's estimates, even if they try to provide their independent assessments.

Strategies for Recognizing and Mitigating Human Factors and Biases:

- **Awareness and Training:** Educate the team and stakeholders about common cognitive biases and human factors that can affect estimation. Simply being aware of these tendencies can help individuals be more mindful of their own biases.

- **Use Multiple Estimation Techniques:** Employing a variety of estimation methods (e.g., analogy, bottom-up, top-down, Planning Poker) can help cross-check estimates and reduce the impact of a single biased approach.

- **Involve Multiple Estimators:** Getting input from different team members with diverse perspectives and levels of experience can help surface and challenge individual biases.

- **Anonymous Estimation:** Techniques like silent estimation or using online tools where estimates are submitted anonymously before discussion can reduce the influence of dominant personalities and anchoring bias.

- **Focus on Relative Estimation (e.g., Story Points):** Relative sizing in Agile can sometimes be less susceptible to optimism bias compared to absolute time estimates.

- **Use Checklists of Common Biases:** Before and during estimation sessions, remind the team of potential biases to be aware of.

- **Encourage "Devil's Advocate" Thinking:** Assign someone the role of challenging assumptions and exploring potential downsides or reasons why an estimate might be too low.

- **Base Estimates on Data:** When historical data is available, use it as a grounding point to counteract optimism and the planning fallacy.

- **Break Down Large Tasks:** Decomposing complex work into smaller, more manageable tasks can make estimation less prone to the planning fallacy.
- **Review Past Estimates and Actuals:** Regularly analyze the accuracy of previous estimates to identify systematic biases within the team or individual estimators.
- **Facilitate Estimation Sessions Effectively:** A skilled facilitator can guide estimation discussions, ensure all voices are heard, and help the team avoid common biases.
- **Seek External Perspectives:** For critical projects, consider bringing in external consultants or experienced estimators to provide an unbiased viewpoint.

My Perspective: We can't eliminate human nature from the estimation process, but we can become more aware of our inherent limitations and implement strategies to mitigate their impact. By fostering a culture of critical thinking, using diverse techniques, and learning from our past mistakes, we can strive for more realistic and reliable software estimates. Recognizing that we are all "imperfect estimators" is the first step towards continuous improvement.

2.11 Managing Client Expectations and Pressure: The External Forces

While we've explored internal factors that can skew our estimates, we can't ignore the significant influence of **external forces**, particularly **client expectations** and the **pressure** they can exert on the estimation process. Clients often have pre-conceived notions about timelines and budgets, driven by their business needs, market pressures, or even experiences with other vendors. Effectively managing these external forces is crucial for setting realistic expectations and avoiding the trap of agreeing to unrealistic estimates that set the project up for failure.

Think of it like negotiating the price of a service. The client might have a target price in mind, and their desire to stay within that budget can put pressure on the service provider to lower their quote, even if it doesn't accurately reflect the effort involved. Similarly, clients often have desired delivery dates and budget constraints that can influence the estimation conversations.

Sources of Client Expectations and Pressure:

- **Budget Constraints:** Clients often have fixed budgets and may push for estimates that fit within those limits, even if the scope and complexity suggest otherwise.
- **Time-to-Market Pressures:** The need to launch a product or feature quickly to capitalize on market opportunities can lead clients to demand aggressive timelines.
- **Perceived Simplicity:** Clients who are not deeply familiar with the technical complexities of software development might underestimate the effort required for certain features.
- **Comparison with Other Vendors:** Clients might have received lower estimates from other vendors (which may be unrealistic or based on a different scope or quality level) and use those as leverage.

- **Internal Stakeholder Demands:** Clients themselves might be under pressure from their own management or stakeholders to deliver quickly and within budget.

- **Past Experiences:** Previous positive or negative experiences with software development can shape a client's expectations, sometimes unrealistically.

- **Lack of Understanding of Agile Principles:** Clients unfamiliar with iterative development might expect fixed timelines and budgets for the entire project upfront, even when the scope is likely to evolve.

The Impact of Unmanaged Client Expectations and Pressure on Estimation:

- **Compromised Accuracy:** The pressure to meet client-imposed deadlines or budgets can lead to rushed or downplayed estimates that don't accurately reflect the work involved.

- **Scope Negotiation Challenges:** It becomes harder to push back on scope requests or highlight the effort implications of "small" additions when there's strong pressure to keep the estimate low.

- **Increased Risk of Overcommitment:** Teams might agree to unrealistic timelines and workloads to satisfy clients, leading to burnout, decreased quality, and missed deadlines.

- **Erosion of Trust:** When projects inevitably run over time or budget due to initially unrealistic estimates driven by client pressure, it can damage the client-vendor relationship.

- **Focus on Speed Over Quality:** The pressure to deliver quickly might lead to shortcuts in testing, documentation, or architectural design, potentially resulting in a less robust and maintainable product.

Code Example (Illustrative - Showing the disconnect between client expectation and realistic effort):

This Python example demonstrates a scenario where a client's desired timeline implies an unrealistic level of developer productivity:

Python

```python
feature_name = "Implement Complex Data Analytics Dashboard"

realistic_estimated_effort_hours = 400


client_desired_timeline_weeks = 4

standard_work_hours_per_week = 40

available_developers = 2


implied_effort_from_client_timeline = client_desired_timeline_weeks * available_developers * standard_work_hours_per_week


productivity_needed_per_developer = realistic_estimated_effort_hours / (client_desired_timeline_weeks * available_developers)
```

```python
print(f"Feature: {feature_name}")

print(f"Realistic Estimated Effort: {realistic_estimated_effort_hours} person-hours")

print(f"\nClient's Desired Timeline: {client_desired_timeline_weeks} weeks")

print(f"Available Developers: {available_developers}")

print(f"Standard Work Hours/Week: {standard_work_hours_per_week}")

print(f"\nImplied Effort from Client Timeline: {implied_effort_from_client_timeline} person-hours")


if implied_effort_from_client_timeline < realistic_estimated_effort_hours:

    effort_gap = realistic_estimated_effort_hours - implied_effort_from_client_timeline

    productivity_gap = productivity_needed_per_developer / standard_work_hours_per_week

    print(f"\nEffort Gap: {effort_gap} person-hours")
```

```
    print(f"Implied Productivity per Developer:
{productivity_needed_per_developer:.2f} hours/week (Requires
{productivity_gap:.2f}x standard productivity)")

else:

    print("\nClient's desired timeline aligns with realistic effort (or is
longer).")
```

Step-by-Step Explanation:

1. **Feature and Realistic Estimate:** We have a feature with a realistic estimated effort based on the team's understanding.
2. **Client's Desired Timeline:** The client expresses a desired completion timeline in weeks.
3. **Implied Effort:** We calculate the total effort that could be delivered within the client's desired timeline given the available developers and standard work hours.
4. **Productivity Comparison:** We compare the realistic estimated effort with the effort implied by the client's timeline to highlight any potential gap and the unrealistic productivity levels that would be required to meet the client's expectations.

Documentation:

This example illustrates how a client's desired timeline, if significantly shorter than what the realistic effort suggests, implies an unsustainable level of productivity for the development team. Clearly presenting such discrepancies to the client is crucial for managing expectations.

Strategies for Managing Client Expectations and Pressure:

- **Early and Transparent Communication:** Engage with clients early in the project lifecycle to discuss the estimation process, the factors influencing estimates, and the potential trade-offs between scope, time, and budget.

- **Educate Clients on Software Development Realities:** Help clients understand the complexities involved in software development, the iterative nature of Agile (if applicable), and the potential for unforeseen challenges.

- **Focus on Value and Trade-offs:** Frame the conversation around delivering the most valuable features within realistic constraints. Discuss potential scope reductions or phased delivery if the client's initial expectations are unrealistic.

- **Provide Clear and Justified Estimates:** Clearly explain how the estimates were derived, highlighting the assumptions made and the effort involved in different aspects of the project (including non-functional requirements).

- **Use Ranges and Confidence Levels:** Instead of single-point estimates, provide a range (e.g., best case, most likely, worst case) to reflect the inherent uncertainty and manage expectations around precision. Communicate the confidence level associated with each range.

- **Emphasize the Importance of Realistic Planning:** Explain that setting achievable goals from the outset leads to a higher likelihood of success and a better quality product in the long run.

- **Establish a Formal Change Management Process:** As discussed in section 2.4, a clear process for handling scope changes is essential for managing client requests and their impact on the timeline and budget.

- **Document Agreements Clearly:** Ensure that the agreed-upon scope, timeline, and budget are clearly documented and signed off by both parties. This provides a reference point when new requests arise.

- **Build Trust and a Collaborative Relationship:** A strong, trusting relationship with the client can make difficult conversations about estimates and scope more manageable. Focus on being a partner in their success.

- **Be Prepared to Say "No" (Professionally):** If a client's demands are truly unrealistic and would jeopardize the project's success, be prepared to push back and explain the reasons why their expectations cannot be met within the given constraints. Offer alternative solutions or compromises.

My Perspective: Managing client expectations is a delicate balancing act. We need to be responsive to their needs and business objectives while also advocating for realistic and achievable plans. Open, honest communication, education, and a focus on delivering value within sustainable constraints are key to navigating these external pressures and setting the stage for a successful project and a positive client relationship. Remember, a project that starts with unrealistic expectations is likely to end in disappointment for everyone involved.

2.12 The Influence of Market Volatility on Estimates: The External Winds

Beyond client pressures, the broader **market volatility** can introduce significant uncertainty and impact the accuracy of our software project estimates. Economic shifts, technological disruptions, changes in resource availability, and evolving competitive landscapes can all act as external winds, buffeting our carefully crafted plans and potentially rendering our initial estimations outdated. Ignoring these macroeconomic factors is akin to sailing without paying attention to the weather forecast – you might be caught off guard by unexpected storms.

Think of a sudden surge in demand for a specific skill set (e.g., cybersecurity experts after a major data breach). This increased demand can drive up the cost of hiring, impacting our budget estimates. Similarly, the emergence of a disruptive technology might alter the scope or approach of our project, affecting both timeline and effort.

Sources of Market Volatility Affecting Estimates:

- **Economic Fluctuations:** Inflation, recession, or changes in currency exchange rates can impact labor costs, software licensing fees, and infrastructure expenses.
- **Technological Disruptions:** The rapid emergence of new technologies can render existing skills obsolete, necessitate retraining, or even change the fundamental approach to the project.

- **Changes in Resource Availability:** Fluctuations in the supply and demand for specific technical skills can affect hiring costs and the time it takes to assemble a team.

- **Competitive Landscape Shifts:** A competitor launching a similar product or a change in market trends might necessitate adjustments to the project scope or timeline.

- **Supply Chain Disruptions:** For projects involving hardware or dependencies on external vendors, disruptions in the supply chain can cause delays and increase costs.

- **Changes in Regulations and Compliance:** New laws or regulations can require unexpected changes to the software, impacting development effort and timelines.

- **Geopolitical Events:** Global events can impact economic stability, resource availability, and even the feasibility of certain project aspects.

The Impact of Market Volatility on Estimates:

- **Increased Labor Costs:** High demand for specific skills can drive up salaries and contractor rates, exceeding initial budget estimates.

- **Fluctuating Infrastructure Costs:** Cloud service pricing or hardware costs can change due to market conditions, impacting operational expenses.

- **Delayed Resource Acquisition:** Difficulty in finding and hiring qualified personnel in a volatile market can lead to project delays.

- **Scope Adjustments:** Market shifts might necessitate adding new features or changing the project's direction, requiring re-estimation of effort and timelines.
- **Increased Project Risk:** Volatile market conditions can introduce unforeseen risks that were not accounted for in the initial risk assessment and contingency planning.
- **Impact on Project Viability:** In extreme cases, significant market changes might even render the original project goals less relevant or financially unviable.

Code Example (Illustrative - Showing the potential impact of fluctuating contractor rates on project cost):

This Python example demonstrates how a sudden increase in the market rate for a specific contractor skill can impact the overall project cost:

Python

```python
project_duration_weeks = 20

estimated_contractor_hours_per_week = 40

initial_contractor_rate_per_hour = 75  # Currency unit


initial_contractor_cost = project_duration_weeks *
estimated_contractor_hours_per_week * initial_contractor_rate_per_hour

print(f"Initial Estimated Contractor Cost: {initial_contractor_cost}")
```

```python
# Scenario: Market demand increases, contractor rate goes up by 15%

market_rate_increase_percentage = 0.15

new_contractor_rate_per_hour = initial_contractor_rate_per_hour * (1 +
market_rate_increase_percentage)

new_contractor_cost = project_duration_weeks *
estimated_contractor_hours_per_week * new_contractor_rate_per_hour

cost_increase = new_contractor_cost - initial_contractor_cost

cost_increase_percentage = (cost_increase / initial_contractor_cost) *
100


print(f"\nNew Contractor Rate (after market shift):
{new_contractor_rate_per_hour:.2f}")

print(f"New Estimated Contractor Cost: {new_contractor_cost:.2f}")

print(f"Cost Increase due to Market Volatility: {cost_increase:.2f}
({cost_increase_percentage:.2f}%)")
```

Step-by-Step Explanation:

1. **Initial Cost Estimate:** We calculate the initial estimated cost for a contractor based on the project duration, estimated hours per week, and the initial hourly rate.

2. **Market Rate Increase:** We simulate a scenario where market demand for the contractor's skills increases, leading to a rise in their hourly rate.

3. **New Cost Calculation:** We recalculate the total contractor cost using the new, higher hourly rate.

4. **Cost Impact:** The code calculates and prints the absolute and percentage increase in the contractor cost due to market volatility.

Documentation:

This simple example illustrates how external market forces, such as increased demand for specific skills, can directly and significantly impact the budget estimates for a software project.

Strategies for Mitigating the Influence of Market Volatility on Estimates:

- **Contingency Planning:** Include a contingency budget and timeline buffer in your estimates to account for potential unforeseen market-related fluctuations. The size of the contingency should be based on the perceived volatility of the relevant market factors.

- **Flexible Resource Planning:** Explore options for flexible resource allocation, such as using a mix of in-house and freelance talent, or having backup plans for key personnel.

- **Short-Term Estimation and Iterative Planning:** In highly volatile markets, consider shorter estimation cycles and more frequent reviews of the project plan. Agile methodologies with their iterative nature can be better suited for adapting to changing circumstances.

- **Negotiate Long-Term Contracts (where feasible):** For critical resources or services, consider negotiating longer-term contracts with fixed rates to mitigate potential price increases.

- **Stay Informed About Market Trends:** Continuously monitor relevant market trends, technological advancements, and economic indicators that could impact your project.

- **Regularly Review and Update Estimates:** As market conditions evolve, revisit your initial estimates and adjust them accordingly. Communicate these adjustments to stakeholders transparently.

- **Consider Outsourcing or Offshoring (with caution):** Depending on the skills required and the market conditions in different regions, outsourcing or offshoring might offer access to a more stable or cost-effective talent pool. However, this comes with its own set of challenges (communication, cultural differences, quality control).

- **Diversify Technology Choices (where appropriate):** Relying on niche or rapidly evolving technologies can increase the risk of cost fluctuations or skill shortages. Consider more widely adopted and stable technologies where feasible.

- **Communicate Risks to Stakeholders:** Clearly articulate the potential impact of market volatility on the project's timeline and budget to manage expectations.

My Perspective: While we can't control the external winds of market volatility, we can certainly prepare our sails and navigate them more effectively. By being aware of potential market influences, building in flexibility and contingency, and maintaining open communication with stakeholders, we can reduce the negative impact of these external forces on our software project estimates and increase our chances of delivering successful outcomes. Ignoring the broader economic and technological landscape is a recipe for unexpected turbulence.

2.13 Improving Data Accessibility and Quality for Estimation: Fueling Accuracy

We've repeatedly emphasized the value of historical data in refining our software project estimates. However, simply *having* data isn't enough. The **accessibility** and **quality** of that data are equally crucial. If our past project information is buried in disparate systems, incomplete, or riddled with inaccuracies, it's like trying to drive with low-grade fuel – the engine might sputter, and you won't get the performance you need. Improving data accessibility and quality is therefore a vital step in **fueling the accuracy** of our estimations.

Think of a well-maintained library versus a disorganized attic. In the library, information is readily available, categorized, and accurate, making research efficient. In the attic, finding what you need is a treasure hunt, and you can't always trust the condition of what you find. Our historical project data should strive to be more like the well-maintained library.

The Pitfalls of Poor Data Accessibility and Quality:

- **Difficulty in Retrieval:** If data is scattered across multiple systems (e.g., spreadsheets, email threads, different project management tools) and not centrally organized, it becomes time-consuming and cumbersome to retrieve the information needed for estimation.

- **Inconsistent Formats:** Data stored in different formats can be challenging to compare and analyze effectively. For example, effort tracked in hours in one project and story points in another requires significant effort to reconcile.

- **Incomplete Information:** Missing data points (e.g., actual effort spent on specific tasks, reasons for delays) limit the insights we can gain from past projects.

- **Inaccuracies and Errors:** Data entry errors, inconsistencies in tracking, or a lack of data validation can lead to unreliable historical information, skewing future estimates.

- **Lack of Context:** Raw data without sufficient context (e.g., project complexity, team experience, technologies used) can be misleading when trying to apply it to new projects.

- **Outdated Information:** Data from very old projects might not be relevant to current technologies, team capabilities, or development processes.

Strategies for Improving Data Accessibility:

1. **Centralized Data Repository:** Implement a centralized system or tool for storing all relevant project data, including estimates, actual effort, timelines, resource allocation, risks, and lessons learned. This could be a dedicated project management platform, a data warehouse, or even a well-structured database.

Practical Implementation: Explore project management tools like Jira, Asana, Trello (with appropriate plugins), or dedicated PPM (Project Portfolio Management) software that offer robust data tracking and reporting capabilities.

Code Example (Illustrative - Showing a simple data structure for a centralized repository):

Python

```python
project_data = {

    "Project Alpha": {

        "tasks": {

            "Task 1": {"estimated_effort": 20, "actual_effort": 25, "status": "Completed"},

            "Task 2": {"estimated_effort": 15, "actual_effort": 12, "status": "Completed"},

            # ... more tasks
```

```python
    },

    "start_date": "2024-01-15",

    "end_date": "2024-03-20",

    "team_size": 5,

    "technologies": ["Python", "Django"],

    "lessons_learned": "Underestimated integration complexity"

    },

    "Project Beta": {

        # ... similar structure

    }

    # ... more projects

}


def get_project_task_data(project_name, task_name,
data_point="actual_effort"):

    if project_name in project_data and task_name in
project_data[project_name]["tasks"]:
```

```
        return
project_data[project_name]["tasks"][task_name].get(data_point)

    return None



print(get_project_task_data("Project Alpha", "Task 1"))
```

Documentation: This simple Python dictionary illustrates a basic structure for centrally storing project data. In a real-world scenario, this would be a more robust database or a feature-rich project management tool.

Standardized Data Entry: Define clear and consistent formats for recording key estimation data across all projects. This includes units of measure (e.g., always use person-hours for effort), status codes, and categorization of tasks.

Practical Implementation: Create data entry guidelines and templates for project plans, progress reports, and post-project reviews. Enforce the use of these standards through training and tool configurations.

Automated Data Collection: Where possible, automate the collection of project data. For example, integrate time-tracking tools with project management software to automatically record actual effort spent on tasks

Practical Implementation: Explore integrations between tools like Toggl Track, Clockify, or Harvest with Jira or other project management platforms.

Strategies for Improving Data Quality:

1. **Data Validation and Cleansing:** Implement processes to regularly review and validate the accuracy and completeness of the collected data. Correct any errors or inconsistencies.

Practical Implementation: Schedule periodic data audits. Use scripts or built-in features of your data repository to identify outliers or inconsistencies (e.g., actual effort significantly exceeding estimates without explanation).

2. **Granular Data Tracking:** Encourage the tracking of effort and progress at a sufficiently granular level (e.g., individual tasks rather than just high-level phases). This provides more detailed insights for future estimations.

   - **Practical Implementation:** Ensure your WBS is detailed enough, and team members are trained to log their time against specific tasks.

3. **Contextual Data Capture:** Go beyond just numbers. Capture the context surrounding the estimates and actuals. This includes information about team experience, technical challenges encountered, scope changes, and any other factors that might have influenced the outcome.

Practical Implementation: Include fields for notes and comments in your project tracking system. Conduct thorough post-project reviews and document lessons learned in a structured way.

4. **Regular Data Review and Analysis:** Don't just collect data; actively analyze it. Look for trends, patterns of underestimation or overestimation in specific areas, and the impact of different factors on project outcomes.

Practical Implementation: Generate regular reports on estimation accuracy. Use data visualization tools to identify trends. Conduct root cause analysis for significant estimation variances.

Code Example (Illustrative - Simple analysis of estimation accuracy):

Python

```python
def analyze_estimation_accuracy(project_data):

    total_variance = 0

    task_count = 0

    for project in project_data.values():

        for task in project.get("tasks", {}).values():

            estimated = task.get("estimated_effort")

            actual = task.get("actual_effort")

            if estimated is not None and actual is not None:
```

```python
        variance = actual - estimated

        total_variance += variance

        task_count += 1


    if task_count > 0:

        average_variance = total_variance / task_count

        print(f"Average Estimation Variance (Actual - Estimated):
{average_variance:.2f} person-hours")

    else:

        print("No task data available for analysis.")



analyze_estimation_accuracy(project_data)
```

Documentation: This simple Python function iterates through the project_data and calculates the average variance between estimated and actual effort, providing a basic measure of estimation accuracy.

Feedback Loops and Continuous Improvement: Use the insights gained from data analysis to refine your estimation processes and techniques. Share learnings with the team and incorporate them into future estimations.

Practical Implementation: Hold regular retrospectives focused on estimation accuracy. Update your estimation guidelines and templates based on data-driven insights.

My Perspective: High-quality, accessible data is the bedrock of accurate software estimation. It transforms estimation from a guessing game into an informed prediction based on your own track record. Investing in the tools, processes, and culture that prioritize data quality and accessibility will yield significant returns in terms of more reliable estimates, better project planning, and increased stakeholder trust.[8] Treat your project data as a valuable asset that needs to be nurtured and maintained.

2.14 Enhancing Communication in the Estimation Process: The Power of Dialogue

While data and techniques are crucial, the software estimation process is fundamentally a **social activity**. The accuracy and buy-in of our estimates heavily rely on effective **communication** among all stakeholders – the development team, project managers, clients, and other relevant parties. Think of it as a symphony orchestra; each instrument (stakeholder) needs to play in harmony (communicate effectively) to produce a beautiful and accurate estimation melody. Poor communication, on the other hand, can lead to a cacophony of misunderstandings, flawed assumptions, and ultimately, inaccurate predictions.

Imagine a scenario where the development team estimates a task based on a vague requirement, without clarifying their assumptions with the product owner. The resulting estimate might be wildly off from what the product owner envisioned, leading to frustration and potential rework down the line.

The Pitfalls of Poor Communication in Estimation:

- **Misunderstood Requirements:** Lack of clear and open dialogue about requirements can lead to different interpretations and estimates that don't align with the actual needs.
- **Unsurfaced Assumptions:** When assumptions are not explicitly communicated and discussed, they can remain unchallenged and potentially flawed, leading to inaccurate estimates.
- **Hidden Risks and Dependencies:** Team members might be aware of potential risks or dependencies that could impact the timeline, but if these aren't communicated, they won't be factored into the estimates.
- **Lack of Buy-in and Ownership:** When the team doesn't feel involved in the estimation process or doesn't understand the rationale behind the estimates, they might lack ownership and commitment to meeting those targets.
- **Stakeholder Disagreements:** If clients or other stakeholders don't understand how the estimates were derived or feel their concerns haven't been heard, it can lead to disagreements and a lack of trust in the process.
- **Delayed Feedback and Course Correction:** Poor communication can hinder the timely identification of estimation

errors or changing circumstances, delaying necessary adjustments to the plan.

- **Erosion of Team Morale:** When teams are held accountable for unrealistic estimates they didn't fully understand or agree with, it can lead to frustration and decreased morale.

Strategies for Enhancing Communication in the Estimation Process:

1. **Early and Frequent Collaboration:** Involve the entire team in the estimation process from the beginning. Encourage open discussions and brainstorming to ensure everyone understands the requirements and can contribute their perspectives.

Practical Implementation: Conduct estimation meetings where developers, testers, designers, and the product owner actively participate.[7] Use collaborative tools (e.g., virtual whiteboards, shared documents) to facilitate the discussion.

2. **Active Listening and Clarification:** Encourage active listening during estimation discussions. Team members should feel comfortable asking clarifying questions to ensure a shared understanding of the scope and requirements.

Practical Implementation: Designate a facilitator for estimation meetings to ensure everyone has a chance to speak and that questions are addressed effectively. Encourage the use of "what if" scenarios to explore different interpretations.

3. **Visual Aids and Shared Understanding:** Use visual aids like diagrams, mockups, and user flow charts to help everyone visualize the requirements and the proposed solution. This can foster a common understanding and lead to more aligned estimates.

Practical Implementation: Share visual representations of the features being estimated. Use story mapping or similar techniques to break down the work visually.

4. **Explicitly Document Assumptions:** Clearly document all key assumptions made during the estimation process. Make these assumptions visible to all stakeholders so they can be reviewed and validated.

Practical Implementation: Create a section in your estimation documentation or project plan to list all relevant assumptions related to scope, technology, dependencies, and team availability.

5. **Communicate the Rationale Behind Estimates:** Explain how the estimates were derived, the techniques used, and the factors considered. This helps build trust and understanding among stakeholders.

Practical Implementation: During estimation reviews, walk stakeholders through the estimation breakdown and the reasoning behind the numbers.

6. **Seek and Incorporate Feedback:** Actively solicit feedback on the estimates from all stakeholders. Be open to challenging your own assumptions and revising estimates based on valid concerns or new information.

Practical Implementation: Schedule review meetings specifically focused on the estimates. Create a mechanism for stakeholders to provide feedback and track how that feedback is addressed.

7. **Use Clear and Consistent Language:** Avoid jargon or overly technical terms when communicating estimates to non-technical stakeholders. Use clear and concise language that everyone can understand.

Practical Implementation: Prepare different levels of estimation summaries for different audiences, focusing on the level of detail relevant to their needs.

8. **Regular Communication of Progress and Changes:** Keep all stakeholders informed about the project's progress and any changes that might impact the original estimates.[8] Promptly communicate any potential deviations and the reasons behind them.

Practical Implementation: Establish regular communication channels (e.g., status meetings, progress reports). Use visual dashboards to track progress against estimates.

9. **Foster a Culture of Openness and Trust:** Create an environment where team members feel comfortable raising

concerns about estimates without fear of reprisal. Encourage honest and transparent communication about potential challenges.

Practical Implementation: Lead by example. Be open about the uncertainties in estimation and acknowledge when estimates need to be revised. Celebrate accurate estimations and learn from inaccuracies in a blameless way.

10. **Document Estimation Decisions:** Record the key decisions made during the estimation process, including the techniques used, the rationale behind the estimates, and any disagreements or concerns raised. This provides a historical record and can be valuable for future reference.

Practical Implementation: Maintain meeting minutes for estimation sessions and store them alongside the project documentation.

My Perspective: Effective communication is the lifeblood of a successful estimation process. It transforms estimation from a solitary task into a collaborative effort where diverse perspectives are valued, assumptions are challenged, and a shared understanding is built. By fostering open dialogue and ensuring that all stakeholders are heard and informed, we can significantly improve the accuracy and acceptance of our software project estimates, paving the way for more predictable and successful outcomes. Remember, estimation is not just about numbers; it's about people talking to each other.

Chapter 3: Expert-Based Estimation Techniques - Wisdom of the Crowd (and the Individual)

Alright, let's dive into a fascinating corner of software estimation: tapping into the knowledge and experience of people – the experts! In many situations, especially when dealing with complex or novel projects, the insights of those who've been there and done that can be invaluable. This chapter will explore several key techniques that harness this "wisdom of the crowd" and the individual expert to arrive at more informed estimates.

Think about it for a moment. Have you ever asked a senior colleague for a rough estimate on a task you've never done before? Their gut feeling, based on past experiences, often gets you surprisingly close. Expert-based techniques formalize this process, adding structure and aiming to mitigate some of the inherent biases that can creep in.

3.1 Planning Poker: Process, Facilitation, and Variations - Let's Play Cards!

Alright, let's talk about a fun and engaging technique that's become a staple in Agile estimation: **Planning Poker**. Don't worry, we won't be gambling away your project budget! Instead, we'll be using a deck of cards to facilitate collaborative and relatively accurate estimation of user stories or backlog items. Think of it as a structured way to have a conversation, leverage the collective wisdom of the team, and arrive at estimates that everyone understands and (hopefully) agrees with.

The Core Idea:

Planning Poker aims to overcome some of the biases we discussed earlier (like anchoring and dominant personalities) by having team members individually and simultaneously provide their estimates. This encourages independent thinking and opens up a dialogue about the reasoning behind different estimates.

The Standard Process - How to Play:

1. **The Backlog Item is Presented:** The Product Owner (or whoever is presenting) describes a user story or backlog item to the team. This should include the acceptance criteria and any relevant context. The goal is to ensure everyone has a basic understanding of what needs to be built.

2. **Clarifying Questions:** The team has an opportunity to ask clarifying questions to ensure they fully grasp the scope and requirements of the item. This is a crucial step to avoid different interpretations.

3. **Individual Silent Estimation:** Each team member privately selects a card from their Planning Poker deck that represents their estimate for the story's complexity or effort (usually in story points or ideal days). The deck typically uses a modified Fibonacci sequence (0, 1, 2, 3, 5, 8, 13, 20, 40, 100) to reflect the increasing uncertainty associated with larger estimates. Some

decks also include cards for "Coffee Break" (unsure, need more info), "?" (completely uncertain), and infinity (unestimable).

4. **Simultaneous Reveal:** Once everyone has chosen a card, they all reveal their cards at the same time. This prevents anchoring, where later estimators are influenced by earlier ones.

5. **Discuss Discrepancies:** If there's a significant difference in the estimates, the team members with the highest and lowest estimates (and sometimes others in between) are asked to briefly explain their reasoning. This is where the real value of Planning Poker lies – the dialogue and shared understanding that emerges.

6. **Re-estimation (If Necessary):** After the discussion, the team may choose to re-estimate the story by repeating steps 3 and 4. This continues until the team reaches a consensus or the differences are deemed acceptable for moving forward. The goal isn't always perfect agreement, but a shared understanding of the effort involved.

7. **Record the Estimate:** Once the team agrees (or comes close to agreeing), the estimate is recorded for the backlog item.

Facilitation - Guiding the Game:

A good facilitator is key to a smooth and productive Planning Poker session. The facilitator's responsibilities include:

- **Keeping the Session Focused:** Ensuring the discussion stays relevant to the story being estimated.
- **Ensuring Everyone Participates:** Encouraging quieter team members to share their perspectives.

- **Managing Time:** Keeping the discussion concise and moving the team through the backlog.
- **Handling Disagreements:** Guiding the conversation towards understanding rather than forcing consensus.
- **Reminding the Team of the Estimation Scale:** Ensuring everyone is using the chosen scale consistently.
- **Documenting Outcomes:** Recording the final estimates.

Variations - Shaking Things Up:

While the standard process is effective, there are variations you can introduce:

- **T-Shirt Sizing:** Instead of numbered cards, teams use t-shirt sizes (XS, S, M, L, XL, XXL) to represent relative effort. This can be a good starting point for teams new to estimation or for very high-level backlog items.
- **Fist of Five:** For quick agreement checks after a discussion, team members can hold up a number of fingers (0 to 5) representing their level of agreement with a proposed estimate.
- **Silent Grouping:** Instead of verbal discussion, team members write down their estimates and then the facilitator groups similar estimates together. The rationale for the clusters can then be discussed.
- **Online Tools:** Numerous online tools simulate Planning Poker, which is especially useful for distributed teams. These tools handle the card selection and reveal process digitally.

Code Example (Illustrative - A simplified simulation of a Planning Poker round):

While we can't fully simulate the nuanced discussion of Planning Poker in code, this Python example shows a basic round with random estimates and highlights the discrepancy that would trigger a discussion:

Python

```python
import random


def planning_poker_round(story_name, team_members):

    print(f"\nEstimating story: {story_name}")

    estimates = {}

    for member in team_members:

        estimates[member] = random.choice([1, 2, 3, 5, 8, 13]) # Simulate card selection

        print(f"{member} played: {estimates[member]}")


    min_estimate = min(estimates.values())

    max_estimate = max(estimates.values())
```

```python
        if min_estimate != max_estimate:

            print("\nSignificant difference in estimates. Discussion needed!")

            high_estimators = [member for member, estimate in
estimates.items() if estimate == max_estimate]

            low_estimators = [member for member, estimate in
estimates.items() if estimate == min_estimate]

            print(f"High estimators ({max_estimate}): {',
'.join(high_estimators)}")

            print(f"Low estimators ({min_estimate}): {',
'.join(low_estimators)}")

            # In a real session, we'd now have them explain their reasoning.

            return "Discussion Needed"
        else:

            consensus_estimate = min_estimate

            print(f"\nConsensus reached: {consensus_estimate}")

            return consensus_estimate


team = ["Alice", "Bob", "Charlie", "David"]

story1_result = planning_poker_round("Implement User Login", team)
```

```
story2_result = planning_poker_round("Update Database Schema", team)
```

Step-by-Step Explanation:

1. `planning_poker_round` **Function:** Takes a story name and a list of team members as input.
2. **Simulate Card Selection:** Each team member "plays" a random card from a simplified Fibonacci sequence.
3. **Identify Discrepancies:** The code checks if the minimum and maximum estimates are different.
4. **Trigger Discussion:** If there's a difference, it indicates that a discussion is needed, and it identifies the team members with the highest and lowest estimates.
5. **Reach Consensus:** If all estimates are the same, it declares a consensus.

Documentation:

This simplified code provides a glimpse into the mechanics of a Planning Poker round. In a real session, the crucial element is the human interaction and the sharing of knowledge that occurs during the discussion phase when estimates diverge.

My Perspective: Planning Poker, when facilitated well, is more than just a game. It's a powerful tool for fostering team understanding, uncovering hidden complexities, and arriving at estimates that are more grounded in the collective experience of the team. The real value lies in the dialogue it sparks, leading to a shared mental model of the work ahead. Don't be afraid to experiment with variations to find what works best for your team's dynamics and the context of your project. Let the cards lead to insightful conversations.

3.2 Leveraging Expert Judgment Effectively - Beyond the Cards

While techniques like Planning Poker harness the collective wisdom of the team, sometimes the complexity or novelty of a task calls for the focused insights of one or more **experts**. **Expert judgment** involves seeking the opinions and estimations of individuals with specialized knowledge or extensive experience relevant to the specific work being estimated. It goes beyond a general team discussion and taps into deep, often tacit, understanding. However, simply asking an expert for a number isn't enough. To leverage expert judgment *effectively*, we need a structured approach that minimizes biases and maximizes the value of their insights.

Think of it like consulting a specialist doctor. You wouldn't just ask for a diagnosis without providing context, history, and undergoing examination. Similarly, to get a reliable estimate from an expert, we need to provide them with sufficient information and engage in a meaningful dialogue.

When to Lean on Expert Judgment:

- **Novel or Highly Complex Tasks:** When the team lacks direct experience with the technology, domain, or complexity involved.

- **High-Risk Areas:** Where potential pitfalls or technical challenges are significant.
- **Early Project Phases:** When high-level estimates are needed and detailed team-based estimation might not be feasible or efficient.
- **Uncertainty and Ambiguity:** When requirements are unclear, and expert intuition based on past experiences can help provide a range or identify key risks.
- **Specialized Skills Required:** When a task demands unique expertise that only a few individuals possess.

The Process of Eliciting Expert Judgment Effectively:

1. **Identify the Right Experts:** Select individuals with demonstrable experience and a strong track record in the specific area relevant to the estimation task. Consider both internal and external experts.
2. **Provide Clear and Comprehensive Information:** Equip the expert(s) with all necessary context, including requirements, design specifications, relevant background information, and any assumptions made so far. The more context they have, the more informed their judgment will be.
3. **Structure the Elicitation Session:** Don't just ask for a single number. Consider using structured techniques to guide the expert's thinking:
   - **Decomposition:** Ask the expert to break down the task into smaller components and estimate each part.
   - **Analogous Reasoning:** Ask them to compare the current task to similar past projects or experiences they've had.

- **Scenario Analysis:** Discuss best-case, worst-case, and most likely scenarios and ask for estimates for each.
- **Risk Identification:** Ask the expert to identify potential risks and their impact on the estimate.

4. **Facilitate a Dialogue:** Engage in a conversation with the expert to understand their reasoning, assumptions, and any uncertainties they foresee. Ask clarifying questions and challenge their thinking constructively. This is where you gain deeper insights beyond just the estimate itself.

5. **Document the Expert's Estimate and Rationale:** Record the expert's estimate(s) along with the key assumptions, considerations, and any caveats they provide. This documentation is crucial for understanding the basis of the estimate and for future reference.

6. **Consider Multiple Perspectives:** If possible, seek input from multiple experts to get a range of opinions and reduce the risk of relying on a single individual's biases or blind spots.

7. **Calibrate and Validate:** Compare the expert's estimate with other available information (e.g., analogous data, initial team estimates). If there are significant discrepancies, investigate the reasons behind them. Over time, track the accuracy of expert judgments to calibrate their future estimations.

Mitigating Biases in Expert Judgment:

Experts, like everyone else, are susceptible to cognitive biases. Here are some strategies to mitigate them:

- **Blind Assessment:** If using multiple experts, consider having them provide their initial estimates independently before discussing them with each other. This can reduce anchoring and groupthink.

- **Devil's Advocate:** Assign someone to challenge the expert's assumptions and reasoning to encourage a more critical evaluation.

- **Use Structured Estimation Techniques (as mentioned above):** These techniques can help guide the expert's thinking and reduce reliance on intuition alone.

- **Document Assumptions and Confidence Levels:** Ask the expert to explicitly state their assumptions and their level of confidence in the estimate.

- **Review Past Accuracy:** If you have a history of estimates from a particular expert, review their past accuracy to identify any consistent biases (e.g., chronic optimism or pessimism).

- **Combine with Other Techniques:** Don't rely solely on expert judgment. Use it in conjunction with other estimation methods (like Planning Poker or analogous estimation) to get a more well-rounded perspective.

Code Example (Illustrative - Simulating the collection and comparison of estimates from multiple experts):

This Python example shows how we might collect estimates from different experts and then analyze the range and average:

Python

```python
import random


def get_expert_estimate(expert_name, task_name, complexity_factor):
    """Simulates an expert providing an estimate based on task
complexity."""
    base_estimate = 10  # Base units of effort
    uncertainty_factor = random.uniform(0.8, 1.2) # Introduce some
variability
    return base_estimate * complexity_factor * uncertainty_factor, f"Based
on {complexity_factor} complexity and past experience."


task = "Implement Complex Algorithm X"
complexity = 3  # Subjective complexity assessment


experts = ["Dr. Algorithm", "Prof. Efficiency", "Master Coder"]
expert_estimates = {}
```

```python
for expert in experts:

    estimate, rationale = get_expert_estimate(expert, task, complexity)

    expert_estimates[expert] = {"estimate": estimate, "rationale":
rationale}

    print(f"{expert} estimates: {estimate:.2f} units. Rationale:
{rationale}")


estimates_only = [data["estimate"] for data in expert_estimates.values()]

range_of_estimates = max(estimates_only) - min(estimates_only)

average_estimate = sum(estimates_only) / len(estimates_only)


print(f"\nRange of expert estimates: {range_of_estimates:.2f} units")

print(f"Average expert estimate: {average_estimate:.2f} units")


# Further analysis could involve looking at the rationale provided by each
expert
```

Step-by-Step Explanation:

1. `get_expert_estimate` **Function:** Simulates an expert providing an estimate based on a task's complexity and a random uncertainty factor. In a real scenario, this would be the expert's actual judgment.
2. **Task and Experts:** We define a task and a list of experts.
3. **Eliciting Estimates:** We loop through the experts, get their estimates and rationales, and store them.
4. **Analyzing Estimates:** We calculate the range and average of the expert estimates to understand the level of agreement and central tendency.

Documentation:

This simplified code demonstrates how collecting estimates from multiple experts can provide a range of opinions. The crucial next step in a real project would be to understand the reasoning behind these different estimates through dialogue with the experts.

My Perspective: Expert judgment is a valuable tool in our estimation arsenal, especially when facing the unknown. However, it's not a magic bullet. To leverage it effectively, we need to approach it systematically, provide adequate context, engage in meaningful dialogue, and be mindful of potential biases. By doing so, we can tap into deep expertise and make more informed and reliable estimates that go beyond what simple card games can provide. Remember, the goal is not just the number, but the understanding behind it.

3.3 The Structured Approach of the Delphi Method - Anonymous Wisdom

Building upon the idea of leveraging expert judgment, the **Delphi Method** offers a more structured and formal approach to collecting and synthesizing expert opinions, particularly when dealing with complex or uncertain estimations. A key characteristic of the Delphi Method is its emphasis on **anonymity** and **iteration**, aiming to mitigate some of the biases inherent in face-to-face group discussions, such as anchoring and the influence of dominant personalities. Think of iht as a way to harness the "wisdom of the crowd" of experts, but in a carefully orchestrated and less confrontational manner.

Imagine trying to estimate the impact of a disruptive new technology on your project timeline. Bringing a group of experts into a room might lead to a lively but potentially swayed discussion. The Delphi Method provides a way to gather their individual insights anonymously, allowing for more independent and considered opinions.

The Core Principles of the Delphi Method:

- **Anonymity:** Experts provide their estimates and justifications anonymously, preventing individuals from being influenced by the opinions of others due to status, personality, or group pressure.
- **Iteration:** The estimation process occurs in multiple rounds. After each round, a summary of the experts' estimates and rationales is provided back to the group.

- **Controlled Feedback:** Experts can revise their estimates in subsequent rounds based on the aggregated feedback, but they remain anonymous, and the feedback is controlled (typically statistical summaries and anonymized justifications).
- **Statistical Group Response:** The final estimate is often derived statistically (e.g., median, interquartile range) from the experts' final round of responses.

The Typical Steps of the Delphi Method in Estimation:

1. **Selection of Experts:** Identify and recruit a panel of experts with relevant knowledge and experience for the estimation task. The number of experts can vary depending on the complexity and scope.

2. **Initial Questionnaire (Round 1):** Each expert receives a questionnaire (often online) asking for their estimate (e.g., effort in person-hours, duration in weeks) for the specific task or project component. They are also asked to provide a brief rationale for their estimate and identify any key assumptions or uncertainties. Responses are submitted anonymously to a facilitator.

3. **Compilation and Summarization (Round 2):** The facilitator compiles the anonymous responses and creates a statistical summary (e.g., median, quartiles, range) of the estimates. The anonymized rationales and assumptions provided by the experts are also summarized and presented.

4. **Distribution of Feedback (Start of Round 2):** The summarized estimates and anonymized rationales from Round 1 are distributed

back to each expert. They can see the range of opinions and the reasoning behind them, but not who provided which estimate.

5. **Revision of Estimates (Round 2):** Experts are asked to reconsider their initial estimates in light of the feedback from the other experts. They are given the opportunity to revise their estimates and, if they deviate significantly from the majority, to provide further justification for their position. These revisions are again submitted anonymously.

6. **Further Rounds (If Necessary):** Steps 3-5 are repeated for several rounds (typically 2-4) until the range of estimates stabilizes or a predetermined stopping criterion is met (e.g., a certain level of consensus is reached, or a fixed number of rounds are completed).

7. **Final Estimate Derivation:** Once the process concludes, the final estimate is typically derived from the statistical summary of the experts' responses in the last round (e.g., the median value is often used as the final estimate). The range (e.g., interquartile range) can also be reported to indicate the level of uncertainty.

Benefits of the Delphi Method in Estimation:

- **Reduces Groupthink and Conformity:** Anonymity encourages independent thinking and prevents individuals from simply aligning with the opinions of more vocal or senior members.

- **Mitigates Anchoring Bias:** Experts are not exposed to initial estimates before forming their own.

- **Allows for Considered Opinions:** The iterative process provides time for reflection and revision based on feedback.

- **Harnesses Diverse Expertise:** It can effectively synthesize the knowledge of geographically dispersed or otherwise unavailable experts.

- **Provides a Statistical Basis for the Estimate:** The final estimate is often data-driven, based on the collective judgment of the experts.

Challenges and Considerations:

- **Time-Consuming:** The iterative nature of the Delphi Method can make it a more time-consuming process than face-to-face estimation techniques.

- **Requires Skilled Facilitation:** A neutral and organized facilitator is crucial for managing the process, summarizing feedback effectively, and keeping the experts engaged.

- **Potential for Compromise to the Median:** While anonymity reduces pressure, there's still a tendency for experts to move their estimates towards the median over rounds, which might not always reflect the most accurate assessment.

- **Difficulty in Achieving True Consensus:** Complete consensus might not always be reached, and the final estimate relies on a statistical measure.

- **Expert Availability and Engagement:** Securing the time and commitment of busy experts can be challenging.

Code Example (Illustrative - A simplified simulation of two Delphi rounds):

This Python example simulates two rounds of the Delphi Method with a small group of simulated experts providing effort estimates:

Python

```python
import random

from collections import defaultdict


def get_initial_estimates(experts):

    estimates = {expert: random.randint(10, 30) for expert in experts}

    rationales = {expert: f"Based on my experience with similar complexity." for expert in experts}

    return estimates, rationales


def summarize_feedback(estimates, rationales):

    median_estimate = sorted(estimates.values())[len(estimates) // 2]

    all_rationales = "\n".join([f"{expert}: {rationale}" for expert, rationale in rationales.items()])

    return median_estimate, all_rationales
```

```python
def revise_estimates(experts, feedback_median):

    revised_estimates = {}

    revised_rationales = {}

    for expert in experts:

        adjustment = random.randint(-5, 5) # Simulate adjustment based on
feedback

        new_estimate = max(1, estimates[expert] + adjustment) # Ensure
estimate is positive

        revised_estimates[expert] = new_estimate

        revised_rationales[expert] = f"Adjusted from {estimates[expert]} to
{new_estimate} after seeing median of {feedback_median}."

    return revised_estimates, revised_rationales


# Simulation parameters

experts = ["Expert A", "Expert B", "Expert C", "Expert D", "Expert E"]

task_name = "Estimate Effort for New Feature Y (in person-days)"
```

```python
# Round 1

print(f"--- Round 1: Initial Estimates for '{task_name}' ---")

estimates, rationales = get_initial_estimates(experts)

for expert, estimate in estimates.items():

    print(f"{expert}: {estimate} days")

print("\n--- Round 1 Feedback Summary ---")

feedback_median, all_rationales = summarize_feedback(estimates,
rationales)

print(f"Median Estimate: {feedback_median} days")

print("Anonymous Rationales:\n", all_rationales)



# Round 2

print(f"\n--- Round 2: Revised Estimates for '{task_name}' ---")

revised_estimates, revised_rationales = revise_estimates(experts,
feedback_median)

for expert, estimate in revised_estimates.items():

    print(f"{expert}: {estimate} days")

print("\n--- Round 2 Feedback Summary ---")
```

```
final_median, final_rationales = summarize_feedback(revised_estimates,
revised_rationales)

print(f"Final Median Estimate: {final_median} days")

print("Anonymous Revised Rationales:\n", final_rationales)


# The final estimate would typically be the median from the last round.

final_estimate = final_median

print(f"\nFinal Estimate (Median of Round 2): {final_estimate}
person-days")
```

Step-by-Step Explanation:

1. **get_initial_estimates:** Simulates experts providing initial anonymous estimates and brief rationales.
2. **summarize_feedback:** Calculates the median estimate and compiles all the anonymous rationales.
3. **revise_estimates:** Simulates experts revising their estimates based on the feedback median from the previous round.
4. **Simulation Execution:** The code runs two rounds of the Delphi process, printing the estimates and feedback at each stage. The final estimate is the median of the second round's responses.

Documentation:

This simplified code illustrates the core mechanics of the Delphi Method: anonymous input, iterative rounds, and controlled feedback. In a real implementation, the questionnaires would be more detailed, the feedback summarization more sophisticated, and the process would likely involve more rounds.

My Perspective: The Delphi Method offers a powerful and structured way to tap into expert knowledge while minimizing the social pressures that can skew group estimations. While it might be more time-intensive than other techniques, its emphasis on anonymity and iteration can lead to more considered and potentially more accurate estimates, especially for complex or highly uncertain tasks where independent expert judgment is paramount. When you need to cut through the noise of group dynamics and harness the collective wisdom of experts in a thoughtful way, the Delphi Method is a valuable tool to consider.

3.4 Advantages and Limitations of Expert Opinions - The Human Element

We've explored techniques like Planning Poker and the Delphi Method that leverage the collective intelligence of a group or the structured input of multiple experts. However, at the heart of many estimation processes lies the fundamental reliance on **expert opinions** – the judgments and predictions provided by individuals with specialized knowledge and experience. While invaluable, it's crucial to recognize both the significant **advantages** and inherent **limitations** of this human element in estimation. Treating expert opinions as infallible can be as detrimental as ignoring them entirely.

Think of consulting a seasoned mechanic about a strange noise in your car. Their experience likely makes their diagnosis more accurate than a novice's guess. However, even the best mechanic can sometimes misdiagnose an issue or be influenced by their own biases. The same holds true for expert opinions in software estimation.

Advantages of Relying on Expert Opinions:

- **Leveraging Experience and Intuition:** Experts often possess tacit knowledge and pattern recognition developed over years of experience. They can draw upon past successes and failures to anticipate potential challenges and provide informed estimates, even when hard data is scarce.

- **Handling Novelty and Complexity:** For tasks involving new technologies, intricate architectures, or ambiguous requirements, expert intuition can provide a valuable starting point where historical data might not exist or be directly applicable.

- **Identifying Hidden Risks and Dependencies:** Experienced individuals are often better at spotting potential roadblocks, integration issues, or dependencies that might be overlooked by less experienced estimators.

- **Providing a Sense of Realism:** Experts who have "been there, done that" can inject a dose of realism into overly optimistic or theoretical estimates.

- **Facilitating Learning and Knowledge Transfer:** Engaging with experts in the estimation process can help less experienced team members develop their own estimation skills and gain a deeper understanding of the work involved.

- **Efficiency for Certain Tasks:** For well-defined or recurring tasks within their area of expertise, a single expert might provide a reasonably accurate estimate more quickly than a lengthy group session.

Limitations and Potential Pitfalls of Expert Opinions:

- **Subjectivity and Bias:** As we've discussed, experts are not immune to cognitive biases like optimism, anchoring, availability bias, and the planning fallacy. Their personal experiences and perspectives can unconsciously skew their judgments.

- **Overconfidence:** Some experts might overestimate their abilities or the predictability of the task, leading to overly optimistic estimates.

- **Underestimation of Complexity:** Conversely, experts might become so familiar with a technology or domain that they underestimate the challenges faced by others or the nuances of a specific implementation.

- **"Halo Effect":** The opinion of a highly respected or senior expert might be given undue weight, even if their expertise isn't directly relevant to the specific task.

- **Limited Perspective:** Even the most knowledgeable expert has a finite perspective based on their individual experiences. They might not be aware of all the constraints, dependencies, or alternative approaches.

- **Difficulty in Articulating Tacit Knowledge:** Experts might struggle to fully articulate the reasoning behind their estimates, making it harder for others to understand and validate them.

- **Time Commitment:** Engaging experts, especially those who are highly sought after, can be time-consuming and potentially costly.

- **Potential for Disagreement:** When multiple experts provide different opinions, reconciling these differences can be challenging and might require further investigation or a structured approach like the Delphi Method.

- **Dependence on the Individual:** The accuracy of the estimate is highly dependent on the specific expertise and judgment of the individual consulted. A different expert might provide a significantly different estimate.

Strategies for Maximizing the Advantages and Mitigating the Limitations:

- **Use Multiple Experts:** Seek input from several experts with diverse backgrounds and perspectives to get a more balanced view.

- **Structure the Elicitation Process:** Employ structured techniques like decomposition, analogy, and scenario analysis to guide the expert's thinking and make their reasoning more transparent.

- **Challenge Assumptions:** Encourage critical questioning of the expert's assumptions and explore potential alternative scenarios.

- **Document Rationale and Confidence Levels:** Ask experts to explicitly state their assumptions and their level of confidence in their estimates.

- **Calibrate Expert Judgment:** Over time, track the accuracy of individual experts' estimates to identify any consistent biases and adjust future reliance accordingly.

- **Combine with Other Estimation Techniques:** Use expert opinions as one input among others. Compare expert estimates with those derived from historical data, team-based methods, or algorithmic models.

- **Facilitate Dialogue and Knowledge Sharing:** Encourage experts to explain their reasoning to the team, fostering learning and a shared understanding.

- **Be Aware of Biases:** Actively look for signs of common cognitive biases in expert opinions and take steps to mitigate their influence (e.g., by using blind assessments or the Delphi Method).

- **Focus on Ranges Rather Than Point Estimates:** Experts are often more accurate when providing a range of possible outcomes (best case, most likely, worst case) rather than a single point estimate.

Code Example (Illustrative - Tracking expert estimation accuracy over time):

This Python example demonstrates a simple way to track the accuracy of estimates provided by different experts:

Python

```python
expert_estimation_history = {

    "Expert Alpha": [

        {"task": "Task A", "estimated": 20, "actual": 22},

        {"task": "Task B", "estimated": 15, "actual": 18},

        {"task": "Task C", "estimated": 30, "actual": 27},

    ],

    "Expert Beta": [

        {"task": "Task D", "estimated": 10, "actual": 15},

        {"task": "Task E", "estimated": 25, "actual": 20},

        {"task": "Task F", "estimated": 40, "actual": 45},

    ],

    # ... more experts

}


def calculate_average_estimation_error(expert_history):

    total_error = 0

    estimation_count = 0
```

```python
    for task_data in expert_history:

        error = task_data["actual"] - task_data["estimated"]

        total_error += error

        estimation_count += 1

    if estimation_count > 0:

        return total_error / estimation_count

    return 0


print("Average Estimation Error per Expert:")

for expert, history in expert_estimation_history.items():

    average_error = calculate_average_estimation_error(history)

    print(f"{expert}: {average_error:.2f} units")


# This data can be used to understand which experts tend to overestimate
or underestimate.
```

Step-by-Step Explanation:

1. **expert_estimation_history:** A dictionary storing the estimated and actual values for tasks estimated by different experts.

2. calculate_average_estimation_error: A function that calculates the average error (actual - estimated) for a given expert's estimation history.

3. **Output:** The code iterates through the expert_estimation_history and prints the average estimation error for each expert. A positive error indicates underestimation, while a negative error indicates overestimation.

Documentation:

Tracking the historical accuracy of expert estimates can help identify patterns of bias and inform how much weight to give their opinions in future estimations.

My Perspective: Expert opinions are a valuable and often indispensable part of the estimation process, especially when venturing into the unknown. However, we must approach them with a critical eye, recognizing their inherent subjectivity and potential for bias. By employing structured elicitation techniques, seeking multiple perspectives, and continuously learning from past estimation accuracy, we can harness the power of expert knowledge while mitigating its limitations, leading to more robust and reliable project predictions. Remember, even the wisest oracle needs to be questioned and validated.

Chapter 4: Algorithmic and Parametric Estimation - The Power of Numbers (and Models)

Welcome to the world of algorithmic and parametric estimation! After exploring the wisdom of experts, we're now shifting gears to a more quantitative approach. This chapter delves into techniques that leverage data, formulas, and models to arrive at estimates. While they might seem more technical, the underlying principles are quite logical, and they offer a valuable counterpoint to the more subjective expert-based methods.

Think of algorithmic and parametric estimation as trying to predict the future of your software project based on measurable characteristics and historical trends. It's like using a recipe – if you know the ingredients and the steps, you can (hopefully!) predict the outcome.

4.1 Function Point Analysis: Identification, Complexity, and Calculation - Measuring Functionality

Let's dive into a more structured and somewhat quantitative approach to software estimation: **Function Point Analysis (FPA)**. Unlike the more subjective methods we've discussed, FPA focuses on measuring the **functionality** delivered to the user, independent of the technology used to implement it. Think of it as counting the "features" from the user's perspective. By quantifying this functionality, we can arrive at a more objective measure of the system's size, which can then be used to estimate effort, cost, and duration.

Imagine you're building two different houses. One is a simple one-bedroom bungalow, and the other is a sprawling mansion with multiple wings and specialized rooms. Intuitively, the mansion is "bigger" in terms of functionality and would likely take longer and cost more to build. FPA provides a systematic way to measure this "bigness" in software.

The Core Idea:

FPA breaks down the software system into five key user-visible components. By identifying these components and assessing their complexity, we can calculate a **Function Point (FP) count**. This FP count then serves as a normalized measure of the system's functional size.

The Five Functional Components:

1. **External Inputs (EI):** Data entering the system from the outside (e.g., data entry screens, files, APIs receiving data). Each unique user-requested input that crosses the boundary of the application should be counted.

2. **External Outputs (EO):** Data leaving the system to the outside (e.g., reports, screens displaying results, files, APIs sending data). Each unique user-requested output that crosses the boundary of the application should be counted.

3. **External Inquiries (EQ):** Requests from the user that result in the retrieval of information from the system without altering any

data (e.g., online queries, search functions). Each unique user-requested inquiry (input-output combination) should be counted.

4. **Internal Logical Files (ILF):** Logical groupings of data that are maintained within the system (e.g., database tables, configuration files managed by the application). Each major logical grouping of data should be counted.

5. **External Interface Files (EIF):** Logical groupings of data that are used by the system but are maintained by another application (e.g., reading data from an external database or file).[7] Each major logical grouping of data referenced should be counted.

Identifying and Counting Functional Components:

The first step in FPA is to meticulously identify each instance of these five component types within the scope of the software being estimated. This requires a good understanding of the user requirements and system design.

Assessing Complexity:

Once the components are identified, each instance is classified into one of three levels of complexity: **Low, Average, or High**. The criteria for determining complexity vary slightly for each component type but generally consider factors like:

- **For EIs, EOs, and EQs:** The number of data elements (fields) and the number of file types referenced.

- **For ILFs and EIFs:** The number of data elements (fields) and the number of record types (logical subgroups of data).

Standard guidelines and matrices are used to determine the complexity level based on these factors.

Calculating Unadjusted Function Points (UFP):

Each identified functional component is assigned a specific number of Function Points based on its type and assessed complexity, according to the following standard weighting factors:

Component Type	Low	Average	High
External Input (EI)	3	4	6
External Output (EO)	4	5	7
External Inquiry (EQ)	3	4	6
Internal Logical File (ILF)	7	10	15
External Interface File (EIF)	5	7	10

The **Unadjusted Function Point (UFP)** count is calculated by multiplying the count of each component type by its corresponding complexity weight and summing the results.

Example Calculation of UFP:

Let's say we have the following counts after identifying components and assessing their complexity:

- EI (Low): 5
- EI (Average): 3
- EO (Average): 7
- EO (High): 2
- EQ (Low): 4
- EQ (Average): 6
- ILF (Average): 2
- ILF (High): 1
- EIF (Low): 3
- EIF (Average): 1

The UFP would be calculated as:

UFP = (5 * 3) + (3 * 4) + (7 * 5) + (2 * 7) + (4 * 3) + (6 * 4) + (2 * 10) + (1 * 15) + (3 * 5) + (1 * 7)

UFP = 15 + 12 + 35 + 14 + 12 + 24 + 20 + 15 + 15 + 7

UFP = 169

Calculating Adjusted Function Points (AFP):

The UFP is then adjusted based on **General System Characteristics (GSCs)**, which represent 14 general characteristics of the system that influence its overall complexity and development effort. Each GSC is rated on a scale from 0 (not applicable) to 5 (essential).

The 14 GSCs are:

1. Data Communications
2. Distributed Data Processing
3. Performance
4. Heavily Used Configuration
5. Transaction Rate
6. Online Data Entry
7. End User Efficiency
8. Online Update
9. Complex Processing
10. Reusability
11. Installation Ease
12. Operational Ease
13. Multiple Sites
14. Facilitate Change

The ratings for each GSC are summed to obtain a **Total Degree of Influence (TDI)**. This TDI is then used to calculate a **Value Adjustment Factor (VAF)** using the formula:

$$VAF = 0.65 + (0.01 * TDI)$$

The **Adjusted Function Point (AFP)** count is then calculated as:

$$AFP = UFP * VAF$$

Example Calculation of AFP:

Let's say the TDI for our example system is 35.

$$VAF = 0.65 + (0.01 * 35) = 0.65 + 0.35 = 1.00$$

$$AFP = 169 * 1.00 = 169$$

In this case, the AFP is the same as the UFP. However, if the TDI were different, the AFP would be adjusted accordingly.

Using Function Points for Estimation:

The final AFP count can then be used in conjunction with historical data on productivity rates (e.g., person-hours per function point) to estimate effort, cost, and duration.These productivity rates vary significantly based on the development team's skills, the technologies used, the complexity of the project, and other environmental factors.

Code Example (Illustrative - A basic Python function to calculate UFP):

Python

```python
def calculate_ufp(ei_low, ei_avg, ei_high,

        eo_low, eo_avg, eo_high,

        eq_low, eq_avg, eq_high,

        ilf_low, ilf_avg, ilf_high,

        eif_low, eif_avg, eif_high):

    """Calculates Unadjusted Function Points (UFP)."""
```

```python
    ufp = (ei_low * 3) + (ei_avg * 4) + (ei_high * 6) + \

        (eo_low * 4) + (eo_avg * 5) + (eo_high * 7) + \

        (eq_low * 3) + (eq_avg * 4) + (eq_high * 6) + \

        (ilf_low * 7) + (ilf_avg * 10) + (ilf_high * 15) + \

        (eif_low * 5) + (eif_avg * 7) + (eif_high * 10)

    return ufp


# Example usage:

ufp_value = calculate_ufp(5, 3, 0, 0, 7, 2, 4, 6, 0, 0, 2, 1, 3, 1, 0)

print(f"Calculated Unadjusted Function Points (UFP): {ufp_value}")
```

Step-by-Step Explanation:

1. **calculate_ufp Function:** Takes the counts of each functional component type at each complexity level as input.
2. **Weighting Factors:** Applies the standard weighting factors to each count.
3. **UFP Calculation:** Sums the weighted values to calculate the total UFP.
4. **Example Usage:** Shows how to call the function with sample counts and prints the resulting UFP.

Documentation:

This basic Python function provides a programmatic way to calculate the UFP once the functional components have been identified and their complexity assessed. Calculating the AFP would require an additional function to handle the GSCs and VAF.

My Perspective: Function Point Analysis offers a valuable, technology-independent way to measure the functional size of a software system. While the process of identifying and classifying components can be subjective and requires a thorough understanding of the system, FPA provides a more objective basis for estimation compared to purely judgmental techniques. When combined with historical productivity data, it can be a powerful tool for forecasting effort and cost. However, it's important to remember that FPA is just one piece of the estimation puzzle and should be used in conjunction with other methods and expert judgment. It excels at measuring the "what" of the system but needs to be complemented by an understanding of the "how" and the "who" involved in building it.

4.2 Use Case Points: Defining Use Cases and Determining Effort - Focusing on User Interactions

Building on the idea of measuring functionality from a user-centric perspective, **Use Case Points (UCP)** offer another estimation technique, particularly well-suited for object-oriented development and projects where use cases are a primary means of capturing requirements. Instead of focusing on data flows and logical files like Function Point Analysis, UCP centers around **user interactions** with the system, as defined by use cases. Think of it as estimating the effort based on the scenarios of how users will achieve their goals through the software.

Imagine a banking application. Instead of counting input screens or reports, UCP would focus on user interactions like "Transfer Funds," "View Account Balance," or "Pay Bills." By analyzing the complexity of these interactions and the technical factors involved in implementing them, we can arrive at an estimate of the project's effort.

The Core Idea:

UCP estimation involves identifying and classifying use cases based on their complexity and actors (external entities interacting with the system). These are then adjusted by technical and environmental factors to arrive at a final Use Case Point count, which can be translated into effort using historical productivity data.

The Steps in Use Case Point Estimation:

1. **Identify Actors:** Actors represent external entities (users, other systems, hardware) that interact with the system. Identify all the distinct actors involved in the use cases.

2. **Identify Use Cases:** Use cases describe the sequences of actions a system performs to yield a result of value to an actor. Identify all the significant use cases that define the system's functionality.

3. **Classify Actors by Complexity:** Actors are typically classified as:

- ○ **Simple:** Representing another system or hardware interface (requiring minimal interaction). Weight = 1.
- ○ **Average:** Representing a human user interacting through a graphical user interface (GUI) or a web interface. Weight = 2.
- ○ **Complex:** Representing a human user interacting through a command-line interface (CLI) or a more intricate interface. Weight = 3.

4. **Classify Use Cases by Complexity:** Use cases are classified based on the number of transactions (unique sequences of interactions) within them:

- ○ **Simple:** 3 or fewer transactions. Weight = 5.
- ○ **Average:** 4 to 7 transactions. Weight = 10.
- ○ **Complex:** More than 7 transactions. Weight = 15.

5. **Calculate Unadjusted Use Case Points (UUCP):** Multiply the number of actors in each complexity category by their respective weights and sum the results (Actor Points). Similarly, multiply the number of use cases in each complexity category by their weights and sum the results (Use Case Points). The UUCP is the sum of Actor Points and Use Case Points.

Actor Points = (Number of Simple Actors * 1) + (Number of Average Actors * 2) + (Number of Complex Actors * 3)

Use Case Points = (Number of Simple Use Cases * 5) + (Number of Average Use Cases * 10) + (Number of Complex Use Cases * 15)

UUCP = Actor Points + Use Case Points

6. **Identify Technical Complexity Factors (TCFs):** These factors assess the technical environment and non-functional requirements that influence the effort. There are typically 13 TCFs, each rated on a scale from 0 (not applicable) to 5 (essential).[7] Examples include:

   - Distributed system
   - Performance requirements
   - End-user efficiency
   - Complex internal processing
   - Reusability
   - Security requirements
   - Reliability
   - Data integrity
   - Adaptability

7. **Calculate Technical Complexity Adjustment Factor (TCAF):** Sum the ratings of all 13 TCFs to get the Total Technical Factor (TTF). Then, calculate the TCAF using the formula:

$$TCAF = 0.6 + (0.01 * TTF)$$

8. **Identify Environmental Factors (EFs):** These factors assess the project team's capabilities and the project environment.[8] There are typically 8 EFs, each rated on a scale from 0 (influential) to 5 (no influence). Note that a higher rating indicates a more favorable environment. Examples include:

   - Familiarity with the development process
   - Application experience
   - Object-oriented experience
   - Team motivation
   - Stable requirements
   - Part-time staff
   - Difficulty of programming language
   - Use of CASE tools

9. **Calculate Environmental Adjustment Factor (EAF):** Sum the ratings of all 8 EFs to get the Total Environmental Factor (TEF). Then, calculate the EAF using the formula:

$$EAF = 1.4 - (0.03 * TEF)$$

10. **Calculate Adjusted Use Case Points (UCP):** Multiply the UUCP by the TCAF and the EAF:[9]

$$UCP = UUCP * TCAF * EAF$$

11. **Estimate Effort:** Multiply the final UCP count by a productivity rate (person-hours per UCP) derived from historical data for similar projects and teams. This productivity rate can vary significantly.

Estimated Effort = UCP * Productivity Rate

Example Calculation of UCP:

Let's say we have:

- Simple Actors: 2
- Average Actors: 3
- Complex Actors: 1
- Simple Use Cases: 4
- Average Use Cases: 6
- Complex Use Cases: 2
- TTF (sum of TCF ratings): 30
- TEF (sum of EF ratings): 25
- Productivity Rate: 15 person-hours per UCP
- **Actor Points:** (2 * 1) + (3 * 2) + (1 * 3) = 2 + 6 + 3 = 11
- **Use Case Points:** (4 * 5) + (6 * 10) + (2 * 15) = 20 + 60 + 30 = 110
- **UUCP:** 11 + 110 = 121
- **TCAF:** 0.6 + (0.01 * 30) = 0.6 + 0.3 = 0.9
- **EAF:** 1.4 - (0.03 * 25) = 1.4 - 0.75 = 0.65
- **UCP:** 121 * 0.9 * 0.65 = 70.785 ≈ 71
- **Estimated Effort:** 71 * 15 = 1065 person-hours

Code Example (Illustrative - A basic Python function to calculate UUCP):

Python

```python
def calculate_uucp(simple_actors, average_actors, complex_actors,

        simple_use_cases, average_use_cases, complex_use_cases):

    """Calculates Unadjusted Use Case Points (UUCP)."""

    actor_points = (simple_actors * 1) + (average_actors * 2) +
(complex_actors * 3)

    use_case_points = (simple_use_cases * 5) + (average_use_cases * 10)
+ (complex_use_cases * 15)

    uucp = actor_points + use_case_points

    return uucp


# Example usage:

uucp_value = calculate_uucp(2, 3, 1, 4, 6, 2)
```

```
print(f"Calculated Unadjusted Use Case Points (UUCP): {uucp_value}")
```

Step-by-Step Explanation:

1. `calculate_uucp` **Function:** Takes the counts of actors and use cases at each complexity level as input.
2. **Actor Points Calculation:** Calculates the total actor points based on the weights.
3. **Use Case Points Calculation:** Calculates the total use case points based on the weights.
4. **UUCP Calculation:** Sums the actor points and use case points to get the UUCP.
5. **Example Usage:** Shows how to call the function with sample counts and prints the resulting UUCP.

Documentation:

This basic Python function helps calculate the initial UUCP. Calculating the final UCP and effort would require additional functions to handle the TCFs, EFs, and the productivity rate.

My Perspective: Use Case Points provide a valuable alternative to Function Point Analysis, particularly for projects driven by user stories and use cases. By focusing on user interactions and incorporating technical and environmental factors, UCP offers a more holistic view of the effort involved. However, the classification of actors and use cases, as well as the rating of TCFs and EFs, can still involve some subjectivity. Therefore, it's crucial to have clear guidelines and involve the entire team in the process to ensure a shared understanding and more reliable estimates. Like FPA, UCP should be used in conjunction with historical data and expert judgment to provide a comprehensive estimation.

4.3 Introduction to COCOMO: Modes and Key Drivers - A Comprehensive Model

Stepping into the realm of more algorithmic estimation models, let's explore the **Constructive Cost Model (COCOMO)**. Developed by Barry Boehm, COCOMO is a suite of models that provide a more structured and mathematically-driven approach to estimating effort, cost, and schedule for software projects. Unlike the functional size-based methods, COCOMO takes into account the **size of the software product** (typically in lines of code or function points) and a set of **cost drivers** that influence the development effort. Think of it as a formula that, when you plug in the size and various project characteristics, spits out a more data-informed estimate.

Imagine you're planning a road trip. Knowing the distance is crucial, but factors like the type of road, traffic conditions, and your driving speed will significantly impact the total travel time. Similarly, COCOMO uses the "distance" (software size) and "driving conditions" (cost drivers) to estimate the "travel time" (effort and schedule).

COCOMO's Three Models (Evolutionary Stages):

COCOMO has evolved through several versions. The most commonly referenced are:

1. **Basic COCOMO:** A static, single-variable model that estimates effort as a function of the estimated size of the software project. It's a good starting point for early, rough estimates.

2. **Intermediate COCOMO:** Expands on the basic model by incorporating a set of 15 **cost drivers** that adjust the effort based on product, hardware, personnel, and project attributes.This provides a more refined estimate.

3. **Detailed COCOMO II:** The most comprehensive model, incorporating the effects of reuse, process maturity, and other factors across different phases of the software lifecycle. It also offers different sub-models for different stages of the project.

For this introduction, we'll primarily focus on the **Intermediate COCOMO model** to understand the core concepts of modes and cost drivers.

COCOMO Modes (Development Environments):

Intermediate COCOMO recognizes three different modes that reflect the nature of the software development environment and project characteristics:

1. **Organic Mode:** Suitable for small to medium-sized projects developed by small, experienced teams in a familiar, stable environment with relatively simple requirements.Examples might

include in-house utility software or well-understood business applications.

2. **Semi-Detached Mode:** Represents projects with a mix of experienced and less experienced team members, dealing with a blend of familiar and new technologies, and having moderately complex requirements. Most medium-sized projects fall into this category.

3. **Embedded Mode:** Typically applies to projects with tight hardware constraints, complex interfaces, real-time requirements, and often developed by teams with less experience in the specific application domain. Examples include embedded systems, aerospace software, or complex operating systems.

Each mode has its own set of nominal effort multipliers (coefficients) used in the effort equation.

The Basic Effort Equation (Intermediate COCOMO):

The core of Intermediate COCOMO is the effort equation:

Effort (Person-Months) = $a * (KLOC)^b * EAF$

Where:

- **a:** Effort adjustment factor (coefficient) specific to the project mode.
- **KLOC:** Estimated size of the software product in thousands of lines of code (or converted from function points).

- **b:** Economies of scale exponent specific to the project mode. Values of 'b' less than 1 indicate increasing returns to scale (larger projects are relatively more efficient per line of code).
- **EAF:** Effort Adjustment Factor, which is the product of the effort multipliers associated with the 15 cost drivers.

Key Cost Drivers (Intermediate COCOMO):

The 15 cost drivers in Intermediate COCOMO are categorized into four groups:

1. Product Attributes:

- **RELY (Required Software Reliability):** The extent to which the software must function without failure.
- **DATA (Database Size):** The size and complexity of the data used by the software.
- **CPLX (Product Complexity):** The intricacy of the software's design, implementation, and interfaces.

2. Computer Attributes:

- **TIME (Execution Time Constraint):** The percentage of available execution time the software will use.
- **STOR (Main Storage Constraint):** The percentage of available main storage the software will use.

- **VIRT (Virtual Machine Volatility):** The frequency of changes to the underlying virtual machine environment.
- **TURN (Computer Turnaround Time):** The responsiveness of the development computer system.

3. Personnel Attributes:

- **ACAP (Analyst Capability):** The experience and skill of the system analysts.
- **PCAP (Programmer Capability):** The experience and skill of the software developers.
- **VEXP (Virtual Machine Experience):** The team's experience with the virtual machine environment.
- **LEXP (Language and Tool Experience):** The team's experience with the programming languages and tools used.

4. Project Attributes:

- **MODP (Use of Modern Programming Practices):** The extent to which modern software development methodologies and techniques are employed.
- **TOOL (Use of Software Tools):** The sophistication and effectiveness of the software development tools used.
- **SCED (Required Development Schedule):** The degree of schedule compression imposed on the project.

Each of these cost drivers has a rating scale (e.g., Very Low, Low, Nominal, High, Very High, Extra High) with an associated effort multiplier.[8] A nominal rating has a multiplier of 1.0. Ratings above nominal increase effort, while ratings below nominal decrease effort.

COCOMO Mode Coefficients:

The 'a' and 'b' coefficients vary based on the project mode:

Mode	'a'	'b'
Organic	3.2	1.05
Semi-Detached	3.0	1.12
Embedded	2.8	1.20

Example Calculation (Illustrative):

Let's consider a Semi-Detached project estimated to be 50 KLOC with the following nominal ratings for all cost drivers (EAF = 1.0).

Effort (Person-Months) = 3.0 * (50)^1.12 * 1.0

Effort ≈ 3.0 * 81.78 ≈ 245.34 Person-Months

If some cost drivers had non-nominal ratings, we would multiply their corresponding effort multipliers into the EAF, adjusting the final effort estimate.

Code Example (Illustrative - Basic COCOMO Effort Calculation in Python):

Python

```python
import math


def calculate_cocomo_effort(kloc, mode, eaf=1.0):

    """Calculates effort in person-months using Intermediate
COCOMO."""

    a_coefficients = {"organic": 3.2, "semi-detached": 3.0, "embedded":
2.8}

    b_exponents = {"organic": 1.05, "semi-detached": 1.12, "embedded":
1.20}


    if mode.lower() not in a_coefficients:

        raise ValueError("Invalid COCOMO mode. Choose from 'organic',
'semi-detached', or 'embedded'.")


    effort = a_coefficients[mode.lower()] * (kloc **
b_exponents[mode.lower()]) * eaf

    return effort
```

```
# Example usage:

size_kloc = 50

project_mode = "semi-detached"

effort = calculate_cocomo_effort(size_kloc, project_mode)

print(f"Estimated Effort for {size_kloc} KLOC in {project_mode} mode
(nominal EAF): {effort:.2f} Person-Months")


# Example with a hypothetical EAF of 1.15 (due to some cost drivers)

effort_adjusted = calculate_cocomo_effort(size_kloc, project_mode,
eaf=1.15)

print(f"Estimated Effort with EAF=1.15: {effort_adjusted:.2f}
Person-Months")
```

Step-by-Step Explanation:

1. **calculate_cocomo_effort Function:** Takes the software size in KLOC, the project mode, and an optional Effort Adjustment Factor (defaulting to 1.0) as input.
2. **Coefficients and Exponents:** Defines dictionaries to store the 'a' coefficients and 'b' exponents for each COCOMO mode.
3. **Mode Validation:** Checks if the provided mode is valid.
4. **Effort Calculation:** Applies the Intermediate COCOMO effort equation.

5. **Example Usage:** Shows how to call the function with sample values and prints the resulting effort estimates.

Documentation:

This basic Python function implements the core effort calculation of Intermediate COCOMO. In a real-world scenario, you would need to determine the appropriate COCOMO mode for your project and carefully assess the ratings of all 15 cost drivers to calculate the EAF.

My Perspective: COCOMO provides a more rigorous and data-driven approach to estimation compared to purely judgmental methods. By considering both the size of the software and the various factors that influence development effort, it offers a more nuanced and potentially more accurate prediction. However, the accuracy of COCOMO heavily relies on the accuracy of the size estimate (KLOC or function points) and the correct assessment of the cost driver ratings, which can still involve some subjectivity.[11] It's a powerful tool when used thoughtfully and calibrated with historical data from your own organization. Understanding the different modes and the impact of the key cost drivers is essential for applying COCOMO effectively.

4.4 Understanding Parametric Models and Statistical Relationships - Beyond Specific Techniques

We've explored various estimation techniques, from expert judgment to algorithmic models like COCOMO. Underlying many of these more structured approaches is the concept of **parametric models** and the leveraging of **statistical relationships**. Instead of relying solely on intuition or high-level analogies, parametric models use historical data to establish mathematical relationships between project characteristics (parameters) and the outcomes we want to estimate (effort, cost, duration). Think of it as building a predictive formula based on past experiences.

Imagine a chef who has baked hundreds of cakes. Over time, they'll notice patterns: more eggs generally lead to a richer cake, a higher oven temperature shortens baking time (up to a point!), and so on. They might even develop a mental "formula" for adjusting ingredients and baking time based on the desired cake size and texture. Parametric models in software estimation aim to do something similar, but with project data.

What are Parametric Models?

At their core, parametric models are statistical models that use project attributes (like size, team experience, complexity) as independent variables to predict dependent variables (like effort, duration, defects). These models are "parametric" because they have a fixed number of parameters (coefficients) that are estimated from historical data.

Key Concepts:

- **Independent Variables (Predictors):** These are the characteristics of the project that we believe influence the outcome we want to estimate.[3] Examples include lines of code, function points, number of developers, team experience level, and complexity ratings.

- **Dependent Variables (Outcomes):** These are the quantities we are trying to predict, such as effort in person-hours, project duration in weeks, or the number of defects expected.

- **Statistical Relationships:** Parametric models aim to uncover and quantify the statistical relationships between the independent and dependent variables. This relationship is often expressed as a mathematical equation.

- **Calibration:** A crucial step in using parametric models is calibrating them with your own organization's historical data. The generic parameters provided by models like COCOMO might not perfectly reflect your team's productivity or the specific nature of your projects.

- **Goodness of Fit:** After building a parametric model, it's important to assess how well it fits the historical data. Statistical measures like R-squared can indicate the proportion of variance in the dependent variable that is predictable from the independent variables.

Common Forms of Statistical Relationships:

- **Linear Regression:** A simple model that assumes a linear relationship between the variables ($y=mx+c$).

- **Power Law Models:** Often used in software estimation (like the basic COCOMO equation), these models capture non-linear relationships where the impact of size on effort changes as the project gets larger ($y=a*xb$).

- **Exponential Models:** Used when the dependent variable increases or decreases at an accelerating rate.

- **Logarithmic Models:** Used when the rate of change of the dependent variable decreases as the independent variable increases.

Building a Simple Parametric Model (Illustrative):

Let's imagine we have historical data on small web development projects, tracking the number of user stories and the total development effort in person-hours. We want to build a simple linear parametric model to predict effort based on the number of user stories.

Python

```python
import pandas as pd

from sklearn.linear_model import LinearRegression

import matplotlib.pyplot as plt


# Sample historical data

data = {'user_stories': [10, 15, 20, 25, 30, 35, 40],

    'effort_hours': [80, 120, 150, 200, 240, 280, 320]}

df = pd.DataFrame(data)


# Independent variable (predictor)
```

```python
X = df[['user_stories']]

# Dependent variable (outcome)

y = df['effort_hours']


# Create a linear regression model

model = LinearRegression()


# Train the model using the historical data

model.fit(X, y)


# Get the model parameters (coefficients)

slope = model.coef_[0]

intercept = model.intercept_


print(f"Parametric Model: Effort (hours) = {slope:.2f} * User Stories + {intercept:.2f}")


# Make a prediction for a new project with 22 user stories
```

```python
new_user_stories = [[22]]

predicted_effort = model.predict(new_user_stories)[0]

print(f"Predicted effort for {new_user_stories[0][0]} user stories: {predicted_effort:.2f} hours")


# Visualize the data and the model

plt.scatter(X, y, color='blue', label='Historical Data')

plt.plot(X, model.predict(X), color='red', label='Linear Regression Model')

plt.scatter(new_user_stories, predicted_effort, color='green', marker='x', s=100, label='Prediction')

plt.xlabel('Number of User Stories')

plt.ylabel('Effort (Hours)')

plt.title('Parametric Effort Estimation Model')

plt.legend()

plt.grid(True)

plt.show()
```

Step-by-Step Explanation:

1. **Import Libraries:** We import pandas for data manipulation, sklearn.linear_model.LinearRegression for building the model, and matplotlib.pyplot for visualization.

2. **Sample Data:** We create a sample dataset of historical projects with the number of user stories and the actual effort.

3. **Define Variables:** We specify the 'user_stories' column as the independent variable (X) and 'effort_hours' as the dependent variable (y).

4. **Create and Train Model:** We create a LinearRegression object and train it using the historical data with the fit() method. This process estimates the model parameters (slope and intercept).

5. **Print Model Equation:** We print the resulting linear equation that represents our parametric model.

6. **Make Prediction:** We use the trained model's predict() method to estimate the effort for a new project with a given number of user stories.

7. **Visualize Results:** We create a scatter plot of the historical data and overlay the linear regression line (our parametric model). We also highlight the prediction for the new project.

Documentation:

This simple example demonstrates how to build a basic linear parametric model using historical project data. In a real-world scenario, you would likely have more complex data, potentially involving multiple independent variables, and you might explore different types of statistical models to find the best fit for your data.

Beyond Specific Techniques:

Understanding parametric models and statistical relationships allows you to move beyond simply applying pre-built techniques like COCOMO. You can:

- **Tailor Models to Your Organization:** Calibrate generic models with your own historical data to make them more accurate for your specific context.
- **Build Custom Models:** Develop your own parametric models based on the specific factors that you've found to be strong predictors of effort or other outcomes in your projects.
- **Evaluate Model Accuracy:** Use statistical measures to assess the reliability of your estimation models and identify areas for improvement.
- **Make Data-Driven Decisions:** Base your estimates on empirical evidence rather than just gut feeling or high-level analogies.

My Perspective: Parametric models offer a powerful way to bring rigor and data-driven insights into software estimation. By understanding the underlying statistical relationships in your project history, you can build more reliable and accurate predictive models. While the initial effort of collecting and analyzing data might seem significant, the long-term benefits of more accurate estimates and better project planning can be substantial. Embrace the power of your historical data – it holds the key to more predictable project outcomes.

4.5 Strengths and Weaknesses of Algorithmic Approaches - A Balanced Perspective

We've delved into the world of algorithmic estimation models like COCOMO and the underlying principles of parametric modeling. These approaches offer a more structured and data-driven way to predict project effort, cost, and duration compared to purely judgmental methods. However, like any tool in our estimation toolkit, algorithmic approaches come with their own set of **strengths** and **weaknesses**. Adopting a **balanced perspective** on when and how to use them is crucial for effective project planning.

Think of relying solely on a GPS for navigation. Its strengths are obvious – precise directions, real-time traffic updates. But its weaknesses (dead zones, outdated maps, inability to account for unexpected road closures) mean you shouldn't discard your general knowledge of the area or the ability to ask for directions. Similarly, algorithmic models are powerful but not infallible.

Strengths of Algorithmic Approaches:

- **Objectivity and Consistency:** Algorithmic models apply the same formulas and parameters to different projects, leading to more consistent and less biased estimates compared to subjective opinions that can vary between individuals or over time.
- **Reliance on Data:** These models are often based on historical data, providing a more empirical foundation for estimates rather than just gut feeling or intuition. This can lead to more defensible and credible predictions.

- **Consideration of Multiple Factors:** Models like Intermediate COCOMO explicitly account for various project attributes (product, hardware, personnel, project) through cost drivers, offering a more comprehensive view of the factors influencing effort.

- **What-If Analysis:** Algorithmic models allow for "what-if" scenarios by easily adjusting input parameters (e.g., team size, project complexity) to see their impact on the estimated outcome. This can be valuable for trade-off analysis and contingency planning.

- **Benchmarking and Comparison:** Using a standardized model allows for benchmarking project estimates against industry averages or historical performance within an organization.

- **Automation and Tool Support:** Many software tools exist that implement algorithmic models, making the calculation and analysis process more efficient.

Weaknesses and Limitations of Algorithmic Approaches:

- **Dependence on Data Quality and Availability:** The accuracy of algorithmic models is heavily reliant on the quality and relevance of the historical data used to calibrate them. Poor or insufficient data can lead to inaccurate predictions.

- **Oversimplification of Complex Realities:** Software development is a complex human endeavor. Algorithmic models, by their nature, simplify this reality into mathematical equations, potentially overlooking nuances and unforeseen challenges.

- **Difficulty in Estimating Input Parameters:** Accurately estimating key input parameters like software size (KLOC, function points) early in the project lifecycle can be challenging and prone to its own set of estimation errors.

- **Lagging Indicator:** Historical data reflects past performance and might not accurately predict effort for projects using new technologies, methodologies, or teams with different skill sets.

- **"Black Box" Perception:** Some stakeholders might view the output of algorithmic models as a "black box" if the underlying formulas and parameters are not well understood or transparent. This can lead to a lack of trust or buy-in.

- **Calibration Challenges:** Generic models often need to be calibrated with an organization's specific historical data to be truly effective. This calibration process can be time-consuming and require statistical expertise.

- **Ignoring Qualitative Factors:** Algorithmic models often struggle to account for qualitative factors like team morale, communication effectiveness, stakeholder relationships, and organizational culture, which can significantly impact project outcomes.

- **The "One Size Fits All" Fallacy:** Different types of projects might require different estimation approaches. Applying the same algorithmic model rigidly to all projects might not yield optimal results.

Code Example (Illustrative - Highlighting the impact of inaccurate size estimation on COCOMO effort):

This Python example shows how a variation in the estimated KLOC (a key input parameter for COCOMO) can significantly affect the resulting effort estimate:

Python

```python
import math


def calculate_cocomo_effort(kloc, mode):

    a_coefficients = {"organic": 3.2, "semi-detached": 3.0, "embedded": 2.8}

    b_exponents = {"organic": 1.05, "semi-detached": 1.12, "embedded": 1.20}

    effort = a_coefficients[mode.lower()] * (kloc ** b_exponents[mode.lower()])

    return effort


# Scenario: Semi-Detached Project

mode = "semi-detached"

best_case_kloc = 40

most_likely_kloc = 50
```

```python
worst_case_kloc = 60


effort_best_case = calculate_cocomo_effort(best_case_kloc, mode)

effort_most_likely = calculate_cocomo_effort(most_likely_kloc, mode)

effort_worst_case = calculate_cocomo_effort(worst_case_kloc, mode)


print(f"COCOMO Effort Estimates (Semi-Detached Mode):")

print(f"Best Case (40 KLOC): {effort_best_case:.2f} Person-Months")

print(f"Most Likely (50 KLOC): {effort_most_likely:.2f}
Person-Months")

print(f"Worst Case (60 KLOC): {effort_worst_case:.2f} Person-Months")


percentage_difference = ((effort_worst_case - effort_best_case) /
effort_most_likely) * 100

print(f"\nPercentage difference between best and worst case effort:
{percentage_difference:.2f}%")
```

Step-by-Step Explanation:

1. calculate_cocomo_effort **Function:** A simplified COCOMO effort calculation for a given KLOC and mode (EAF assumed to be 1.0 for simplicity).

2. **Size Variation:** We define best-case, most likely, and worst-case estimates for the software size (KLOC).

3. **Effort Calculation for Each Scenario:** We calculate the estimated effort for each size scenario using the COCOMO formula.

4. **Output:** We print the effort estimates for each case and the percentage difference between the best and worst cases, highlighting how sensitive the model is to the input size estimate.

Documentation:

This example illustrates that even with a sophisticated algorithmic model like COCOMO, the accuracy of the output is highly dependent on the accuracy of the input parameters, particularly the software size. A significant variation in the size estimate can lead to a substantial difference in the predicted effort.

My Perspective: Algorithmic approaches provide valuable structure and a data-driven foundation for software estimation. They excel at consistency and considering multiple influencing factors. However, they should not be treated as a silver bullet. It's crucial to be aware of their limitations, particularly their dependence on data quality and their potential to oversimplify complex realities. The most effective estimation often involves a blend of algorithmic techniques, expert judgment, and a deep understanding of the specific project context. Use algorithms as a powerful tool, but always apply them with critical thinking and a healthy dose of real-world awareness.

Chapter 5: Agile Estimation Strategies - Embracing Uncertainty with Flexibility

Welcome to the dynamic world of Agile estimation! If the previous chapter felt like meticulously measuring ingredients for a precise recipe, this one is more about the art of cooking with a focus on adaptability and continuous feedback. Agile methodologies, with their iterative nature and emphasis on delivering value incrementally, require estimation techniques that are lightweight, collaborative, and responsive to change.

Think about it: in an Agile environment, requirements can evolve, priorities can shift, and the understanding of the product deepens with each iteration. Rigid, upfront estimates often become outdated quickly. Agile estimation strategies embrace this inherent uncertainty, focusing on relative sizing and team velocity to forecast delivery.

5.1 Story Points: Relative Estimation and Velocity - Size Matters (Relatively Speaking)

Let's shift gears and talk about a cornerstone of Agile estimation: **Story Points**. Unlike absolute estimations in hours or days, story points are about **relative estimation**. Instead of asking "How long will this take?", we ask "How big is this compared to something else?". This subtle shift in perspective can often lead to more accurate and less contentious estimates, especially in the face of uncertainty. Think of it as comparing the sizes of different mountains rather than trying to guess their exact heights in meters from a distance.

Imagine you're asked to estimate the time it will take to drive to three different cities you've never visited. Guessing the exact travel time in hours for each might be difficult. However, you could probably say, with more confidence, that City B is roughly twice as far as City A, and City C is a bit further than City B. Story points leverage this intuitive ability to make relative comparisons.

The Core Idea of Relative Estimation:

With story points, the team assigns a numerical value to each user story (or backlog item) that represents its **relative size**, considering factors like:

- **Complexity:** How intricate is the work? Are there many dependencies or edge cases?
- **Effort:** How much work (in terms of person-days or hours) do we anticipate?
- **Risk:** How uncertain are we about the implementation? Are there unknown technologies or potential roadblocks?

The actual unit of a story point is abstract and doesn't directly translate to a specific number of hours. What matters is the *relative* difference between story point values. A story estimated at 5 points is considered roughly twice as "big" as a 3-point story, and five times as "big" as a 1-point story.

The Fibonacci Sequence (Often Used):

Many Agile teams use a modified Fibonacci sequence (0, 1, 2, 3, 5, 8, 13, 20, ...) for assigning story points. This sequence helps to highlight the increasing uncertainty associated with larger estimates. The jumps between numbers become more significant as the values increase, discouraging the illusion of precision for larger, more complex items.

The Process of Assigning Story Points:

Teams typically use techniques like **Planning Poker** (which we discussed earlier) to collaboratively assign story points. The process involves:

1. **Presenting a User Story:** The Product Owner explains the story and its acceptance criteria.
2. **Discussion:** The team asks clarifying questions to ensure a shared understanding.
3. **Silent Voting:** Each team member privately selects a story point value from their deck (or an online tool).
4. **Revealing Votes:** All team members reveal their votes simultaneously.
5. **Discussing Discrepancies:** If there are significant differences, the team members with the highest and lowest votes explain their reasoning.
6. **Re-voting (If Necessary):** The team re-votes until a consensus is reached or the differences are deemed acceptable.

Velocity: Measuring the Team's Capacity:

Once stories are estimated in points and the team starts working in sprints, we can track **velocity**. Velocity is the total number of story points the team successfully completes in a single sprint.

Velocity = Sum of Story Points of Completed Stories in a Sprint

Velocity becomes a crucial metric for:

- **Predicting Future Capacity:** By observing the team's velocity over several sprints, we can get a reliable understanding of how many story points they are likely to complete in future sprints.
- **Sprint Planning:** During sprint planning, the team can use their historical velocity as a guideline for how many story points they can realistically commit to.
- **Monitoring Progress:** Tracking velocity over time can help identify trends and potential issues affecting the team's output.

Using Velocity for Forecasting:

To forecast how long it will take to complete the remaining backlog, we can divide the total remaining story points by the team's average velocity:

Estimated Number of Sprints = Total Remaining Story Points / Average Velocity

Code Example (Illustrative - Tracking velocity and forecasting):

Python

```python
import statistics
```

```python
# Sample sprint data (story points completed per sprint)

sprint_velocities = [25, 30, 28, 32, 27, 31]


# Calculate average velocity

average_velocity = statistics.mean(sprint_velocities)

print(f"Average Team Velocity: {average_velocity:.2f} story points per sprint")


# Remaining backlog in story points

remaining_backlog = 210


# Forecast the number of sprints needed

estimated_sprints = remaining_backlog / average_velocity

print(f"Estimated Sprints to Complete Backlog ({remaining_backlog} points): {estimated_sprints:.2f} sprints")


# Simulate adding a new sprint and recalculating average velocity

new_velocity = 33
```

```python
sprint_velocities.append(new_velocity)

new_average_velocity = statistics.mean(sprint_velocities)

new_estimated_sprints = remaining_backlog / new_average_velocity

print(f"\nAfter one more sprint (velocity {new_velocity}), new average
velocity: {new_average_velocity:.2f}")

print(f"New Estimated Sprints: {new_estimated_sprints:.2f} sprints")
```

Step-by-Step Explanation:

1. **sprint_velocities List:** Represents the total story points completed by the team in each of the past sprints.

2. **Calculate Average Velocity:** We use the statistics.mean() function to calculate the average velocity based on the historical data.

3. **remaining_backlog:** Represents the total number of story points remaining in the product backlog.

4. **Forecast Sprints:** We divide the remaining_backlog by the average_velocity to estimate the number of sprints required to complete the work.

5. **Simulate New Sprint:** We simulate the completion of one more sprint with a new velocity and recalculate the average velocity and the estimated number of remaining sprints.

Documentation:

This simple Python example demonstrates how to calculate a team's average velocity based on historical sprint data and how to use this velocity to forecast the time needed to complete the remaining work in the backlog. As more sprints are completed, the average velocity becomes a more reliable predictor.

My Perspective: Story points and velocity provide a powerful and flexible way to estimate and track progress in Agile projects. The focus on relative size reduces the pressure for precise upfront estimations and encourages valuable discussions within the team. Velocity, as a measure of the team's actual output, provides a realistic basis for forecasting. It's crucial to remember that story points are a unit of work, not time, and velocity is a measure of the team's capacity, not individual performance. Embrace the "relative" nature of story points – it's about understanding the size and complexity of the work in relation to each other, allowing for more adaptable and realistic planning.

5.2 T-Shirt Sizing and Its Mapping to Effort - High-Level Simplicity

Sometimes, when dealing with a large backlog or in the early stages of a project, the granularity of story points might feel too detailed. That's where **T-Shirt Sizing** comes in. It's a high-level, intuitive relative estimation technique that uses familiar t-shirt sizes (XS, S, M, L, XL, XXL) to represent the relative size and complexity of backlog items. Think of it as sorting tasks into broad categories before getting down to the nitty-gritty of individual point values. It's like organizing your closet by general size before meticulously folding each item.

The Core Idea:

T-shirt sizing simplifies relative estimation by using easily understandable categories. The team collectively assigns a size to each backlog item based on a gut feeling of its overall magnitude, considering factors like complexity, effort, and risk, just like with story points. The key difference is the level of abstraction.

The Typical Sizes and Their Meaning (Qualitative):

- **XS (Extra Small):** Very small effort, likely a quick and simple task.
- **S (Small):** Relatively small effort, might involve a few straightforward steps.
- **M (Medium):** Moderate effort, likely involves several tasks and some complexity.
- **L (Large):** Significant effort, could involve multiple developers or a considerable amount of work.
- **XL (Extra Large):** Substantial effort, likely a complex undertaking with potential risks.
- **XXL (Extra Extra Large):** Very large and complex effort, might need to be broken down further. Often indicates an epic rather than a single story.

The Process of T-Shirt Sizing:

Similar to Planning Poker, the team collaborates to assign sizes:

1. **Presenting a Backlog Item:** The Product Owner describes the item.
2. **Discussion:** The team clarifies any questions.
3. **Silent Voting:** Each team member privately selects a t-shirt size.
4. **Revealing Votes:** Everyone reveals their chosen size simultaneously.
5. **Discussing Discrepancies:** The team discusses the reasoning behind significantly different sizes.
6. **Re-sizing (If Necessary):** The team re-votes until a consensus is reached.

Mapping T-Shirt Sizes to Effort (Quantitative):

The real power of t-shirt sizing for estimation comes when we **map these qualitative sizes to quantitative measures** like story points or estimated time ranges. This mapping allows us to use the high-level estimates for forecasting and capacity planning.

The mapping can be team-specific and should be based on the team's historical data and understanding of their own velocity or effort patterns. A common example of a mapping to story points using a modified Fibonacci sequence is:

T-Shirt Size	Typical Story Points Range	Representative Story Point

XS	1	1
S	2-3	2
M	5-8	5
L	13-20	13
XL	20-40	20
XXL	40+ (Needs Breakdown)	-

Using the Mapping for Forecasting:

Once the mapping is established, we can:

1. **Estimate the entire backlog using t-shirt sizes.**
2. **Convert the t-shirt sizes to their corresponding story point values (or representative values).**
3. **Use the total estimated story points and the team's velocity to forecast the number of sprints required.**

Alternatively, teams can directly map t-shirt sizes to estimated time ranges (e.g., S = 1-2 days, M = 3-5 days), although this brings back some of the challenges of absolute estimation. Mapping to story points and then using velocity is generally preferred in Agile.

Code Example (Illustrative - Mapping T-Shirt Sizes to Story Points and Forecasting):

Python

```python
import statistics


# Define the T-Shirt size to Story Point mapping

size_mapping = {"XS": 1, "S": 2, "M": 5, "L": 13, "XL": 20}


# Sample backlog estimated using T-Shirt sizes

backlog_sizes = ["M", "S", "L", "XS", "M", "XL", "S", "M"]


# Convert backlog sizes to story points

backlog_points = [size_mapping.get(size, 0) for size in backlog_sizes]

total_points = sum(backlog_points)
```

```python
print(f"Backlog estimated in T-Shirt sizes: {backlog_sizes}")

print(f"Mapped story points for the backlog: {backlog_points}")

print(f"Total estimated story points: {total_points}")


# Sample average velocity of the team

average_velocity = 25


# Forecast the number of sprints

estimated_sprints = total_points / average_velocity

print(f"Average team velocity: {average_velocity} story points per
sprint")

print(f"Estimated sprints to complete the backlog: {estimated_sprints:.2f}
sprints")


# Function to get a representative point for a size (handling XXL)

def get_representative_points(size):

    return size_mapping.get(size, 0) if size != "XXL" else None
```

```
# Example of handling XXL - indicating need for breakdown

xxl_item = "XXL"

representative_points_xxl = get_representative_points(xxl_item)

if representative_points_xxl is None:

    print(f"\nItem sized '{xxl_item}' needs to be broken down into smaller
stories.")
```

Step-by-Step Explanation:

1. **size_mapping Dictionary:** Defines the mapping between t-shirt sizes and representative story point values.

2. **backlog_sizes List:** Represents a sample product backlog where each item has been estimated using t-shirt sizes.

3. **Convert to Story Points:** We use a list comprehension and the get() method of the dictionary to convert the t-shirt sizes in the backlog to their corresponding story point values. If a size is not found in the mapping, it defaults to 0.

4. **Calculate Total Points:** We sum the mapped story points to get the total estimated size of the backlog.

5. **Forecast Sprints:** We use a sample average_velocity to estimate the number of sprints required to complete the total story points.

6. **get_representative_points Function:** This function handles the "XXL" size, returning None to indicate that such large items

should be broken down further rather than being directly mapped to a point value for forecasting.

Documentation:

This Python example demonstrates how to map t-shirt sizes to story points and use the resulting point estimates along with the team's velocity to forecast project completion. It also highlights the importance of breaking down very large items (like those sized "XXL") into smaller, more manageable stories.

My Perspective: T-shirt sizing offers a valuable entry point to relative estimation, especially when dealing with a large and somewhat undefined backlog. Its simplicity makes it easy for all stakeholders to understand and participate in the estimation process. The key is to establish a clear and consistent mapping to a more granular unit like story points to enable meaningful forecasting and capacity planning. Think of t-shirt sizing as a first pass – a way to get a general sense of the "bigness" before diving into the more precise measurements. It's a great way to start the conversation and build a shared understanding of the relative effort involved.

5.3 Affinity Estimating for Rapid Backlog Assessment - Grouping for Insight

When faced with a large backlog of user stories or features that need to be estimated quickly at a high level, techniques like detailed Planning Poker for every item can become time-consuming and inefficient. That's where **Affinity Estimating** shines. It's a rapid, collaborative technique that leverages the team's collective intuition to group backlog items into relative size categories. Think of it as a quick sorting exercise where the "size" emerges from the grouping rather than being explicitly assigned to each item individually at the outset. It's like organizing a messy room by first creating general piles (clothes, books, electronics) before meticulously sorting within each pile.

The Core Idea:

Affinity Estimating involves the team collectively placing backlog items (typically written on sticky notes) into groups based on their perceived relative size or effort. These groups often correspond to t-shirt sizes or broad story point ranges. The process emphasizes speed and shared understanding over precise individual estimates.

The Steps in Affinity Estimating:

1. **Prepare the Backlog Items:** Write each user story or backlog item on a separate sticky note. Ensure the descriptions are concise and understandable to the entire team.

2. **Establish the Scale:** Define the relative size categories you'll be using. This could be t-shirt sizes (XS, S, M, L, XL), broad story point ranges (e.g., 1, 2-3, 5-8, 13+), or even just relative terms (Small, Medium, Large). Place labeled cards representing these categories across a whiteboard or table.

3. **Silent Placement:** The team members silently take turns placing sticky notes under the category that they feel best represents the item's relative size. There's typically no discussion during this initial placement phase to avoid anchoring.

4. **Review and Adjust:** Once all items are placed, the team reviews the groupings. This is where the discussion begins. If an item seems misplaced, anyone can move it to a different category, and a brief discussion ensues to understand the different perspectives. The goal is to reach a shared understanding of the relative sizes.

5. **Finalize the Groupings:** After the discussion and adjustments, the team agrees on the final placement of the backlog items within the categories.

6. **Assign Representative Values (Optional but Recommended):** Once the items are grouped, the team can assign a representative story point value (or a range) to each category (as we saw with t-shirt sizing). This allows for quantitative forecasting using velocity.

Benefits of Affinity Estimating:

- **Speed and Efficiency:** It's much faster than estimating each item individually with Planning Poker, especially for large backlogs.
- **Collaborative and Engaging:** It encourages the entire team to participate and build a shared understanding of the backlog size.
- **High-Level Overview:** It provides a quick, high-level assessment of the relative size of the entire backlog.
- **Identifies Outliers:** Items that are consistently placed in the "too big" category (like XL or XXL equivalents) quickly become apparent and can be flagged for further breakdown.
- **Reduces Anchoring:** The initial silent placement helps to minimize the influence of the first person to estimate.

- **Facilitates Discussion:** The movement and discussion phase surfaces different interpretations and assumptions.

Limitations of Affinity Estimating:

- **Lower Precision:** It doesn't provide the same level of granularity as individual story point estimation.
- **Potential for Subjectivity:** The initial placement relies on the team's gut feeling, which can be subjective.
- **Requires a Shared Understanding of Size:** The team needs to have a relatively consistent understanding of what each size category represents.
- **Less Detail for Individual Items:** While it gives a sense of the overall size, it doesn't delve into the specific complexities of each item as deeply as Planning Poker.

Code Example (Illustrative - Simulating Affinity Grouping and Point Assignment):

Python

```python
import random

from collections import defaultdict


# Sample backlog items

backlog = [f"Feature {i}" for i in range(20)]
```

```python
# Define size categories and representative points

size_categories = {"XS": 1, "S": 2, "M": 5, "L": 13}


# Simulate team members placing items into categories (randomly for demonstration)

initial_grouping = defaultdict(list)

team_members = ["Alice", "Bob", "Charlie"]

for item in backlog:

    category = random.choice(list(size_categories.keys()))

    initial_grouping[category].append(item)


print("Initial Item Grouping:")

for category, items in initial_grouping.items():

    print(f"{category}: {', '.join(items)}")


# Simulate a simplified review and adjustment (no actual logic here)

# In a real session, the team would discuss and move items.
```

```python
final_grouping = {

    "XS": [item for item in backlog if "Feature" in item and
int(item.split()[-1]) < 3],

    "S": [item for item in backlog if 3 <= int(item.split()[-1]) < 8],

    "M": [item for item in backlog if 8 <= int(item.split()[-1]) < 15],

    "L": [item for item in backlog if 15 <= int(item.split()[-1]) < 20],

}


print("\nFinal Item Grouping after Review:")

for category, items in final_grouping.items():

    print(f"{category}: {', '.join(items)}")


# Calculate total estimated story points based on the final grouping

total_points = 0

for category, items in final_grouping.items():

    total_points += len(items) * size_categories.get(category, 0)


print(f"\nTotal Estimated Story Points for the Backlog: {total_points}")
```

Step-by-Step Explanation:

1. backlog **List:** Represents a sample backlog of user stories.
2. size_categories **Dictionary:** Defines the size categories (XS, S, M, L) and their corresponding representative story point values.
3. initial_grouping: This uses defaultdict(list) to simulate the initial silent placement of backlog items into random size categories by the team members.
4. **Print Initial Grouping:** Shows the initial, potentially scattered, placement of items.
5. final_grouping: This simulates the outcome after the team has reviewed and adjusted the groupings through discussion. The logic here is arbitrary for demonstration; in a real session, it would be based on team consensus.
6. **Print Final Grouping:** Shows the refined groupings after the collaborative adjustment.
7. **Calculate Total Estimated Points:** We iterate through the final_grouping and multiply the number of items in each category by its representative story point value to get a total estimated size of the backlog in story points.

Documentation:

This Python example provides a simplified illustration of how backlog items might be initially grouped and then refined through a collaborative affinity estimating process. It also shows how the final groupings can be used with a defined mapping to calculate a total estimated story point value for the backlog.

My Perspective: Affinity Estimating is a valuable technique for quickly gaining a high-level understanding of the relative size of a large backlog. Its collaborative nature fosters shared understanding and can highlight items that need further discussion or breakdown. While it sacrifices the precision of individual story point estimation, its speed and efficiency make it ideal for initial backlog grooming and release planning. Think of it as a first-pass filter that helps the team quickly see the "big picture" before zooming in on the details of individual stories. Combining it with more granular techniques like Planning Poker for the top priority items can create a well-rounded estimation strategy.

5.4 The Bucket System for Categorizing Effort - Sorting into Levels

Another rapid and collaborative technique for high-level backlog estimation is the **Bucket System**. Similar to Affinity Estimating, it focuses on quickly categorizing backlog items based on their relative size or effort. However, instead of freely grouping items, the Bucket System uses predefined "buckets" representing different levels of effort or story point ranges. Think of it as sorting items into labeled containers to get a quick overview of the distribution of work. It's like organizing your tasks for the week by assigning them to "Quick Wins," "Medium Effort," and "Major Projects" buckets.

The Core Idea:

The Bucket System involves the team placing backlog items into predefined categories or "buckets," each representing a specific range of effort or story points. This allows for a quick and shared understanding of the relative size of the backlog without getting bogged down in detailed estimation of individual items.

The Typical Steps of the Bucket System:

1. **Define the Buckets:** The team first agrees on the number and range of the buckets. These buckets should represent distinct levels of effort or story points that are meaningful to the team. Common examples include:

   - **T-Shirt Sizes:** XS, S, M, L, XL
   - **Story Point Ranges:** 1-2, 3-5, 8-13, 20+
   - **Effort Levels:** Very Small, Small, Medium, Large, Very Large
   - **Numerical Ranges (e.g., Ideal Days):** 0.5-1, 2-3, 4-7, 8+

Label these buckets clearly on a whiteboard or using an online collaboration tool.

2. **Prepare the Backlog Items:** Write each user story or backlog item on a separate sticky note.

3. **Silent Placement:** Team members silently take turns placing sticky notes into the bucket that they believe best represents the item's relative size or effort. Similar to Affinity Estimating, this initial silent phase helps to avoid anchoring.

4. **Review and Discuss:** Once all items are placed, the team reviews the distribution across the buckets. Items that seem misplaced or

where there are significant disagreements can be discussed. The goal is to reach a shared understanding and move items to the appropriate buckets based on the team's collective judgment.

5. **Finalize Placement:** After the discussion, the team agrees on the final placement of all backlog items within the buckets.

6. **Assign Representative Values (Optional but Recommended):** For forecasting purposes, the team can assign a representative story point value (or the midpoint of the range) to each bucket.

Benefits of the Bucket System:

- **Speed and Efficiency:** It's a quick way to get a high-level estimate for a large backlog.
- **Collaborative and Inclusive:** It involves the entire team in the estimation process.
- **Provides a Shared Understanding:** The act of discussing and placing items in buckets helps the team align on the relative size of the work.
- **Highlights Large Items:** Items consistently placed in the "Large" or "Very Large" buckets become visible and can be flagged for potential splitting.
- **Structured Categorization:** The predefined buckets provide a clearer structure compared to the free-form grouping of Affinity Estimating.

Limitations of the Bucket System:

- **Lower Granularity:** It provides a less precise estimate than individual story pointing.
- **Reliance on Consistent Bucket Definitions:** The effectiveness depends on the team having a shared understanding of what each bucket represents.
- **Potential for Boundary Disputes:** Items near the boundaries of buckets might lead to more discussion and potential disagreements on which bucket is most appropriate.
- **Still Relies on Relative Judgment:** The initial placement is based on the team's subjective assessment of relative size.

Code Example (Illustrative - Simulating the Bucket System and Point Calculation):

Python

```python
import random

from collections import defaultdict



# Sample backlog items

backlog = [f"Feature {i}" for i in range(20)]



# Define the buckets and their representative story points

buckets = {
```

```python
    "Small (1-2)": 1.5,

    "Medium (3-5)": 4,

    "Large (8-13)": 10.5,

    "X-Large (20+)": 20,

}


bucket_labels = list(buckets.keys())


# Simulate team members placing items into buckets (randomly for
demonstration)

item_placement = defaultdict(list)

team_members = ["Alice", "Bob", "Charlie"]

for item in backlog:

    bucket = random.choice(bucket_labels)

    item_placement[bucket].append(item)


print("Initial Item Placement in Buckets:")

for bucket, items in item_placement.items():
```

```python
    print(f"{bucket}: {', '.join(items)}")



# Simulate a simplified review and adjustment (no actual logic here)

# In a real session, the team would discuss and move items.

final_placement = {

    "Small (1-2)": [item for item in backlog if int(item.split()[-1]) < 5],

    "Medium (3-5)": [item for item in backlog if 5 <= int(item.split()[-1])
< 12],

    "Large (8-13)": [item for item in backlog if 12 <= int(item.split()[-1])
< 18],

    "X-Large (20+)": [item for item in backlog if 18 <= int(item.split()[-1])
< 20],

}



print("\nFinal Item Placement after Review:")

for bucket, items in final_placement.items():

    print(f"{bucket}: {', '.join(items)}")
```

```python
# Calculate total estimated story points based on the final placement

total_points = 0

for bucket, items in final_placement.items():

    representative_point = buckets.get(bucket, 0)

    total_points += len(items) * representative_point



print(f"\nTotal Estimated Story Points for the Backlog: {total_points}")
```

Step-by-Step Explanation:

1. **backlog List:** Represents a sample backlog of user stories.
2. **buckets Dictionary:** Defines the effort/story point buckets (e.g., "Small (1-2)") and their representative story point values (e.g., 1.5 for "Small (1-2)").
3. **bucket_labels:** A list of the bucket labels for random selection in the initial placement.
4. **item_placement:** This defaultdict(list) simulates the initial silent placement of backlog items into random buckets by team members.
5. **Print Initial Placement:** Shows the initial distribution of items across the buckets.

6. **final_placement:** This simulates the outcome after the team has reviewed and adjusted the placement through discussion. The logic here is arbitrary for demonstration.

7. **Print Final Placement:** Shows the refined distribution of items after the collaborative adjustment.

8. **Calculate Total Estimated Points:** We iterate through the final_placement and multiply the number of items in each bucket by its representative story point value to get a total estimated size of the backlog in story points.

Documentation:

This Python example illustrates the basic mechanics of the Bucket System. Backlog items are placed into predefined buckets representing effort levels or story point ranges. After a collaborative review, the final distribution can be used with the representative point values of each bucket to calculate a total estimated size of the backlog.

My Perspective: The Bucket System offers a good balance between speed and structure for high-level backlog estimation. The predefined buckets provide a clearer framework than the free grouping of Affinity Estimating, making it easier for teams to align on relative sizes. It's particularly useful during initial backlog grooming sessions or when a quick, overall estimate is needed. By assigning representative values to the buckets, teams can also leverage velocity for forecasting. Remember that the key to an effective Bucket System is having well-defined and consistently understood buckets that resonate with the team's experience.

5.5 Connecting Agile Estimates to Release Planning - From Points to Timelines

We've explored various Agile estimation techniques, primarily focusing on sizing work relative to each other using story points or t-shirt sizes. But these relative measures need to be translated into something more tangible for release planning: **timelines**. Connecting our Agile estimates to a release schedule involves understanding the team's capacity (velocity) and the total scope of work (estimated story points) to predict when we can deliver a set of features. Think of it as using the "size" of the work and the "speed" of the team to calculate the "travel time" to reach our release destination.

Imagine you're planning a multi-stage hike. You've estimated the difficulty of each segment using a relative scale (easy, moderate, hard). To figure out when you'll reach the final destination, you need to know your hiking pace (miles per day) and the total "difficulty" converted into a comparable unit. Similarly, in Agile release planning, we convert story points into a timeline using the team's velocity.

The Key Steps in Connecting Agile Estimates to Release Planning:

1. **Backlog Prioritization and Scope Definition:** The Product Owner, in collaboration with stakeholders, prioritizes the backlog and defines the scope of the initial release. This involves selecting the user stories and features that are essential for the first release.

2. **Estimate the Release Backlog:** The prioritized backlog items for the release are estimated using story points (or t-shirt sizes

converted to points).[2] This gives us the total estimated size of the release in story points.

3. **Determine Team Velocity:** As discussed earlier, velocity is the average number of story points the team completes in a sprint. This is typically calculated based on the team's performance over the last few sprints. It's crucial to use a stable and representative velocity.

4. **Calculate the Number of Sprints:** Divide the total estimated story points for the release by the team's average velocity:

Estimated Number of Sprints for Release = Total Release Story Points / Average Velocity

5. **Translate Sprints to a Timeline:** Multiply the estimated number of sprints by the duration of each sprint (e.g., 2 weeks) to get an estimated release duration:

Estimated Release Duration = Estimated Number of Sprints * Sprint Length

6. **Factor in Buffer and Contingencies:** It's wise to add a buffer to the estimated release timeline to account for unforeseen issues, dependencies, team capacity fluctuations (e.g., holidays, sick days), and potential scope changes. The size of the buffer can be based on historical experience and the level of risk associated with the release.

7. **Communicate and Iterate:** Share the estimated release timeline with stakeholders, highlighting any assumptions and uncertainties. Release plans are not set in stone and should be revisited and adjusted as the project progresses and the team's velocity becomes more stable.[3]

Code Example (Illustrative - Calculating Release Timeline):

Python

```python
import statistics


# Estimated story points for the initial release backlog

total_release_points = 280


# Sample of the team's velocity over the last 5 sprints

sprint_velocities = [25, 30, 28, 32, 27]


# Calculate average velocity

average_velocity = statistics.mean(sprint_velocities)

print(f"Average Team Velocity: {average_velocity:.2f} story points per sprint")
```

```python
# Standard sprint length in weeks

sprint_length_weeks = 2


# Calculate the estimated number of sprints for the release

estimated_sprints = total_release_points / average_velocity

print(f"Estimated Sprints for Release ({total_release_points} points): {estimated_sprints:.2f} sprints")


# Calculate the estimated release duration in weeks

estimated_release_duration_weeks = estimated_sprints * sprint_length_weeks

print(f"Estimated Release Duration: {estimated_release_duration_weeks:.2f} weeks")


# Add a buffer (e.g., 1 sprint)

buffer_sprints = 1

adjusted_release_duration_weeks = (estimated_sprints + buffer_sprints) * sprint_length_weeks
```

```
print(f"Estimated Release Duration (with {buffer_sprints} sprint buffer):
{adjusted_release_duration_weeks:.2f} weeks")


# Assuming a start date, we can calculate the estimated release date

from datetime import datetime, timedelta


start_date_str = "2025-05-05"  # Example start date (Monday)

start_date = datetime.strptime(start_date_str, "%Y-%m-%d").date()

estimated_release_date = start_date +
timedelta(weeks=adjusted_release_duration_weeks)

print(f"Estimated Release Date (starting {start_date_str}):
{estimated_release_date.strftime('%Y-%m-%d')}")
```

Step-by-Step Explanation:

1. **total_release_points:** Represents the sum of story points for all the user stories included in the initial release scope.
2. **sprint_velocities:** A list of the team's completed story points in recent sprints.
3. **Calculate Average Velocity:** We calculate the average velocity using statistics.mean().
4. **sprint_length_weeks:** Defines the duration of a single sprint in weeks.

5. **Calculate Estimated Sprints:** We divide the total_release_points by the average_velocity to estimate how many sprints it will take to complete the release scope.

6. **Calculate Estimated Release Duration:** We multiply the estimated_sprints by the sprint_length_weeks to get the estimated release duration in weeks.

7. **Add Buffer:** We introduce a buffer_sprints variable and add it to the estimated number of sprints to account for contingencies.

8. **Calculate Estimated Release Date:** We use the datetime and timedelta objects to calculate a potential release date based on a hypothetical start date and the adjusted release duration.

Documentation:

This Python example demonstrates how to use the total estimated story points for a release and the team's average velocity to forecast the number of sprints and the overall release duration. It also shows how to incorporate a buffer and calculate a potential release date based on a starting point.

Key Considerations for Agile Release Planning:

- **Velocity Stability:** Use a velocity that is relatively stable over several sprints. Significant fluctuations might indicate underlying issues that need to be addressed.
- **Team Capacity:** Account for team member availability (vacations, training) when projecting velocity for future sprints.

- **Definition of Done:** Ensure a consistent "Definition of Done" so that story points completed in each sprint represent truly finished work.

- **Scope Changes:** Be prepared for scope changes during the release. These will impact the total story points and the projected timeline. Regularly review and adjust the plan as needed.

- **Dependencies:** Identify and manage dependencies between stories, as these can affect the order in which work can be completed and potentially the overall timeline.[4]

- **Stakeholder Communication:** Maintain open and transparent communication with stakeholders about the release plan, including assumptions, risks, and any changes to the projected timeline.

My Perspective: Connecting Agile estimates to release planning is about turning our relative sizing of work into a tangible timeline. Velocity acts as the crucial link, translating the "size" of the backlog into the "speed" at which the team can deliver.[5] By understanding our velocity, the total scope of the release, and factoring in realistic buffers, we can create a roadmap that provides valuable insights for stakeholders. Remember that release plans are living documents that should be continuously reviewed and adjusted based on the team's progress and any changes in the project landscape. It's about providing a realistic expectation while remaining flexible and adaptive.

Chapter 6: Data-Driven and Emerging Techniques - Learning from the Past, Looking to the Future

We've explored expert opinions and the structured world of algorithms. Now, let's step into an era where data takes center stage. Data-driven estimation leverages the wealth of information from past projects to make more informed predictions about the future. And as technology continues to evolve, exciting new techniques, including machine learning, are beginning to reshape the landscape of software estimation.

Think about it: every software project generates a treasure trove of data – effort spent, timelines, team composition, defect rates, and much more. By systematically collecting and analyzing this information, we can identify patterns, understand influencing factors, and build more accurate estimation models.

6.1 Utilizing Historical Project Data for Improved Accuracy - Mining Your Project Archives

We've explored various estimation techniques, but arguably one of the most powerful tools in our arsenal is our own **historical project data**. Just like a seasoned gold prospector sifts through earth to find valuable nuggets, we can "mine" our project archives for insights that can significantly improve the accuracy of our future estimates. Think of it as learning from our past successes and mistakes, allowing us to make more informed predictions about the future.

Imagine a weather forecaster who only relied on general meteorological principles without looking at past weather patterns in their specific region. Their predictions would likely be less accurate than someone who analyzes years of local temperature, rainfall, and wind data. Similarly, ignoring our own project history means we're missing out on valuable context that can make our estimates far more reliable.

The Value of Historical Project Data:

Our completed projects hold a wealth of information that can inform future estimations, including:

- **Actual Effort vs. Estimated Effort:** Identifying patterns of underestimation or overestimation for different types of tasks or projects.
- **Actual Duration vs. Estimated Duration:** Understanding how long similar projects actually took.
- **Team Velocity Trends:** Observing how the team's capacity has evolved over time.
- **Impact of Project Characteristics:** Correlating project attributes (e.g., size, complexity, technology) with actual outcomes.
- **Frequency and Impact of Risks:** Learning from past challenges and incorporating contingency planning into future estimates.
- **Productivity Rates:** Calculating actual person-hours per story point, function point, or line of code for different contexts.

The Process of Mining Your Project Archives:

1. **Identify Relevant Data Sources:** Determine where your historical project data is stored. This might include project management tools, timesheets, issue tracking systems, post-project reviews, and even team communication logs.

2. **Extract and Clean the Data:** Gather the necessary data points and ensure its quality. This might involve cleaning up inconsistencies, handling missing values, and standardizing formats.

3. **Define Key Metrics:** Decide which metrics you want to analyze to improve your estimations (e.g., estimation accuracy, productivity, velocity).

4. **Analyze the Data:** Use statistical methods and visualization techniques to identify trends, patterns, and correlations in your historical data.

5. **Calibrate Estimation Models:** Use the insights gained from the data analysis to calibrate your chosen estimation techniques (e.g., adjusting COCOMO coefficients, refining story point mappings, establishing more realistic velocity ranges).

6. **Incorporate Lessons Learned:** Document the key findings and integrate them into your estimation guidelines and processes. Regularly review and update these guidelines as more data becomes available.

Code Example (Illustrative - Analyzing Estimation Accuracy):

This Python example demonstrates how to analyze historical data to calculate the estimation accuracy for past tasks:

Python

```python
import pandas as pd

import matplotlib.pyplot as plt


# Sample historical estimation data

data = {'task': ['Task A', 'Task B', 'Task C', 'Task D', 'Task E', 'Task F'],

    'estimated_hours': [20, 15, 30, 25, 18, 35],

    'actual_hours': [25, 12, 33, 28, 15, 40]}

df = pd.DataFrame(data)


# Calculate the estimation error (actual - estimated)

df['error'] = df['actual_hours'] - df['estimated_hours']


# Calculate the percentage error

df['percentage_error'] = (df['error'] / df['estimated_hours']) * 100
```

```python
print("Historical Estimation Accuracy:")

print(df)


# Visualize the percentage error

plt.figure(figsize=(10, 6))

plt.bar(df['task'], df['percentage_error'], color=['red' if x > 0 else 'green'
for x in df['percentage_error']])

plt.ylabel('Percentage Error (%)')

plt.xlabel('Task')

plt.title('Estimation Accuracy for Past Tasks')

plt.axhline(0, color='black', linewidth=0.8)

plt.grid(axis='y', linestyle='--')

plt.show()


# Calculate overall average percentage error

average_percentage_error = df['percentage_error'].mean()

print(f"\nOverall Average Percentage Error:
{average_percentage_error:.2f}%")
```

```python
if average_percentage_error > 0:

    print("On average, we tend to underestimate.")

elif average_percentage_error < 0:

    print("On average, we tend to overestimate.")

else:

    print("On average, our estimations are quite accurate.")
```

Step-by-Step Explanation:

1. **Import Libraries:** We import pandas for data manipulation and matplotlib.pyplot for visualization.
2. **Sample Data:** We create a sample DataFrame containing historical task estimations and actual effort.
3. **Calculate Error:** We calculate the absolute error (actual - estimated hours) for each task.
4. **Calculate Percentage Error:** We calculate the percentage error to normalize the error based on the initial estimate.
5. **Print Data:** We display the DataFrame showing the estimation accuracy for each task.
6. **Visualize Error:** We create a bar chart visualizing the percentage error for each task, using different colors for overestimation and underestimation.

7. **Calculate Average Percentage Error:** We calculate the mean of the percentage error to understand the overall trend in our estimations.

8. **Interpret Average Error:** We provide a basic interpretation of the average percentage error.

Documentation:

This Python example demonstrates a simple analysis of historical estimation accuracy. By calculating and visualizing the estimation error, we can identify if there's a consistent tendency to under- or overestimate. This insight can then be used to adjust future estimates.

Key Considerations for Utilizing Historical Data:

- **Data Consistency:** Ensure that your historical data is recorded consistently across projects.
- **Context is Key:** Understand the context surrounding past projects (e.g., team experience, technology used, project complexity) when applying historical data to new estimations.
- **Data Volume:** The more historical data you have, the more reliable your analysis will be.
- **Regular Analysis:** Make analyzing historical data a regular part of your estimation process.
- **Tooling:** Consider using data analysis tools and techniques to efficiently process and visualize your project archives.
- **Don't Just Look at Averages:** Explore the distribution of errors and identify patterns for specific types of tasks or projects.

My Perspective: Mining your project archives is like having a crystal ball that shows you the patterns of your past. By systematically analyzing this data, we can move beyond guesswork and intuition to make more informed and accurate estimations. It's an investment that pays off in more realistic project plans, better resource allocation, and increased stakeholder trust. Don't let your valuable project history gather dust – actively mine it for the gold of improved estimation accuracy.

6.2 Introduction to Statistical Concepts in Estimation - Understanding the Numbers

As we aim for more accurate and reliable estimations, moving beyond simple averages and gut feelings towards a more data-driven approach becomes essential. This is where understanding basic **statistical concepts** comes into play. These concepts provide us with the tools to analyze our historical data, quantify uncertainty, and make more informed predictions. Think of it as moving from simply saying "it will probably take a while" to being able to say "based on past projects, there's an 80% chance this will take between X and Y weeks."

Imagine a doctor diagnosing a patient. They don't just rely on a single measurement like blood pressure. They consider a range of factors, compare them to typical values and distributions, and might even calculate probabilities of different outcomes. Similarly, in estimation, understanding statistical concepts helps us interpret our data more effectively and make more nuanced predictions.

Key Statistical Concepts for Estimation:

1. **Data Distribution:** Understanding how our historical data (e.g., actual effort, estimation errors) is spread out. Is it clustered around an average, or is it more spread out? Common distributions include the normal distribution (bell curve) and skewed distributions. Visualizing data with histograms or box plots can be very helpful here.

2. **Measures of Central Tendency:** These tell us about the "typical" value in our data.

   - **Mean (Average):** The sum of all values divided by the number of values. Useful for symmetrical distributions without significant outliers.
   - **Median:** The middle value when the data is ordered. Less affected by outliers than the mean.
   - **Mode:** The most frequently occurring value.

3. **Measures of Dispersion (Variability):** These tell us how spread out our data is, indicating the level of uncertainty.
   - **Range:** The difference between the maximum and minimum values. Simple but sensitive to outliers.
   - **Variance:** The average of the squared differences from the mean. Provides a measure of overall spread.
   - **Standard Deviation:** The square root of the variance. Easier to interpret as it's in the same units as the data. A higher standard deviation indicates greater variability and thus higher uncertainty in our estimates.

4. **Percentiles and Quartiles:** These divide our data into segments. For example, the 25th percentile (Q1) is the value below which 25% of the data falls. The 50th percentile is the median (Q2), and the 75th percentile (Q3) is the value below which 75% of the data falls. These can help us understand the range of likely outcomes (e.g., "80% of similar tasks were completed within X days").

5. **Confidence Intervals:** A range of values within which we are reasonably confident (e.g., 90% confident) that the true value of a parameter (like the average estimation error) lies. Confidence intervals provide a way to quantify the uncertainty in our estimates.

6. **Correlation:** A statistical measure that describes the strength and direction of a linear relationship between two variables (e.g., project size and actual effort). A positive correlation means that as one variable increases, the other tends to increase as well. Correlation doesn't imply causation.

7. **Regression Analysis:** A statistical technique used to model the relationship between a dependent variable (the one we want to predict, like effort) and one or more independent variables (predictors, like size or complexity). Linear regression is a common type. Regression models can be used to build parametric estimation models.

Code Example (Illustrative - Basic Statistical Analysis of Historical Effort Data):

Python

```python
import pandas as pd

import numpy as np

import matplotlib.pyplot as plt

from scipy import stats


# Sample historical effort data (in person-hours) for similar tasks

effort_data = [25, 30, 28, 35, 22, 40, 32, 27, 38, 31]


# Create a Pandas Series for easier analysis

effort_series = pd.Series(effort_data)


# Calculate measures of central tendency

mean_effort = effort_series.mean()

median_effort = effort_series.median()
```

```python
mode_effort = effort_series.mode()


print(f"Mean Effort: {mean_effort:.2f} hours")

print(f"Median Effort: {median_effort:.2f} hours")

print(f"Mode Effort: {mode_effort.tolist()} hours")


# Calculate measures of dispersion

range_effort = effort_series.max() - effort_series.min()

variance_effort = effort_series.var()

std_dev_effort = effort_series.std()


print(f"\nRange of Effort: {range_effort} hours")

print(f"Variance of Effort: {variance_effort:.2f}")

print(f"Standard Deviation of Effort: {std_dev_effort:.2f}")


# Calculate percentiles

percentile_25 = effort_series.quantile(0.25)
```

```python
percentile_75 = effort_series.quantile(0.75)

print(f"\n25th Percentile (Q1): {percentile_25:.2f} hours")

print(f"75th Percentile (Q3): {percentile_75:.2f} hours")


# Visualize the distribution with a histogram

plt.hist(effort_series, bins=5, edgecolor='black')

plt.xlabel('Effort (Hours)')

plt.ylabel('Frequency')

plt.title('Distribution of Historical Effort')

plt.grid(axis='y', alpha=0.75)

plt.show()


# (Illustrative) Calculate a 90% confidence interval (assuming normal
distribution)

confidence_level = 0.90

alpha = 1 - confidence_level

degrees_freedom = len(effort_series) - 1

t_critical = stats.t.ppf(1 - alpha/2, degrees_freedom)
```

```
margin_of_error = t_critical * (std_dev_effort /
np.sqrt(len(effort_series)))

confidence_interval = (mean_effort - margin_of_error, mean_effort +
margin_of_error)

print(f"\n90% Confidence Interval for Mean Effort:
({confidence_interval[0:.2f]}, {confidence_interval[1:.2f]}) hours")
```

Step-by-Step Explanation:

1. **Import Libraries:** We import pandas for data handling, numpy for numerical operations, matplotlib.pyplot for plotting, and scipy.stats for statistical functions.
2. **Sample Data:** We create a list of historical effort data.
3. **Pandas Series:** We convert the list to a Pandas Series for easier statistical analysis.
4. **Central Tendency:** We calculate the mean, median, and mode of the effort data.
5. **Dispersion:** We calculate the range, variance, and standard deviation to understand the spread of the data.
6. **Percentiles:** We calculate the 25th and 75th percentiles (quartiles).
7. **Histogram:** We create a histogram to visualize the distribution of the effort data.
8. **Confidence Interval (Illustrative):** We demonstrate how to calculate a 90% confidence interval for the mean effort, assuming a normal distribution (which might not always be the case with real-world data, but serves as an example).

Documentation:

This Python example provides a basic introduction to calculating and interpreting key statistical measures from historical effort data. Understanding these concepts allows us to describe the central tendency and variability of our past performance, which can inform our future estimates and help us quantify the associated uncertainty.

My Perspective: Embracing statistical concepts in estimation empowers us to move beyond simple averages and gain a deeper understanding of the underlying patterns and uncertainties in our project data. By visualizing distributions, calculating measures of central tendency and dispersion, and even exploring confidence intervals, we can make more informed and defensible estimates. It's about adding a layer of analytical rigor to our estimation process, ultimately leading to more realistic and predictable project outcomes. Don't be intimidated by the numbers – they tell a story about your past performance that can significantly improve your future predictions.

6.3 Exploring Machine Learning Applications in Estimation (Overview) - The Rise of Intelligent Predictions

The field of software estimation is constantly evolving, and one of the most exciting frontiers is the application of **Machine Learning (ML)**. By leveraging algorithms that can learn from vast amounts of historical project data, ML offers the potential to create more sophisticated and accurate estimation models than traditional methods. Think of it as moving from manually analyzing patterns in our project history to having an intelligent assistant that can automatically identify complex relationships and make predictions.

Imagine recommendation systems that suggest movies or products based on your past behavior and the behavior of millions of other users. Machine learning in estimation aims to do something similar: predict project effort, duration, or cost based on patterns learned from numerous past projects.

The Promise of Machine Learning in Estimation:

ML algorithms can analyze complex datasets with many variables and potentially uncover non-linear relationships that might be missed by traditional statistical methods. This opens up possibilities for:

- **Improved Accuracy:** By learning from large datasets, ML models can potentially make more accurate predictions than human experts or simpler algorithmic models.
- **Automated Estimation:** Once trained, ML models can provide estimates quickly based on project characteristics, reducing the manual effort involved.
- **Personalized Models:** ML models can be trained on an organization's specific historical data, creating estimation models that are tailored to their unique context and project types.
- **Identifying Key Predictors:** ML techniques can help identify the most influential factors (features) that impact project outcomes.
- **Handling Uncertainty:** Some ML methods can provide probabilistic estimates, giving a range of likely outcomes and quantifying uncertainty.

Common Machine Learning Techniques Applicable to Estimation:

1. **Regression Algorithms:** These algorithms are used to predict continuous values, such as effort, cost, or duration. Examples include:

   - **Linear Regression:** A foundational algorithm that models a linear relationship between variables (as seen in basic parametric models).
   - **Polynomial Regression:** Can model non-linear relationships by fitting a polynomial curve to the data.
   - **Support Vector Regression (SVR):** Effective in high-dimensional spaces and can handle non-linear relationships.
   - **Decision Tree Regression:** Creates a tree-like structure to make predictions based on data features.
   - **Random Forest Regression:** An ensemble method that combines multiple decision trees to improve accuracy and reduce overfitting.
   - **Gradient Boosting Regression:** Another ensemble method that builds models sequentially, with each new model correcting the errors of the previous ones.
   - **Neural Networks (Deep Learning):** Complex models with multiple layers that can learn intricate patterns in very large datasets.

2. **Clustering Algorithms:** These can be used to group similar past projects together based on their characteristics. New projects can

then be compared to these clusters, and estimates from similar past projects can be used as a starting point. Examples include:

- **K-Means Clustering:** Partitions data into K distinct clusters.

A High-Level Workflow for Applying ML in Estimation:

1. **Data Collection and Preparation:** Gather a comprehensive dataset of historical projects, including features like project size, team experience, complexity metrics, technology used, and the actual effort, cost, and duration. Clean and preprocess the data, handling missing values and encoding categorical features.

2. **Feature Engineering:** Select and transform relevant features from the historical data that the ML model can learn from. This might involve creating new features or combining existing ones.

3. **Model Selection:** Choose an appropriate ML regression algorithm based on the characteristics of your data and the desired outcome.

4. **Model Training:** Train the chosen ML model using a portion of your historical data (the training set). The algorithm learns the relationships between the features and the target variable (e.g., effort).

5. **Model Evaluation:** Evaluate the performance of the trained model on a separate portion of the data (the test set) to assess its accuracy and generalization ability. Use metrics like Mean Absolute Error (MAE), Mean Squared Error (MSE), or R-squared.

6. **Model Deployment and Prediction:** Once a satisfactory model is trained and evaluated, it can be deployed to predict effort, cost, or duration for new projects based on their features.

7. **Monitoring and Retraining:** Continuously monitor the model's performance and retrain it with new data as it becomes available to maintain accuracy and adapt to evolving project patterns.

Code Example (Illustrative - Simple Linear Regression for Effort Prediction using scikit-learn):

Python

```python
import pandas as pd

from sklearn.model_selection import train_test_split

from sklearn.linear_model import LinearRegression

from sklearn.metrics import mean_squared_error


# Sample historical project data

data = {'size_loc': [1000, 1500, 2000, 2500, 3000, 3500],

    'team_exp_years': [2, 3, 4, 2.5, 3.5, 4.5],

    'complexity_score': [3, 4, 5, 4, 5, 6],

    'actual_effort_hours': [800, 1200, 1600, 1900, 2400, 2800]}

df = pd.DataFrame(data)
```

```python
# Features (independent variables)

X = df[['size_loc', 'team_exp_years', 'complexity_score']]

# Target variable (dependent variable)

y = df['actual_effort_hours']


# Split data into training and testing sets

X_train, X_test, y_train, y_test = train_test_split(X, y, test_size=0.2,
random_state=42)


# Create a linear regression model

model = LinearRegression()


# Train the model

model.fit(X_train, y_train)


# Make predictions on the test set

y_pred = model.predict(X_test)
```

```
# Evaluate the model

mse = mean_squared_error(y_test, y_pred)

print(f"Mean Squared Error on Test Set: {mse:.2f}")


# Predict effort for a new project

new_project_data = pd.DataFrame({'size_loc': [2200], 'team_exp_years':
[3.2], 'complexity_score': [4.8]})

predicted_effort = model.predict(new_project_data)[0]

print(f"Predicted Effort for New Project: {predicted_effort:.2f} hours")
```

Step-by-Step Explanation:

1. **Import Libraries:** We import pandas for data handling, train_test_split for splitting data, LinearRegression for the ML model, and mean_squared_error for evaluation.
2. **Sample Data:** We create a sample DataFrame of historical projects with size, team experience, complexity, and actual effort.
3. **Define Features and Target:** We specify the independent variables (features) and the dependent variable (target).
4. **Split Data:** We split the data into training and testing sets to evaluate the model's performance on unseen data.

5. **Create and Train Model:** We create a LinearRegression model and train it using the training data.

6. **Make Predictions:** We use the trained model to make predictions on the test set.

7. **Evaluate Model:** We calculate the Mean Squared Error to assess the model's prediction accuracy.

8. **Predict New Project:** We demonstrate how to use the trained model to predict the effort for a new, unseen project.

Documentation:

This basic Python example demonstrates a simple application of linear regression for effort prediction using the scikit-learn library. Real-world applications would likely involve more complex datasets, more sophisticated ML algorithms, and more rigorous data preprocessing and evaluation.

My Perspective: Machine learning holds immense potential to revolutionize software estimation by uncovering complex patterns in historical data and providing more accurate and automated predictions. While still an evolving field in this context, the increasing availability of project data and the advancements in ML algorithms make it a promising avenue for improving our estimation capabilities. However, it's crucial to remember that ML models are only as good as the data they are trained on, and human expertise remains essential for feature engineering, model selection, and interpreting the results. The rise of intelligent predictions doesn't mean the end of human judgment, but rather its augmentation with powerful data-driven insights.

6.4 Considerations and Challenges of Data-Driven Methods - Not a Perfect Crystal Ball

While the allure of using historical data and even machine learning for estimation is strong, it's crucial to approach these **data-driven methods** with a realistic understanding of their **considerations and challenges**. They are powerful tools, but they are not perfect crystal balls that can predict the future with absolute certainty. Over-reliance or a naive application of these techniques can lead to flawed estimates and unrealistic expectations. Think of it like using a weather model – it's based on vast amounts of data and sophisticated algorithms, but it can still be wrong due to unforeseen factors or limitations in the model itself.

Imagine a company that has meticulously tracked its sales data for years and uses a sophisticated algorithm to forecast future sales. While this data-driven approach is undoubtedly valuable, it can be thrown off by unexpected events like a sudden economic downturn or a competitor launching a disruptive product. Similarly, in software estimation, historical data and ML models are susceptible to various limitations.

Key Considerations and Challenges of Data-Driven Estimation:

1. **Data Availability and Quality:** The effectiveness of data-driven methods hinges on having a sufficient volume of high-quality, relevant historical project data.

   - **Challenge:** Many organizations lack comprehensive and consistently tracked historical data. Data might be incomplete, inconsistent in format, or contain errors. "Garbage in, garbage out" is a critical concern.

- **Consideration:** Invest time and effort in establishing robust data collection processes and ensuring data quality. This might involve standardizing data formats, defining clear metrics, and implementing data validation procedures.

2. **Data Relevance and Context:** Past projects might not perfectly reflect the characteristics of future projects.

- **Challenge:** Technology evolves, team compositions change, methodologies shift, and project complexities vary. Applying data from significantly different past projects can lead to inaccurate estimates.
- **Consideration:** Carefully select historical data that is most relevant to the project being estimated. Consider factors like technology stack, team experience, application domain, and project size. Be cautious when extrapolating from very different projects.

3. **Feature Selection and Engineering:** In machine learning, choosing the right features (project characteristics) that the model learns from is crucial.

- **Challenge:** Identifying the most influential factors and engineering meaningful features can be complex and require domain expertise. Irrelevant or poorly engineered features can lead to poor model performance.

- **Consideration:** Involve experienced project managers and technical leads in the feature selection process. Experiment with different feature combinations and transformations to find the most predictive ones.

4. **Model Complexity and Overfitting:** Machine learning models can become overly complex and "memorize" the training data, performing well on past projects but poorly on new, unseen ones (overfitting).

- **Challenge:** Striking the right balance between model complexity and generalization ability is crucial. Overfit models can give a false sense of accuracy on historical data.
- **Consideration:** Use techniques like cross-validation and regularization during model training to prevent overfitting, Evaluate model performance on a separate test set that the model has never seen before.

5. **The "Black Box" Problem:** Some complex machine learning models (like deep neural networks) can be difficult to interpret, making it hard to understand why they are making certain predictions.

- **Challenge:** Lack of transparency can make it difficult to trust the model's output and identify potential biases or errors.
- **Consideration:** Consider using more interpretable models (like linear regression or decision trees) or employing

techniques to understand the feature importance in more complex models.

6. **Handling Novelty and Uncertainty:** Data-driven models are primarily trained on past experiences. They might struggle to accurately estimate projects involving entirely new technologies, domains, or highly uncertain requirements where there is little or no relevant historical data.

   - **Challenge:** Relying solely on historical data might not adequately capture the risks and unknowns associated with truly innovative projects.
   - **Consideration:** Supplement data-driven estimates with expert judgment and qualitative risk assessments for novel projects. Acknowledge the higher uncertainty in such cases.

7. **The Human Element Still Matters:** Estimation is not just a mathematical exercise. Factors like team dynamics, communication effectiveness, stakeholder relationships, and unforeseen external events can significantly impact project outcomes and are often difficult to capture in historical data or ML models.

   - **Challenge:** Over-reliance on data-driven models can lead to neglecting these crucial human and contextual factors.
   - **Consideration:** Use data-driven methods as one input among others. Combine them with expert judgment,

team-based estimation, and ongoing monitoring to create a more holistic and realistic view.

8. **Maintenance and Evolution:** Data-driven models need to be continuously maintained and updated with new project data to remain accurate as the organization and its projects evolve.

   - **Challenge:** Building and maintaining a robust data pipeline and retraining models can require ongoing effort and resources.
   - **Consideration:** Establish a process for regularly updating your historical data and retraining your estimation models. Monitor their performance over time and be prepared to adapt them as needed.

Code Example (Illustrative - Demonstrating the impact of irrelevant data on a simple linear regression model):

Python

```python
import pandas as pd

from sklearn.linear_model import LinearRegression

import matplotlib.pyplot as plt


# Relevant historical data (size vs. effort)

relevant_data = {'size': [100, 150, 200, 250, 300],
```

```python
            'effort': [200, 300, 400, 500, 600]}

df_relevant = pd.DataFrame(relevant_data)

model_relevant = LinearRegression().fit(df_relevant[['size']],
df_relevant['effort'])


# Irrelevant historical data (feature X vs. effort)

irrelevant_data = {'feature_x': [10, 20, 15, 25, 30],

                'effort': [220, 310, 410, 520, 610]} # No clear linear
relationship

df_irrelevant = pd.DataFrame(irrelevant_data)

model_irrelevant = LinearRegression().fit(df_irrelevant[['feature_x']],
df_irrelevant['effort'])


# Predict effort for a new project with size 220

new_size = pd.DataFrame({'size': [220]})

predicted_relevant = model_relevant.predict(new_size)[0]


# Predict effort for the same (conceptual) new project using the irrelevant
feature (value assumed)
```

```python
new_feature_x = pd.DataFrame({'feature_x': [22]}) # Arbitrary value

predicted_irrelevant = model_irrelevant.predict(new_feature_x)[0]


print(f"Predicted effort (relevant data): {predicted_relevant:.2f}")

print(f"Predicted effort (irrelevant data): {predicted_irrelevant:.2f}")


# Visualize the models

plt.figure(figsize=(12, 5))


plt.subplot(1, 2, 1)

plt.scatter(df_relevant['size'], df_relevant['effort'], color='blue',
label='Relevant Data')

plt.plot(df_relevant['size'], model_relevant.predict(df_relevant[['size']]),
color='red', label='Relevant Model')

plt.scatter(new_size['size'], predicted_relevant, color='green', marker='x',
s=100, label='Prediction')

plt.xlabel('Size')

plt.ylabel('Effort')
```

```python
plt.title('Prediction with Relevant Data')

plt.legend()


plt.subplot(1, 2, 2)

plt.scatter(df_irrelevant['feature_x'], df_irrelevant['effort'], color='orange',
label='Irrelevant Data')

plt.plot(df_irrelevant['feature_x'],
model_irrelevant.predict(df_irrelevant[['feature_x']]), color='purple',
label='Irrelevant Model')

plt.scatter(new_feature_x['feature_x'], predicted_irrelevant, color='green',
marker='x', s=100, label='Prediction')

plt.xlabel('Irrelevant Feature X')

plt.ylabel('Effort')

plt.title('Prediction with Irrelevant Data')

plt.legend()


plt.tight_layout()

plt.show()
```

Step-by-Step Explanation:

1. **Relevant Data and Model:** We create a dataset with a clear linear relationship between size and effort and train a linear regression model.
2. **Irrelevant Data and Model:** We create a dataset with a feature that has no clear linear relationship with effort and train another linear regression model.
3. **Prediction:** We predict the effort for a new project (conceptualized by its size) using both models.
4. **Visualization:** We plot the data and the regression lines for both scenarios, highlighting the prediction. The plot clearly shows that the model trained on irrelevant data provides a meaningless prediction.

Documentation:

This example illustrates the critical importance of using relevant data for training data-driven estimation models. A model trained on features that have no meaningful correlation with the target variable will produce unreliable predictions.

My Perspective: Data-driven methods offer a powerful avenue for improving estimation accuracy, but they are not a panacea. A critical and thoughtful approach is essential. We must be mindful of the quality and relevance of our data, the potential for overfitting, and the limitations in capturing the full complexity of software development. The most effective estimation strategies often involve a blend of data-driven insights and human expertise, recognizing that while data can illuminate the past, the future still holds a degree of inherent uncertainty. Treat data-driven methods as valuable tools that augment, but do not replace, sound judgment and experience.

6.5 Hybrid Approaches: Combining Techniques for Better Results - The Best of Both Worlds

By now, we've explored a spectrum of estimation techniques, from the subjective wisdom of expert opinions to the data-driven rigor of algorithmic models and machine learning. Each approach has its own strengths and weaknesses. Recognizing this, the most effective estimation strategies often involve **hybrid approaches**, strategically combining different techniques to leverage their individual advantages and mitigate their limitations. Think of it as assembling a well-rounded toolbox, where you select the best tool for each specific task, rather than relying on a single, potentially inadequate one.

Imagine a chef preparing a complex dish. They might rely on their experience and intuition for flavor combinations (expert judgment), follow precise measurements from a recipe (algorithmic approach), and even use data from past attempts to adjust cooking times (historical data). This multi-faceted approach leads to a more reliable and delicious outcome than relying solely on one method. Similarly, in software estimation, combining techniques can lead to more robust and accurate predictions.

Why Combine Estimation Techniques?

- **Increased Accuracy:** Different techniques can provide complementary perspectives on the estimation problem. Combining them can help to cross-validate estimates and identify potential biases or oversights in any single method.

- **Improved Confidence:** When multiple approaches yield similar estimates, our confidence in the prediction increases. Conversely, significant discrepancies can trigger further investigation and refinement.

- **Addressing Different Project Phases:** Certain techniques might be more suitable for different stages of a project. For example, high-level techniques like t-shirt sizing might be used for initial backlog grooming, while more detailed methods like story points or function points are applied as requirements become clearer.

- **Mitigating Individual Limitations:** Combining a technique that excels at capturing complexity (e.g., function points) with one that accounts for team velocity (e.g., story points) can provide a more comprehensive estimate.

- **Tailoring to Project Characteristics:** The optimal combination of techniques might vary depending on the size, complexity, novelty, and criticality of the project.

Common Hybrid Approaches in Software Estimation:

1. **Expert Judgment Combined with Decomposition:** Start with a high-level estimate based on expert intuition, then decompose the project into smaller tasks or features and have the team estimate

these components using techniques like Planning Poker. The bottom-up estimate can then be compared to the initial top-down estimate for consistency.

2. **Function Points (or Use Case Points) Calibrated with Historical Data:** Use a functional size measurement technique to get an objective measure of the software's size, then calibrate the resulting FP count with historical productivity data (e.g., person-hours per FP) from similar past projects within the organization.

3. **Story Points Informed by Analogous Projects:** When estimating user stories, the team might refer to similar stories from past projects and use their actual effort as a reference point to inform the assignment of story points.

4. **Algorithmic Models Adjusted by Expert Opinion:** Use the output of an algorithmic model like COCOMO as a baseline, and then have experienced project managers or technical leads review and adjust the estimate based on their qualitative knowledge of the specific project's risks, team capabilities, or unique challenges.

5. **T-Shirt Sizing Mapped to Story Points and Validated with Velocity:** Use t-shirt sizing for a quick initial estimate of a large backlog, map the sizes to story point ranges, and then use the team's historical velocity to project a timeline. This high-level projection can then be validated as the team refines the backlog

and provides more detailed story point estimates for upcoming sprints.

6. **Machine Learning Models Combined with Expert Review:** Use a machine learning model trained on historical data to generate an initial estimate, and then have experienced estimators review the output, identify potential anomalies or overlooked factors, and make adjustments based on their expertise.

Code Example (Illustrative - Combining Function Points with Historical Productivity):

Python

```python
import pandas as pd


# Estimated Unadjusted Function Points (UFP)

ufp = 150


# Value Adjustment Factor (VAF) based on General System
Characteristics

vaf = 1.10


# Calculate Adjusted Function Points (AFP)
```

```python
afp = ufp * vaf

print(f"Adjusted Function Points (AFP): {afp:.2f}")


# Historical productivity data (AFP vs. Actual Effort in Person-Hours)

historical_data = {'afp': [120, 180, 150, 200, 130],

            'actual_effort': [900, 1400, 1150, 1550, 1000]}

df_history = pd.DataFrame(historical_data)


# Calculate average productivity (Person-Hours per AFP)

productivity = df_history['actual_effort'].sum() / df_history['afp'].sum()

print(f"Average Historical Productivity: {productivity:.2f} Person-Hours
per AFP")


# Estimate effort based on AFP and historical productivity

estimated_effort = afp * productivity

print(f"Estimated Effort (based on AFP and historical productivity):
{estimated_effort:.2f} Person-Hours")
```

```
# Incorporating expert adjustment (e.g., +10% due to new technology)

expert_adjustment = 0.10

adjusted_estimated_effort = estimated_effort * (1 + expert_adjustment)

print(f"Estimated Effort (with +{expert_adjustment*100:.0f}% expert
adjustment): {adjusted_estimated_effort:.2f} Person-Hours")
```

Step-by-Step Explanation:

1. **Calculate AFP:** We first calculate the Adjusted Function Points based on the UFP and a Value Adjustment Factor.
2. **Historical Productivity Data:** We have a sample of historical projects with their AFP and actual effort.
3. **Calculate Average Productivity:** We calculate the average person-hours spent per AFP based on the historical data.
4. **Estimate Effort:** We multiply the AFP of the current project by the average historical productivity to get an initial effort estimate.
5. **Expert Adjustment:** We then apply an expert adjustment (in this case, an increase of 10% due to the perceived impact of a new technology) to the initial estimate.

Documentation:

This example demonstrates a hybrid approach by combining a functional size measurement (Function Points) with historical productivity data and expert judgment to arrive at a final effort estimate.

My Perspective: The most mature and reliable estimation practices often involve a thoughtful combination of different techniques. There's no one-size-fits-all solution, and the optimal blend will depend on the specific context of the project, the available data, the expertise of the team, and the level of precision required at different stages. By strategically leveraging the strengths of various methods and acknowledging their limitations, we can create a more robust and adaptable estimation process that leads to more accurate and trustworthy predictions. Embrace the "best of both worlds" philosophy to build an estimation toolkit that serves your specific needs effectively.

Chapter 7: Managing Uncertainty and Risk in Estimates - Expect the Unexpected (and Plan for It!)

Let's face it: software development is rarely a smooth, predictable journey. Unexpected challenges, unforeseen complexities, and plain old bad luck can throw even the most meticulously planned projects off course. That's why mastering software estimation isn't just about predicting the ideal scenario; it's also about understanding and managing the inherent uncertainty and risks that can impact our estimates.

Think of your initial estimate as the best guess in a perfect world. This chapter is about acknowledging that our world is far from perfect and equipping you with strategies to account for the "what ifs" that inevitably arise.

7.1 Identifying and Analyzing Project Risks Affecting Estimates - Spotting the Potential Storm Clouds

We've spent considerable time exploring various estimation techniques. However, even the most meticulously crafted estimate can be derailed by unforeseen events – **project risks**. These are uncertain events or conditions that, if they occur, can have a negative impact on our project goals, including our estimates for effort, cost, and schedule. Ignoring or underestimating these risks is like setting sail without checking the weather forecast; you might encounter a storm you weren't prepared for.

Think of planning a weekend trip. You estimate the travel time, budget for gas and food, and book accommodation. But what if your car breaks down, there's unexpected traffic, or your hotel overbooks? These are risks that could significantly impact your timeline and budget. Similarly, software projects are rife with potential risks that can throw our estimates off track.

Why Focus on Risks in Estimation?

Integrating risk management into our estimation process is crucial for several reasons:

- **More Realistic Estimates:** By identifying potential risks, we can factor in contingency buffers (additional time, effort, or budget) to account for their potential impact.
- **Improved Planning:** Understanding risks allows us to develop mitigation strategies to prevent them from occurring or to minimize their impact if they do.
- **Enhanced Communication:** Explicitly discussing risks with stakeholders helps to manage expectations and fosters a shared understanding of potential challenges.
- **Better Decision-Making:** Risk analysis can inform decisions about project scope, technology choices, and resource allocation.

Identifying Project Risks:

The first step is to systematically identify potential risks that could affect our project estimates. Common techniques for risk identification include:

- **Brainstorming:** A collaborative session where the team generates a list of potential risks.
- **Checklists:** Using predefined lists of common software project risks (e.g., requirements changes, technical difficulties, team turnover).
- **Lessons Learned from Past Projects:** Reviewing risks that occurred in previous similar projects.
- **Risk Workshops:** Facilitated sessions involving stakeholders to identify and discuss potential risks.
- **SWOT Analysis:** Analyzing Strengths, Weaknesses, Opportunities, and Threats related to the project.
- **Expert Interviews:** Consulting with experienced individuals who can offer insights into potential risks.

Categories of Risks Affecting Estimates:

Risks can be broadly categorized, and understanding these categories can help in a more systematic identification process:

- **Technical Risks:** Issues related to the technology being used (e.g., performance problems, integration difficulties, technology obsolescence).
- **Requirements Risks:** Problems with the project requirements (e.g., unclear, incomplete, changing requirements, scope creep).

- **Resource Risks:** Issues related to the project team and resources (e.g., lack of skilled personnel, team turnover, resource unavailability).

- **Schedule Risks:** Factors that could delay the project timeline (e.g., underestimated task durations, dependencies, external delays).

- **External Risks:** Factors outside the project team's direct control (e.g., changes in regulations, vendor issues, market shifts).

- **Management Risks:** Issues related to project management (e.g., poor communication, inadequate planning, lack of stakeholder involvement).

Analyzing Project Risks:

Once risks are identified, the next step is to analyze them to understand their potential impact and likelihood. A common approach involves:

1. **Assessing Likelihood:** Estimating the probability of each risk occurring (e.g., Very Low, Low, Medium, High, Very High).

2. **Assessing Impact:** Evaluating the potential consequences if the risk occurs, particularly on the project estimates (e.g., Minor Delay, Moderate Delay, Major Delay; Small Cost Increase, Significant Cost Increase, Budget Overrun).

3. **Prioritizing Risks:** Based on their likelihood and impact, risks are prioritized. A common method is using a **Risk Matrix** (Likelihood vs. Impact) to categorize risks as Low, Medium, or High priority. High-priority risks require the most attention in terms of mitigation and contingency planning.

Incorporating Risk into Estimates:

There are several ways to incorporate the impact of identified and analyzed risks into our estimates:

- **Contingency Buffers:** Adding extra time, effort, or budget to the base estimate to cover potential risks. The size of the buffer should be proportional to the likelihood and impact of the identified risks.
- **Expected Value Analysis:** For each risk, calculate the expected impact (Impact x Likelihood). Summing the expected impacts of all identified risks can provide an overall contingency value to add to the estimate.
- **Scenario Planning:** Developing "best-case," "most likely," and "worst-case" scenarios based on the potential occurrence of key risks. The final estimate can be presented as a range reflecting these scenarios.
- **Monte Carlo Simulation:** A more sophisticated technique that uses probabilistic models to simulate a range of possible project outcomes based on the likelihood and impact of various risks. This can provide a probability distribution of potential estimates.

Code Example (Illustrative - Simple Expected Value Calculation):

Python

```
import pandas as pd
```

```python
# Sample identified risks, their likelihood, and estimated impact (in days)

risks_data = {'risk': ['Requirement Change', 'Key Person Leaves',
'Integration Issues'],

        'likelihood': [0.6, 0.2, 0.4],  # Probability between 0 and 1

        'impact_days': [10, 20, 15]}

df_risks = pd.DataFrame(risks_data)


# Calculate the expected impact of each risk

df_risks['expected_impact'] = df_risks['likelihood'] *
df_risks['impact_days']


# Calculate the total expected impact

total_expected_impact = df_risks['expected_impact'].sum()


print("Identified Project Risks and Expected Impact:")

print(df_risks)
```

```python
print(f"\nTotal Expected Impact on Schedule:
{total_expected_impact:.2f} days")


# Base schedule estimate (without considering risks)

base_schedule_days = 100


# Schedule estimate including expected risk impact

schedule_with_risk = base_schedule_days + total_expected_impact

print(f"\nBase Schedule Estimate: {base_schedule_days} days")

print(f"Schedule Estimate Including Expected Risk Impact:
{schedule_with_risk:.2f} days")
```

Step-by-Step Explanation:

1. risks_data **Dictionary:** Contains sample risks, their estimated likelihood (as a probability), and their potential impact on the project schedule in days.
2. **Create DataFrame:** We create a Pandas DataFrame to easily work with the risk data.
3. **Calculate Expected Impact:** For each risk, we multiply its likelihood by its impact to get the expected impact in days.

4. **Calculate Total Expected Impact:** We sum the expected impacts of all identified risks to get a total expected delay.

5. **Base and Risk-Adjusted Schedule:** We define a base schedule estimate and then add the total expected impact to get a schedule estimate that accounts for the identified risks.

Documentation:

This simple Python example demonstrates how to calculate the expected impact of project risks and how this can be used to adjust a base schedule estimate. Similar calculations can be applied to effort and cost estimates.

My Perspective: Identifying and analyzing project risks is not just a separate activity; it's an integral part of responsible estimation. By proactively spotting potential "storm clouds," we can develop more realistic estimates that include contingency for potential setbacks. Ignoring risks is akin to wishful thinking, while actively managing them allows us to navigate the uncertainties of software development with greater confidence and predictability. Remember, a well-considered risk analysis can be the difference between a project that barely survives a crisis and one that weathers the storms and reaches its goals successfully.

7.2 Incorporating Contingency and Buffers Effectively - Building in Breathing Room

We've just discussed the importance of identifying and analyzing project risks. The natural next step is to figure out how to account for these potential pitfalls in our estimates. This is where the concepts of **contingency** and **buffers** come into play. They represent the "breathing room" we build into our estimates to absorb the impact of identified risks and the inherent uncertainty of software development. Think of it as adding a safety margin to your travel time to account for unexpected delays or packing extra supplies for a long hike.

Imagine you're estimating the time to complete a complex coding task. Based on your experience, you might estimate 8 hours. However, you also know there's a risk of encountering a tricky bug or needing to refactor some existing code. Incorporating contingency means adding some extra time – perhaps 2 additional hours – to your estimate to account for these possibilities.

Understanding Contingency vs. Buffers:

While often used interchangeably, there's a subtle distinction:

- **Contingency:** Typically tied to **specific identified risks**. It's a planned allowance (in time, effort, or cost) to address the potential impact of a particular risk if it occurs. For example, if we identify a high risk of integration issues that could take up to 3 extra days to resolve, we might add a 3-day contingency to the schedule.
- **Buffers:** Often more **general allowances** added to the overall project schedule or budget to account for the inherent uncertainty and the accumulation of smaller, less predictable delays across multiple tasks. Think of a project buffer at the end of the schedule or a phase buffer between critical stages.

Why Incorporate Contingency and Buffers?

- **More Realistic Estimates:** They acknowledge the inherent uncertainty in software development and the potential for things to go wrong.

- **Improved Project Stability:** Having built-in allowances helps the project stay on track when minor delays or issues arise.

- **Better Stakeholder Management:** It's better to proactively include a buffer and potentially deliver early than to constantly report delays.

- **Reduced Stress:** Knowing there's some "breathing room" can reduce pressure on the team.

Effective Strategies for Incorporating Contingency and Buffers:

1. **Risk-Based Contingency:** The most effective approach is to directly link contingency to the identified and analyzed risks. For each significant risk, estimate the potential impact on schedule, effort, and cost, and include a corresponding contingency in the plan. The higher the likelihood and impact of a risk, the larger the contingency should be.

2. **Expected Value as Contingency:** As we saw in the previous section, calculating the expected value of each risk (Likelihood x Impact) and summing these values can provide a data-driven basis for the overall contingency.

3. **Percentage-Based Buffers (Use with Caution):** Some organizations use a fixed percentage (e.g., 10-20%) as a buffer on top of the total estimate. While simple, this approach can be

arbitrary and might not be directly related to the actual risks. It's generally better to base buffers on risk analysis.

4. **Phase Buffers and Project Buffers (Critical Chain Method):** In critical chain project management, buffers are strategically placed at the end of the project (project buffer) and at the end of critical chains of tasks (feeding buffers) to absorb delays.

5. **Buffer Management:** It's crucial to actively manage the buffers. Track how much of the buffer is being consumed and why. This provides valuable insights into the types of risks that are materializing and helps in making informed decisions about the remaining buffer.

6. **Transparency with Stakeholders:** Be transparent about the contingency and buffers included in the estimates and the rationale behind them. Explain that these are not "padding" but rather planned allowances for potential issues.

Code Example (Illustrative - Calculating Contingency Based on Risk Impact):

Python

```python
import pandas as pd
```

```python
# Base effort estimates for project tasks (in hours)

base_estimates = {'Task A': 40, 'Task B': 60, 'Task C': 80}

df_estimates = pd.DataFrame.from_dict(base_estimates, orient='index',
columns=['base_effort'])



# Identified risks and their potential impact on task effort (in additional
hours)

risk_impacts = {'Task A': {'Integration Issue': 10},

        'Task B': {'Database Problem': 15, 'Requirement Clarification':
5},

        'Task C': {'External Dependency Delay': 20}}



# Incorporate contingency into the estimates based on identified risks

df_estimates['contingency'] = 0.0

for task, risks in risk_impacts.items():

    total_risk_contingency = sum(risks.values())

    if task in df_estimates.index:

        df_estimates.loc[task, 'contingency'] = total_risk_contingency
```

```python
# Calculate total estimated effort including contingency

df_estimates['total_estimated_effort'] = df_estimates['base_effort'] +
df_estimates['contingency']


print("Effort Estimates with Risk-Based Contingency:")

print(df_estimates)


# Calculate total base effort and total estimated effort

total_base_effort = df_estimates['base_effort'].sum()

total_estimated_effort = df_estimates['total_estimated_effort'].sum()


print(f"\nTotal Base Effort: {total_base_effort} hours")

print(f"Total Estimated Effort (including contingency):
{total_estimated_effort} hours")

print(f"Total Contingency: {total_estimated_effort - total_base_effort}
hours")
```

Step-by-Step Explanation:

1. base_estimates **Dictionary:** Contains the initial effort estimates for different project tasks.

2. risk_impacts **Dictionary:** Defines the identified risks for each task and their potential impact on effort (in additional hours).

3. **Create DataFrame:** We create a Pandas DataFrame from the base estimates.

4. **Incorporate Contingency:** We iterate through the risk_impacts. For each task, we sum the potential impact of all identified risks and add this sum as the contingency for that task in the DataFrame.

5. **Calculate Total Estimated Effort:** We calculate the total estimated effort for each task by adding the base effort and the contingency.

6. **Print Results:** We display the effort estimates with the incorporated contingency and the overall total base effort, total estimated effort, and total contingency.

Documentation:

This Python example demonstrates how to incorporate contingency into task-level effort estimates based on the potential impact of identified risks. This risk-based approach provides a more justifiable and transparent way to build in "breathing room" compared to arbitrary percentage-based buffers.

My Perspective: Incorporating contingency and buffers is not about padding estimates or being pessimistic; it's about being realistic and responsible in our planning. By proactively accounting for potential risks and the inherent uncertainty of software development, we create more stable projects and manage stakeholder expectations more effectively. The key is to base these allowances on a thorough understanding of the risks involved and to manage them transparently throughout the project lifecycle. Building in "breathing room" is an act of foresight that can significantly increase the likelihood of project success.

7.3 Range-Based Estimation and PERT Analysis - Embracing the Spectrum of Possibilities

Up to this point, we've often talked about single-point estimates – a single number representing our best guess for effort, duration, or cost. However, the reality of software development is rarely so precise. Recognizing this inherent uncertainty, **range-based estimation** encourages us to think in terms of a spectrum of possibilities rather than a single definitive value. **PERT (Program Evaluation and Review Technique) analysis** is a specific statistical method that builds upon this idea by using weighted averages of these ranges to provide a more probabilistic estimate. Think of it as acknowledging that a weather forecast isn't just one temperature, but a range with a most likely scenario.

Imagine estimating the time to fix a complex bug. You might have a "best-case" scenario if the fix is straightforward, a "most likely" scenario based on similar past bugs, and a "worst-case" scenario if the bug is deeply rooted or introduces regressions. Range-based estimation captures this spectrum. PERT analysis then uses a formula to weigh these scenarios and provide a more statistically informed estimate.

The Core Idea of Range-Based Estimation:

Instead of providing a single estimate, range-based estimation involves providing three values for each task or project:

- **Optimistic Estimate (O or Best Case):** The most favorable scenario, assuming no significant problems or delays. Everything goes smoothly and efficiently.
- **Most Likely Estimate (M):** The most realistic estimate, considering the typical challenges and efficiencies encountered on similar projects. This is often the estimate we'd provide as a single point.
- **Pessimistic Estimate (P or Worst Case):** The least favorable scenario, assuming significant problems, delays, and potential risks materialize.

This range (from O to P) acknowledges the uncertainty and provides stakeholders with a better understanding of the potential variability in the estimate.

PERT Analysis: Adding Statistical Weight:

PERT analysis goes a step further by applying a weighted average to these three estimates to arrive at an **expected value (E)**.[5] The traditional PERT formula gives more weight to the most likely estimate:

$$E = (O + 4M + P) / 6$$

The rationale behind this formula is that the most likely scenario is more probable than either the best or worst case. The weights (1 for O, 4 for M, 1 for P) reflect this assumption, approximating a beta distribution.

PERT analysis can also provide a measure of the **standard deviation (SD)** of the estimate, which helps quantify the uncertainty:

$$SD = (P - O) / 6$$

A larger standard deviation indicates a wider range of possibilities and thus higher uncertainty.

Finally, we can use the expected value and standard deviation to estimate a range within which the actual outcome is likely to fall, often using a 68-95-99.7 rule (assuming a normal distribution):

- Approximately 68% probability that the actual value will be within +/- 1 standard deviation of the expected value (E).
- Approximately 95% probability that the actual value will be within +/- 2 standard deviations of the expected value (E).

The Process of Range-Based Estimation and PERT Analysis:

1. **Identify Tasks:** Break down the project into smaller, manageable tasks.

2. **Elicit Three-Point Estimates:** For each task, the estimator (often the person responsible for the work) provides optimistic (O), most likely (M), and pessimistic (P) estimates. Encourage the estimator

to think about best-case and worst-case scenarios realistically.

3. **Calculate Expected Value (E):** Apply the PERT formula to calculate the expected duration (or effort, cost) for each task.

4. **Calculate Standard Deviation (SD):** Use the PERT formula for standard deviation to quantify the uncertainty for each task.

5. **Aggregate Estimates:** Sum the expected values (E) of the individual tasks to get the total expected project duration (or effort, cost).

6. **Aggregate Standard Deviations (Optional):** If tasks are independent, the standard deviation of the total project duration can be estimated as the square root of the sum of the squared standard deviations of the individual tasks:

$$SD\_project = sqrt(SD\_task1^2 + SD\_task2^2 + ... + SD\_taskN^2)$$

7. **Determine Probability Ranges:** Use the total expected value and the project standard deviation to estimate probability ranges for project completion (e.g., 68% chance of finishing within E +/- SD_project).

Code Example (Illustrative - PERT Analysis for Task Duration):

Python

```python
import math

def calculate_pert(optimistic, most_likely, pessimistic):
    """Calculates the PERT expected value and standard deviation."""
    expected_value = (optimistic + 4 * most_likely + pessimistic) / 6
    standard_deviation = (pessimistic - optimistic) / 6
    return expected_value, standard_deviation


# Sample task estimates (in days)
tasks_data = {
    'Task A': {'O': 2, 'M': 3, 'P': 5},
    'Task B': {'O': 4, 'M': 5, 'P': 7},
    'Task C': {'O': 1, 'M': 2, 'P': 4},
    'Task D': {'O': 3, 'M': 4, 'P': 6},
}


project_expected_duration = 0
```

```python
    project_squared_sd_sum = 0

    print("PERT Analysis for Task Durations (in days):")

    for task, estimates in tasks_data.items():

        expected, sd = calculate_pert(estimates['O'], estimates['M'],
    estimates['P'])

        print(f"{task}: Expected = {expected:.2f}, Standard Deviation =
    {sd:.2f}")

        project_expected_duration += expected

        project_squared_sd_sum += sd ** 2

    project_standard_deviation = math.sqrt(project_squared_sd_sum)

    print(f"\nTotal Expected Project Duration:
    {project_expected_duration:.2f} days")

    print(f"Project Standard Deviation: {project_standard_deviation:.2f}
    days")

    # Estimate probability ranges (assuming normal distribution)
```

```python
    confidence_68_lower = project_expected_duration -
    project_standard_deviation

    confidence_68_upper = project_expected_duration +
    project_standard_deviation

    confidence_95_lower = project_expected_duration - 2 *
    project_standard_deviation

    confidence_95_upper = project_expected_duration + 2 *
    project_standard_deviation


    print(f"\nEstimated Duration Range (68% confidence):
    {confidence_68_lower:.2f} - {confidence_68_upper:.2f} days")

    print(f"Estimated Duration Range (95% confidence):
    {confidence_95_lower:.2f} - {confidence_95_upper:.2f} days")
```

Step-by-Step Explanation:

1. **calculate_pert Function:** Takes optimistic, most likely, and pessimistic estimates as input and returns the PERT expected value and standard deviation.

2. **tasks_data Dictionary:** Contains sample tasks with their three-point estimates for duration (in days).

3. **Iterate and Calculate:** We loop through each task, calculate its expected duration and standard deviation using the calculate_pert function, and print the results.

4. **Aggregate Expected Duration:** We sum the expected durations of all tasks to get the total expected project duration.

5. **Aggregate Standard Deviations:** We sum the squared standard deviations of individual tasks and then take the square root to estimate the project standard deviation (assuming task independence).

6. **Estimate Probability Ranges:** We use the total expected duration and the project standard deviation to estimate ranges within which the project is likely to be completed with 68% and 95% confidence, assuming a normal distribution.

Documentation:

This Python example demonstrates how to perform PERT analysis for project duration. It calculates the expected duration and standard deviation for individual tasks based on three-point estimates and then aggregates these values to provide an expected project duration and probability ranges.

My Perspective: Range-based estimation and PERT analysis provide a more realistic and statistically grounded approach to dealing with the inherent uncertainty in software projects. By moving beyond single-point estimates, we acknowledge the spectrum of possibilities and provide stakeholders with a more comprehensive understanding of potential outcomes. PERT analysis, with its weighted average and standard deviation, offers a valuable way to quantify this uncertainty and communicate probabilities of meeting certain targets. While the assumption of a beta or normal distribution might not always perfectly hold true in software development, the underlying principle of considering a range of outcomes leads to more robust and defensible estimates. Embrace the spectrum of possibilities – it's a more accurate reflection of the complex world of software development.

7.4 The Interplay Between Risk Management and Estimation - A Symbiotic Relationship

We've explored risk management as a way to identify potential threats to our project estimates and techniques like contingency and PERT to account for uncertainty. Now, let's explicitly delve into the **symbiotic relationship** between risk management and estimation. They aren't separate activities but rather interconnected processes that feed and strengthen each other. Think of it like the circulatory system in the human body – risk management identifies potential "blockages" or "weaknesses," while estimation provides the "flow" and "pressure" metrics that can be affected. They work together to ensure the project's overall health and viability.

Imagine a construction project. Before estimating the cost and timeline, the project manager would assess potential risks like weather delays, material price fluctuations, or subcontractor issues. This risk assessment directly influences the contingency added to the budget and schedule. Conversely, the initial cost and timeline estimates might highlight areas of significant financial or schedule pressure, prompting a deeper dive into the risks that could exacerbate these vulnerabilities.

How Risk Management Informs Estimation:

- **Identifying Potential Impacts:** Risk identification helps us pinpoint the specific areas of our estimates (tasks, resources, schedule) that are most vulnerable to disruptions. For example, identifying a risk of key personnel leaving might lead to increased effort estimates for knowledge transfer and onboarding new team members.

- **Quantifying Uncertainty:** Risk analysis (assessing likelihood and impact) provides the data needed to quantify the potential range of our estimates. Techniques like expected value analysis and PERT rely heavily on understanding the probability and magnitude of risks.

- **Determining Contingency:** A thorough risk assessment provides a rational basis for determining the appropriate level of contingency to include in our estimates. Instead of arbitrary padding, contingency becomes a calculated allowance for specific potential problems.

- **Scenario Planning for Estimates:** Risk analysis can drive the development of different estimation scenarios (best-case, most likely, worst-case) based on the occurrence or non-occurrence of key risks.

- **Prioritizing Estimation Efforts:** High-priority risks often warrant more detailed estimation and closer monitoring. For example, if a technical risk has a high likelihood and significant impact on a critical path task, we might invest more effort in refining the estimate for that task and developing mitigation plans.

How Estimation Informs Risk Management:

- **Highlighting Areas of Vulnerability:** Tight estimates with little built-in buffer can signal areas where the project is particularly vulnerable to delays or cost overruns if risks materialize. This can prompt a more proactive approach to risk mitigation.

- **Assessing the Cost of Risks:** The potential impact of risks is often expressed in terms of deviations from the baseline estimates (e.g., a delay of X days, a cost increase of Y dollars). The initial estimates provide the yardstick against which the cost of risks is measured.

- **Identifying Costly Risks:** Estimation can help pinpoint risks with the most significant potential financial impact, allowing for focused risk mitigation efforts. For example, a risk of major rework identified during estimation might trigger a more rigorous review process early on.

- **Evaluating Mitigation Strategies:** When considering different risk mitigation strategies, the cost and effort estimates associated with each strategy are crucial factors in the decision-making process. We need to weigh the cost of mitigation against the potential cost of the risk occurring.

- **Tracking Risk Exposure:** As the project progresses and actual effort and schedule are tracked against the estimates, deviations can indicate that certain risks might be materializing or that new risks are emerging. This triggers a review of the risk management plan.

Code Example (Illustrative - Linking Risk Likelihood to Contingency Percentage):

Python

```python
import pandas as pd


# Base effort estimate for a task (in hours)

base_effort = 100


# Identified risks and their likelihood

risks_data = {'risk': ['External API Unstable', 'Unclear Requirements Section'],

        'likelihood': ['High', 'Medium']}

df_risks = pd.DataFrame(risks_data)


# Define a mapping of risk likelihood to contingency percentage

contingency_mapping = {'Low': 0.05, 'Medium': 0.10, 'High': 0.20}
```

```python
# Function to apply contingency based on likelihood

def apply_contingency(row):

    likelihood = row['likelihood']

    contingency_percentage = contingency_mapping.get(likelihood, 0)

    return row['base_effort'] * contingency_percentage


# Add base effort to the risks DataFrame (for demonstration)

df_risks['base_effort'] = base_effort


# Calculate contingency for each risk

df_risks['contingency'] = df_risks.apply(apply_contingency, axis=1)


# Calculate total estimated effort including risk-based contingency

total_estimated_effort = df_risks['base_effort'].iloc[0] +
df_risks['contingency'].sum()


print("Risk Analysis and Contingency Calculation:")
```

```
print(df_risks)

print(f"\nBase Effort: {base_effort} hours")

print(f"Total Risk-Based Contingency:
{df_risks['contingency'].sum():.2f} hours")

print(f"Total Estimated Effort (including risk):
{total_estimated_effort:.2f} hours")
```

Step-by-Step Explanation:

1. **base_effort:** Defines the initial effort estimate for a task.
2. **risks_data:** Contains identified risks and their qualitative likelihood.
3. **contingency_mapping:** A dictionary that maps risk likelihood levels to corresponding contingency percentages.
4. **apply_contingency Function:** Takes a row from the DataFrame (containing likelihood and base effort) and returns the calculated contingency based on the mapping.
5. **Add Base Effort to DataFrame:** We add the base_effort to the df_risks for easier calculation.
6. **Calculate Contingency:** We apply the apply_contingency function to each risk to determine the contingency amount.
7. **Calculate Total Estimated Effort:** We sum the base effort and the total contingency to get the final estimated effort that accounts for the identified risks.

Documentation:

This Python example illustrates a simple way to link the qualitative likelihood of identified risks to a quantitative contingency percentage that is then added to the base effort estimate. This demonstrates how risk analysis directly informs the estimation process.

My Perspective: Risk management and estimation are two sides of the same coin in project planning. Effective risk management provides the insights needed to create more realistic and robust estimates, while thoughtful estimation can highlight areas of risk and inform risk mitigation strategies. This symbiotic relationship is essential for navigating the inherent uncertainties of software development and increasing the likelihood of project success. By integrating these two disciplines, we move beyond simply predicting the future to actively shaping it by understanding and preparing for potential challenges.

Chapter 8: Communicating and Refining Estimates - Telling the Story Behind the Numbers

You've diligently applied various estimation techniques, considered risks, and built in buffers. But your work isn't over yet. The ability to clearly communicate your estimates and the reasoning behind them is just as crucial as the accuracy of the numbers themselves. This chapter focuses on how to effectively convey your estimates to stakeholders, manage their expectations, and continuously refine your estimation process based on feedback and experience.

Think about it: an estimate, no matter how well-crafted, is just a number (or a range) until you can articulate the assumptions, uncertainties, and potential implications behind it. Effective communication builds trust, fosters understanding, and sets the stage for realistic expectations.

8.1 Strategies for Clear and Transparent Communication - Painting a Picture with Words

We've spent considerable time diving into the intricacies of estimation techniques, risk management, and data analysis. However, even the most accurate and well-reasoned estimate is only as effective as its communication. **Clear and transparent communication** is the crucial bridge that connects our analysis to the understanding and buy-in of our stakeholders – the project team, clients, management, and anyone else invested in the outcome. Think of it as the frame around a masterpiece; a poorly chosen or presented frame can detract from the beauty of the artwork itself.

Imagine a meteorologist who has meticulously analyzed weather patterns and developed a highly accurate forecast. If they present their findings using jargon-filled charts and technical terms that the general public doesn't understand, their valuable insights will be lost. Similarly, in software estimation, we need to "paint a picture with words" that clearly conveys our estimates, the assumptions behind them, and the associated uncertainties.

Why Clear and Transparent Communication Matters in Estimation:

- **Builds Trust and Credibility:** When stakeholders understand how an estimate was derived and the factors considered, they are more likely to trust its validity.

- **Manages Expectations:** Clear communication helps to set realistic expectations about project timelines, budgets, and potential challenges.

- **Facilitates Informed Decision-Making:** When stakeholders understand the basis of the estimates, they can make better decisions about scope, priorities, and resource allocation.

- **Encourages Collaboration:** Transparent communication fosters open dialogue and allows stakeholders to provide valuable input and feedback on the estimates.

- **Reduces Conflict and Misunderstandings:** Clear explanations minimize ambiguity and the potential for misinterpretations that can lead to conflict later in the project.

Strategies for Clear and Transparent Communication of Estimates:

1. **Know Your Audience:** Tailor your communication style and level of detail to the specific needs and understanding of your audience. A technical team might appreciate more granular details, while executive stakeholders might need a high-level summary with key takeaways.

2. **Explain the "Why" Behind the Numbers:** Don't just present the estimate itself. Clearly articulate the techniques used, the data sources relied upon, the key assumptions made, and any significant factors that influenced the estimate (e.g., complexity, team experience, identified risks).

3. **Use Clear and Concise Language:** Avoid technical jargon or overly complex terminology that your audience might not understand. Use plain language and explain any necessary technical terms simply.

4. **Visualize Your Estimates:** Use charts, graphs, and other visual aids to present estimates and related information in an easily digestible format. For example, a burndown chart can clearly show the projected timeline based on the estimated velocity.

5. **Present Ranges and Uncertainty:** Instead of always providing single-point estimates, communicate the inherent uncertainty by presenting estimates as ranges (e.g., using PERT analysis) or by explicitly stating the confidence level associated with the

estimate.

6. **Document Your Assumptions and Risks:** Clearly document all the key assumptions underlying your estimates and the significant risks that could impact them. This provides context and allows for revisiting the estimates if the assumptions change or risks materialize.

7. **Be Prepared to Explain and Defend:** Be ready to answer questions about how the estimates were derived and to justify your reasoning. This requires a solid understanding of the estimation techniques used and the data behind them.

8. **Seek Feedback and Iterate:** Share your estimates early and solicit feedback from stakeholders. Be open to revising your estimates based on valid input and new information.

9. **Regularly Review and Communicate Updates:** As the project progresses and more information becomes available, review and update your estimates and communicate any significant changes to stakeholders promptly.

10. **Tell a Story with the Data:** Frame your estimates within the context of the project goals and business value. Explain how the estimated timeline and cost align with the desired outcomes.

Code Example (Illustrative - Generating a Simple Report of Estimates with Assumptions and Risks):

Python

```python
import pandas as pd

from datetime import datetime, timedelta


def generate_estimation_report(project_name, total_story_points,
average_velocity, sprint_length_weeks, key_assumptions, key_risks):

    """Generates a simple text-based estimation report."""

    estimated_sprints = total_story_points / average_velocity

    estimated_duration_weeks = estimated_sprints * sprint_length_weeks

    today = datetime.now().date()

    estimated_end_date = today +
timedelta(weeks=estimated_duration_weeks)


    report = f"""

    Project Estimation Report: {project_name}

    Generated on: {today.strftime("%Y-%m-%d")}
```

```
Scope: {total_story_points} Story Points

Average Team Velocity: {average_velocity:.2f} points per sprint

Sprint Length: {sprint_length_weeks} weeks


Estimated Number of Sprints: {estimated_sprints:.2f} sprints

Estimated Project Duration: {estimated_duration_weeks:.2f} weeks

Estimated Project End Date (from today):
{estimated_end_date.strftime('%Y-%m-%d')}


Key Assumptions:

-----------------

"""

for i, assumption in enumerate(key_assumptions):

    report += f"{i+1}. {assumption}\n"


report += "\nKey Risks and Potential Impact on Estimate:\n"

report += "-------------------------------------------\n"
```

```python
    for i, risk in enumerate(key_risks):

        report += f"{i+1}. {risk}\n"


    return report


# Example Usage

project = "New Mobile App Development"

points = 150

velocity = 25

sprint_len = 2

assumptions = [

    "Team velocity remains consistent.",

    "No significant scope changes.",

    "Key resources remain available."

]

risks = [

    "Potential delays in API integration.",
```

```
    "Risk of performance issues requiring rework.",

    "Possible delays due to third-party library dependencies."

]



estimation_report = generate_estimation_report(project, points, velocity,
sprint_len, assumptions, risks)

print(estimation_report)
```

Step-by-Step Explanation:

1. **generate_estimation_report Function:** Takes project details,
   estimates, key assumptions, and key risks as input.
2. **Calculates Timeline:** Calculates the estimated number of sprints,
   project duration in weeks, and a potential end date based on the
   provided data.
3. **Formats Report:** Creates a formatted text report including the
   project name, generation date, key estimates, assumptions, and
   risks.
4. **Example Usage:** Provides sample data for a project and calls the
   function to generate and print the estimation report.

Documentation:

This Python example demonstrates how to generate a simple text-based report that not only presents the estimated timeline but also explicitly includes the key assumptions underlying the estimate and the significant risks that could affect it. This kind of transparency is crucial for effective communication.

My Perspective: Clear and transparent communication is not just a "nice-to-have" in software estimation; it's a fundamental requirement for building trust, managing expectations, and fostering collaboration.By taking the time to explain our estimates clearly, articulate our assumptions and risks, and use visuals where appropriate, we empower our stakeholders to understand and engage with the estimation process effectively. Remember, a well-communicated estimate, even if it's not perfectly accurate, is far more valuable than a precise estimate that remains locked in the estimator's head. Let's strive to be effective storytellers with our data.

8.2 Managing Stakeholder Expectations and Concerns - Navigating the Human Element

While accurate estimation and clear communication are crucial, the human element plays a significant role in how our estimates are received and acted upon. **Managing stakeholder expectations and concerns** is an essential skill for anyone involved in software estimation. Stakeholders – be they clients, managers, or the development team itself – often have their own perspectives, priorities, and anxieties related to project timelines and budgets. Effectively navigating these human dynamics is key to building trust, securing buy-in, and ensuring a smoother project journey. Think of it as being a skilled diplomat, understanding different viewpoints and finding common ground.

Imagine presenting an estimate that exceeds a client's initial expectations. Their immediate reaction might be disappointment or even resistance. Simply defending the numbers might not be enough. Understanding their underlying concerns (e.g., budget constraints, time-to-market pressures) and addressing them empathetically is crucial for a productive conversation.

Understanding Stakeholder Perspectives and Concerns:

Before even presenting an estimate, it's beneficial to understand the different stakeholders involved and their potential concerns:

- **Clients:** Often focused on cost, delivery timelines, and the realization of business value. They might be concerned about estimates exceeding their budget or delaying their market entry.
- **Management:** Typically concerned with resource allocation, project profitability, and alignment with strategic goals. They might scrutinize estimates for efficiency and ROI.
- **Development Team:** Concerned with the feasibility of the estimates, the potential for unrealistic deadlines leading to burnout, and the impact on code quality. They need to feel the estimates are achievable.
- **Sales/Business Development:** Focused on securing the deal, they might have set initial expectations with the client that need to be reconciled with the actual estimates.

Strategies for Managing Stakeholder Expectations and Concerns:

1. **Early and Frequent Engagement:** Involve stakeholders in the estimation process as early as possible. Seek their input, understand their needs, and manage expectations proactively rather than presenting a final estimate as a fait accompli.

2. **Transparency and Explanation (Revisited):** As emphasized before, clearly explain the basis of your estimates, the assumptions made, and the inherent uncertainties. This helps stakeholders understand the rationale behind the numbers and reduces the perception of arbitrariness.

3. **Presenting Ranges and Scenarios:** Instead of a single number, present estimates as a range (e.g., based on PERT or scenario planning) to illustrate the potential variability and acknowledge uncertainty. This helps manage the expectation of pinpoint accuracy.

4. **Highlighting Trade-offs:** Be prepared to discuss the trade-offs between scope, time, and cost. If a stakeholder has a fixed deadline or budget, explain the potential impact on the scope or quality of the deliverable.

5. **Focusing on Value and Benefits:** Frame the estimates in the context of the value and benefits the project will deliver. This can help stakeholders see the investment in a more positive light.

6. **Active Listening and Empathy:** When stakeholders express concerns, listen actively to understand their underlying reasons. Acknowledge their perspective and show empathy for their situation.

7. **Addressing Concerns Directly:** Don't avoid difficult conversations. Address concerns head-on with clear explanations and data where possible. If a concern is valid, be willing to re-evaluate the estimates.

8. **Building Trust Over Time:** Consistent communication, transparency, and a track record of delivering on commitments (or explaining deviations clearly) build trust with stakeholders, making them more receptive to future estimates.

9. **Visual Communication:** Use visual aids like charts and graphs to present estimates and progress in a clear and understandable way, highlighting trends and potential deviations early.

10. **Collaboration and Negotiation:** View the estimation process as a collaborative effort rather than a confrontation. Be open to negotiation and finding mutually acceptable solutions that balance project goals with stakeholder constraints.

11. **Managing Scope Creep:** Clearly define the project scope and communicate the impact of any scope changes on the original estimates. Having a formal change management process is crucial.

12. **Celebrating Successes and Learning from Challenges:** When projects are delivered successfully within the estimated parameters (or when deviations are managed effectively), highlight these successes to build confidence. Also, openly discuss lessons learned from estimation challenges to improve future processes.

Code Example (Illustrative - Tracking and Visualizing Estimate vs. Actual Progress):

Python

```python
import pandas as pd

import matplotlib.pyplot as plt

import datetime


# Sample data: Planned vs. Actual effort over time (in story points completed)

data = {'week': [1, 2, 3, 4, 5, 6],

    'planned': [20, 40, 60, 80, 100, 120],

    'actual': [18, 35, 58, 75, 92, 110]}

df = pd.DataFrame(data)
```

```python
# Calculate variance

df['variance'] = df['actual'] - df['planned']


# Create a line chart of planned vs. actual progress

plt.figure(figsize=(10, 6))

plt.plot(df['week'], df['planned'], label='Planned Progress', marker='o')

plt.plot(df['week'], df['actual'], label='Actual Progress', marker='x')

plt.xlabel('Week')

plt.ylabel('Story Points Completed')

plt.title('Planned vs. Actual Progress')

plt.legend()

plt.grid(True)

plt.axhline(0, color='black', linewidth=0.5) # X-axis


# Display variance (optional - can be a separate bar chart)

plt.figure(figsize=(10, 4))
```

```python
plt.bar(df['week'], df['variance'], color=['green' if v >= 0 else 'red' for v in
df['variance']])

plt.xlabel('Week')

plt.ylabel('Variance (Actual - Planned)')

plt.title('Variance in Progress')

plt.axhline(0, color='black', linewidth=0.5)

plt.grid(axis='y', linestyle='--')

plt.tight_layout()

plt.show()


print("\nProgress Tracking:")

print(df)
```

Step-by-Step Explanation:

1. **Import Libraries:** Import pandas for data manipulation and matplotlib.pyplot for visualization.
2. **Sample Data:** Create a DataFrame with planned and actual progress (in story points completed) over several weeks.
3. **Calculate Variance:** Calculate the difference between actual and planned progress.

4. **Line Chart:** Create a line chart to visually compare the planned and actual progress over time. This helps stakeholders see if the project is on track, ahead, or behind schedule.

5. **Variance Bar Chart (Optional):** Create a bar chart to specifically highlight the variance (positive or negative) in progress each week.

6. **Print Data:** Display the DataFrame showing the planned, actual, and variance data.

Documentation:

This Python example demonstrates how to track planned versus actual progress and visualize the variance. Regularly sharing such visuals with stakeholders helps manage expectations by providing a clear and objective view of the project's status against the initial estimates.

My Perspective: Managing stakeholder expectations is as much about emotional intelligence and communication skills as it is about estimation accuracy. By understanding different perspectives, communicating transparently, and actively addressing concerns, we can build strong relationships and foster a collaborative environment. Remember that stakeholders are people with their own pressures and priorities. Approaching them with empathy and a willingness to engage in open dialogue is crucial for navigating the human element successfully and ensuring that our estimates are not just numbers, but a foundation for shared understanding and project success.

8.3 The Role of Visual Aids in Presenting Estimates - Showing is Often Better Than Telling

We've emphasized the importance of clear and transparent communication when presenting estimates. One of the most powerful tools in our communication arsenal is the use of **visual aids**. In many situations, "showing" information through charts, graphs, and diagrams is far more effective than simply "telling" it with words and numbers. Visuals can make complex data more accessible, highlight key trends, and engage our audience more effectively.Think of it as the difference between reading a description of a beautiful landscape and actually seeing a photograph – the visual experience is often more impactful and easier to grasp.

Imagine presenting a project timeline with just a list of tasks and dates. It can be difficult for stakeholders to quickly understand the overall duration, dependencies, and critical path. However, presenting the same information as a Gantt chart provides an immediate visual overview that is much easier to interpret.

Why Visual Aids Enhance the Presentation of Estimates:

- **Improved Comprehension:** Visuals can simplify complex information and make it easier for stakeholders to understand the key aspects of the estimates.
- **Enhanced Engagement:** Well-designed visuals can capture and maintain the audience's attention more effectively than dense text or tables of numbers.

- **Highlighting Trends and Patterns:** Charts and graphs can clearly illustrate trends in estimated effort, cost, or schedule over time or across different project components.
- **Facilitating Comparisons:** Visuals make it easier to compare different scenarios, such as planned vs. actual progress or estimates using different techniques.
- **Concise Communication:** A well-chosen visual can often convey a significant amount of information in a compact and easily digestible format.
- **Increased Retention:** Visual information is often processed and remembered more effectively than purely textual or numerical data.

Effective Types of Visual Aids for Presenting Estimates:

1. **Gantt Charts:** Excellent for visualizing project timelines, task durations, dependencies, and milestones. They provide a clear overview of the project schedule.

2. **Burndown Charts:** Ideal for tracking progress against estimated effort or story points over time within a sprint or release. They visually show if the team is on track to meet the goals.

3. **Burnup Charts:** Another way to visualize progress, showing the cumulative work completed against the total estimated scope. They are particularly useful for tracking scope changes.

4. **Histograms and Bar Charts:** Useful for comparing estimated effort or cost across different tasks, project phases, or risk categories.

5. **Line Charts:** Effective for showing trends over time, such as cumulative estimated cost or effort, or for comparing planned vs. actual values.

6. **Scatter Plots:** Can be used to explore relationships between different project variables, such as project size and actual effort from historical data.

7. **Pie Charts:** Useful for showing the distribution of estimated effort or cost across different categories (e.g., development, testing, deployment). However, use them sparingly as they can sometimes be harder to interpret accurately than bar charts.

8. **Risk Matrices:** Visual representations of the likelihood and impact of identified risks, helping to prioritize which risks need the most attention in terms of contingency planning.

9. **Cumulative Flow Diagrams:** Provide insights into the flow of work through different stages of the development process, highlighting potential bottlenecks and helping to forecast completion based on historical throughput.

Code Example (Illustrative - Generating a Simple Burndown Chart):

Python

```python
import pandas as pd

import matplotlib.pyplot as plt

import datetime


# Sample sprint data: Estimated vs. Remaining Story Points

data = {'day': [1, 2, 3, 4, 5, 6, 7, 8, 9, 10],

    'estimated': [100, 90, 80, 70, 60, 50, 40, 30, 20, 10],

    'remaining': [95, 82, 71, 65, 52, 40, 35, 25, 15, 5]}

df = pd.DataFrame(data)


# Create a burndown chart

plt.figure(figsize=(10, 6))

plt.plot(df['day'], df['estimated'], label='Ideal Burndown', linestyle='--')

plt.plot(df['day'], df['remaining'], label='Actual Remaining', marker='o')

plt.xlabel('Day of Sprint')
```

```
plt.ylabel('Story Points Remaining')

plt.title('Sprint Burndown Chart')

plt.legend()

plt.grid(True)

plt.gca().invert_yaxis() # Invert y-axis so down is "better"

plt.tight_layout()

plt.show()
```

Step-by-Step Explanation:

1. **Import Libraries:** Import pandas for data handling and matplotlib.pyplot for plotting.
2. **Sample Data:** Create a DataFrame with the day of the sprint, the ideal (linear) burndown of story points, and the actual remaining story points.
3. **Create Plot:** Create a line chart with the day on the x-axis and story points remaining on the y-axis.
4. **Plot Lines:** Plot the 'estimated' burndown as a dashed line representing the ideal scenario and the 'remaining' story points as a solid line with markers showing the actual progress.
5. **Add Labels and Title:** Set appropriate labels for the x and y axes and add a title to the chart.
6. **Add Legend and Grid:** Include a legend to identify the lines and a grid for better readability.

7. **Invert Y-Axis:** Invert the y-axis so that a downward trend visually represents progress (fewer remaining points are better).

8. **Show Plot:** Display the generated burndown chart.

Documentation:

This Python example demonstrates how to generate a simple burndown chart using Matplotlib. This visual aid provides a clear and concise way to communicate sprint progress against the initial estimates.

My Perspective: In the realm of presenting estimates, visual aids are not just decorative elements; they are powerful communication tools that can significantly enhance understanding and engagement. By thoughtfully selecting the right type of visual for the information we want to convey, we can make our estimates more accessible, memorable, and impactful. Remember the adage: "A picture is worth a thousand words." Let's leverage the power of visuals to effectively "show" the story behind our estimates, making them clearer and more persuasive than just "telling" the numbers.

8.4 Negotiation and Agreement on Realistic Timelines - Finding Common Ground

After diligently estimating, clearly communicating, and visually presenting our timelines, the next crucial step is often **negotiation and agreement** with stakeholders. Rarely will our initial estimates be accepted without discussion. Stakeholders may have their own constraints, expectations, or priorities that lead to a need for finding common ground and agreeing on realistic timelines. Think of it as a dialogue, not a monologue, where different parties come together to align on a shared understanding of what's achievable.

Imagine presenting a project timeline that extends beyond a client's desired launch date. Their initial reaction might be to push for a faster delivery. A successful negotiation involves understanding their urgency, explaining the rationale behind your estimate, and exploring potential trade-offs or alternative solutions to reach a mutually agreeable timeline.

The Importance of Negotiation:

- **Alignment of Expectations:** Negotiation ensures that all stakeholders have a shared understanding of the project timeline and the factors influencing it.
- **Realistic Commitments:** Through discussion, unrealistic expectations can be addressed, leading to more achievable timelines and reducing the risk of project failure.
- **Building Stronger Relationships:** A collaborative negotiation process fosters trust and strengthens relationships between the project team and stakeholders.
- **Exploring Creative Solutions:** Negotiation can uncover alternative approaches, scope adjustments, or resource allocations that might lead to a more acceptable timeline.
- **Securing Buy-in:** When stakeholders feel their concerns have been heard and addressed, they are more likely to buy into the agreed-upon timeline and support the project.

Strategies for Effective Negotiation on Timelines:

1. **Understand Stakeholder Needs and Constraints:** Before negotiating, take the time to understand why a stakeholder might be pushing for a different timeline. What are their business drivers, deadlines, or dependencies?

2. **Be Prepared to Explain and Justify:** Reiterate the basis of your estimates, the assumptions made, and the risks considered. Use data and visuals to support your reasoning.

3. **Focus on Trade-offs:** Clearly articulate the potential consequences of accelerating the timeline, such as reduced scope, lower quality, increased risk, or higher cost. Help stakeholders understand the trade-offs involved in different timeline scenarios.

4. **Explore Alternatives and Compromises:** Be open to exploring alternative solutions that might partially address stakeholder concerns without jeopardizing the project's success. This could involve phasing the release, prioritizing key features, or adjusting resource allocation.

5. **Listen Actively and Empathize:** Pay close attention to the stakeholder's perspective and acknowledge their concerns. Show empathy for their situation, even if you can't fully meet their initial demands.

6. **Be Collaborative, Not Confrontational:** Approach the negotiation as a joint problem-solving exercise rather than an

adversarial battle. The goal is to find a mutually agreeable solution.

7. **Focus on Data and Facts:** Ground the discussion in the data and analysis that underpin your estimates. Avoid emotional arguments or purely subjective opinions.

8. **Document Agreements Clearly:** Once a timeline is agreed upon, ensure it is clearly documented, along with any assumptions, dependencies, and agreed-upon trade-offs.

9. **Manage Scope Rigorously:** Once a timeline is set, establish a robust change management process to control scope creep, as this is a common cause of timeline slippage.

10. **Regularly Review and Communicate Progress:** Throughout the project, regularly communicate progress against the agreed-upon timeline. If deviations occur, explain the reasons and discuss potential impacts and mitigation strategies proactively.

Code Example (Illustrative - Simulating Timeline Negotiation Scenarios):

Python

```python
def analyze_timeline_scenario(initial_estimate_weeks,
desired_reduction_weeks, potential_impacts):
```

```python
    """Analyzes the potential impacts of reducing the estimated
timeline."""

    revised_estimate = initial_estimate_weeks - desired_reduction_weeks

    print(f"Initial Timeline Estimate: {initial_estimate_weeks:.2f} weeks")

    print(f"Desired Timeline Reduction: {desired_reduction_weeks:.2f}
weeks")

    print(f"Potential Revised Timeline: {revised_estimate:.2f} weeks\n")


    if revised_estimate <= 0:

        print("Warning: Desired reduction is too aggressive and results in a
non-positive timeline.")

        return


    print("Potential Impacts of Timeline Reduction:")

    for area, impact_level in potential_impacts.items():

        print(f"- {area}: {impact_level}")


# Scenario 1: Client wants a 2-week reduction
```

```python
initial_timeline = 10

reduction = 2

impacts_scenario_1 = {

    "Scope": "Minor reduction in non-critical features",

    "Quality": "Increased risk of minor bugs",

    "Team Overtime": "Potential for increased team workload"

}

print("Scenario 1: Client wants a 2-week reduction")

analyze_timeline_scenario(initial_timeline, reduction,
impacts_scenario_1)

print("-" * 30)


# Scenario 2: Management wants a 4-week reduction

reduction = 4

impacts_scenario_2 = {

    "Scope": "Significant reduction in key features",

    "Quality": "Higher risk of critical defects",

    "Team Overtime": "Likely significant and unsustainable",
```

```
    "Project Risk": "Substantially increased"

}

print("\nScenario 2: Management wants a 4-week reduction")

analyze_timeline_scenario(initial_timeline, reduction,
impacts_scenario_2)
```

Step-by-Step Explanation:

1. **analyze_timeline_scenario Function:** Takes the initial timeline estimate, the desired reduction, and a dictionary of potential impacts as input.
2. **Calculates Revised Timeline:** Subtracts the desired reduction from the initial estimate.
3. **Warns of Aggressive Reduction:** Checks if the revised timeline is non-positive and issues a warning if so.
4. **Prints Potential Impacts:** Iterates through the potential_impacts dictionary and prints the consequences of the timeline reduction in different areas.
5. **Example Scenarios:** Demonstrates two different negotiation scenarios with varying desired timeline reductions and their potential impacts.

Documentation:

This Python example illustrates a simple way to analyze the potential impacts of reducing the estimated project timeline. By explicitly outlining the consequences in terms of scope, quality, team workload, and risk, it provides a framework for a more informed negotiation with stakeholders.

My Perspective: Reaching agreement on realistic timelines is a collaborative process that requires not only accurate estimation but also strong communication and negotiation skills. By understanding stakeholder needs, clearly articulating the basis of our estimates, and being open to exploring trade-offs, we can navigate the human element effectively and build consensus around achievable timelines. Remember that a timeline agreed upon through mutual understanding and negotiation is far more likely to be met than one imposed without dialogue. Let's strive to find that common ground where project goals align with realistic expectations.

8.5 Tracking Actuals and Comparing Against Estimates - Learning in Real-Time

Even with the most diligent estimation and effective communication, the real test of our predictions comes during project execution. **Tracking actuals** – the real effort, time, and cost spent – and **comparing them against our initial estimates** is a crucial practice for several reasons. It's not about pointing fingers or dwelling on discrepancies, but rather about **learning in real-time**, identifying trends, and making necessary adjustments to stay on track and improve future estimations. Think of it as a pilot constantly monitoring the aircraft's instruments, comparing them to the flight plan, and making corrections to stay on course.

Imagine you estimated a task would take 8 hours, but after completion, it actually took 12. Simply noting this difference isn't enough. Understanding *why* it took longer (e.g., unexpected technical challenges, unclear requirements) provides valuable insights that can inform your approach to similar tasks in the future.

Why Track Actuals and Compare Against Estimates?

- **Early Identification of Issues:** Significant deviations between actuals and estimates can signal potential problems early in the project, allowing for timely intervention and corrective actions.
- **Improved Project Control:** By monitoring performance against the plan, project managers can make informed decisions about resource allocation, scope adjustments, and schedule revisions.
- **Enhanced Forecasting Accuracy:** Tracking trends in variances can help refine future forecasts and provide more realistic projections for the remainder of the project.
- **Learning and Process Improvement:** Analyzing the reasons for estimation inaccuracies provides valuable lessons learned that can be incorporated into future estimation processes, leading to greater accuracy over time.
- **Increased Accountability and Transparency:** Comparing actuals against estimates provides a transparent view of project performance for all stakeholders.

Strategies for Effective Tracking and Comparison:

1. **Establish Clear Tracking Mechanisms:** Implement systems and processes for accurately capturing actual effort, time spent on tasks, and costs incurred.This might involve timesheets, project management software, or regular progress reports.

2. **Define Key Metrics:** Identify the key metrics you will track and compare, such as estimated vs. actual effort per task, estimated vs. actual duration per task, estimated vs. actual cost, and planned vs. actual progress (e.g., story points completed per sprint).

3. **Regularly Monitor and Report Variances:** Establish a cadence for reviewing actuals against estimates (e.g., daily, weekly).Calculate and report variances clearly, highlighting significant deviations.

4. **Analyze the Root Causes of Variances:** Don't just focus on the numbers. Investigate the reasons behind significant variances. Was the initial estimate flawed? Did unexpected issues arise? Were there changes in scope or requirements?

5. **Update Estimates Based on Trends:** If consistent patterns of underestimation or overestimation are observed, or if significant risks materialize, be prepared to revise the remaining estimates and forecasts accordingly.

6. **Communicate Variances and Revised Forecasts:** Transparently communicate any significant variances and the reasons behind them to stakeholders, along with any necessary adjustments to the project plan.

7. **Use Visual Aids (Again!):** Charts and graphs are excellent for visualizing the comparison between planned and actual progress, effort, and cost over time. Burndown charts, burnup charts, and trend lines can be particularly effective.

8. **Focus on Learning, Not Blame:** Frame the analysis of variances as an opportunity for learning and improvement, rather than a fault-finding exercise. Encourage open discussion and a culture of continuous improvement.

9. **Document Lessons Learned:** Capture the key insights gained from comparing actuals against estimates and incorporate them into your organization's estimation guidelines and training materials.

Code Example (Illustrative - Tracking and Visualizing Planned vs. Actual Effort):

Python

```python
import pandas as pd

import matplotlib.pyplot as plt
```

```python
import datetime

# Sample task data with estimated and actual effort (in hours)
data = {'task': ['Task A', 'Task B', 'Task C', 'Task D', 'Task E'],
        'estimated_effort': [20, 30, 40, 25, 35],
        'actual_effort': [22, 35, 38, 30, 42]}
df = pd.DataFrame(data)

# Calculate the variance in effort
df['effort_variance'] = df['actual_effort'] - df['estimated_effort']

# Create a bar chart comparing estimated and actual effort
plt.figure(figsize=(10, 6))
plt.bar(df['task'], df['estimated_effort'], label='Estimated Effort', alpha=0.7)
plt.bar(df['task'], df['actual_effort'], label='Actual Effort', alpha=0.7)
plt.xlabel('Task')
plt.ylabel('Effort (Hours)')
```

```python
plt.title('Estimated vs. Actual Effort per Task')

plt.legend()

plt.grid(axis='y', linestyle='--')

plt.tight_layout()

plt.show()



# Create a bar chart showing the effort variance

plt.figure(figsize=(8, 5))

plt.bar(df['task'], df['effort_variance'], color=['red' if v > 0 else 'green' for
v in df['effort_variance']])

plt.xlabel('Task')

plt.ylabel('Effort Variance (Actual - Estimated)')

plt.title('Effort Variance per Task')

plt.axhline(0, color='black', linewidth=0.8)

plt.grid(axis='y', linestyle='--')

plt.tight_layout()

plt.show()
```

```
print("\nEffort Tracking:")

print(df)
```

Step-by-Step Explanation:

1. **Import Libraries:** Import pandas for data handling and matplotlib.pyplot for plotting.
2. **Sample Data:** Create a DataFrame with tasks, their estimated effort, and their actual effort.
3. **Calculate Variance:** Calculate the difference between actual and estimated effort for each task.
4. **Bar Chart (Estimated vs. Actual):** Create a bar chart to visually compare the estimated and actual effort for each task side-by-side.
5. **Bar Chart (Variance):** Create another bar chart specifically showing the effort variance for each task, using different colors to indicate overestimation (green) and underestimation (red).
6. **Print Data:** Display the DataFrame showing the estimated effort, actual effort, and the calculated variance.

Documentation:

This Python example demonstrates how to compare estimated and actual effort for project tasks and visualize the variances using bar charts. Regularly tracking and visualizing such comparisons helps in identifying areas where our estimates were accurate or where there were significant deviations, facilitating learning for future projects.

My Perspective: Tracking actuals against estimates is the feedback loop that allows us to learn and improve our estimation skills over time. It transforms estimation from a one-time prediction into an ongoing process of learning and adaptation. By embracing this real-time learning, we can refine our techniques, identify our blind spots, and ultimately become more accurate and reliable in our future project estimations. It's about viewing deviations not as failures, but as valuable data points on the path to continuous improvement.

8.6 Conducting Post-Project Reviews for Estimation Improvement - Hindsight is 20/20 (Use It!)

We've diligently estimated, tracked actuals, and compared them along the way. But the learning journey doesn't end with project completion. **Conducting post-project reviews (PPRs)** with a specific focus on estimation is a crucial final step in the feedback loop. It's our opportunity to look back with "hindsight being 20/20" and systematically analyze what went well, what didn't, and most importantly, how we can improve our estimation processes for future endeavors. Think of it as an archaeological dig after a major event, carefully excavating the layers to understand what truly happened and why.

Imagine a sports team that finishes a season. They don't just move on to the next one without analyzing their performance. They review game tapes, discuss strategies, and identify areas for improvement. Similarly, a post-project review focused on estimation allows us to dissect our predictions and learn from our successes and shortcomings.

Why Conduct Post-Project Reviews for Estimation Improvement?

- **Identify Systemic Biases:** PPRs can reveal consistent patterns of underestimation or overestimation across different types of tasks or projects, indicating potential biases in our estimation techniques or assumptions.

- **Uncover Unexpected Factors:** Analyzing deviations between estimates and actuals can highlight unforeseen factors (e.g., technical complexities, dependencies, team dynamics) that significantly impacted the project.

- **Validate Estimation Techniques:** PPRs provide an opportunity to assess the effectiveness of the estimation techniques used on the project and determine if they were appropriate for the context.

- **Share Lessons Learned:** The insights gained from PPRs can be shared across the organization to improve estimation practices on future projects, preventing the repetition of past mistakes.

- **Foster a Culture of Continuous Improvement:** Regularly conducting PPRs focused on estimation reinforces a commitment to learning and continuous improvement within the team and the organization.

Key Areas to Focus on During an Estimation-Focused PPR:

1. **Review Initial Estimates:** Examine the original estimates for key tasks, milestones, and the overall project.

2. **Compare with Actual Outcomes:** Compare the initial estimates with the actual effort, time, and cost spent. Quantify the variances.

3. **Analyze Significant Variances:** Deeply investigate the reasons behind significant deviations (both positive and negative). What factors contributed to these inaccuracies?

4. **Evaluate Estimation Techniques:** Assess the effectiveness of the estimation techniques used. Were they appropriate? Were they applied correctly?

5. **Examine Assumptions:** Review the key assumptions that underpinned the estimates. Which assumptions held true, and which did not? How did deviations from assumptions impact the actual outcomes?

6. **Identify Risks and Their Impact:** Analyze the risks that were identified during planning and their actual impact on the project timeline and budget. Were there any significant risks that were missed?

7. **Assess Contingency Effectiveness:** If contingency was included in the estimates, evaluate how effectively it absorbed the impact of realized risks or unforeseen issues.

8. **Gather Team Feedback:** Solicit feedback from the project team members who were involved in both the estimation and execution phases. Their insights into the accuracy and challenges of the estimates are invaluable.

9. **Document Lessons Learned:** Systematically document the key findings, insights, and recommendations for improving future estimation processes.

The Post-Project Review Meeting:

A structured meeting is often the most effective way to conduct a PPR. Consider the following steps:

1. **Preparation:** Distribute relevant data (e.g., initial estimates vs. actuals, variance reports) to participants in advance.
2. **Facilitation:** Assign a facilitator to guide the discussion and ensure it remains focused and productive.
3. **Open and Honest Discussion:** Encourage open and honest feedback from all participants. Emphasize that the goal is learning and improvement, not blame.
4. **Focus on Facts and Data:** Ground the discussion in the data and analysis of the project's performance.
5. **Identify Actionable Insights:** The goal is to identify concrete steps that can be taken to improve future estimation processes.
6. **Document Outcomes and Action Items:** Clearly document the key findings, lessons learned, and any agreed-upon action items with assigned owners and deadlines.
7. **Follow Up:** Ensure that the identified action items are implemented and their effectiveness is reviewed in future projects.

Code Example (Illustrative - Analyzing and Reporting on Estimation Variance):

Python

```python
import pandas as pd
```

```python
def analyze_estimation_variance(estimates_df):

    """Analyzes the variance between estimated and actual effort."""

    estimates_df['variance'] = estimates_df['actual_effort'] -
estimates_df['estimated_effort']

    estimates_df['percentage_variance'] = (estimates_df['variance'] /
estimates_df['estimated_effort']) * 100

    return estimates_df


def generate_variance_report(variance_df, threshold_percentage=20):

    """Generates a report highlighting significant estimation variances."""

    significant_variance =
variance_df[abs(variance_df['percentage_variance']) >
threshold_percentage].sort_values(by='percentage_variance',
ascending=False)


    report = "\n--- Significant Estimation Variance Report ---\n\n"

    if significant_variance.empty:

        report += "No significant estimation variances found (above
{}%).\n".format(threshold_percentage)

    else:
```

```python
    report += "The following tasks had significant variances (above
{}%):\n\n".format(threshold_percentage)

    for index, row in significant_variance.iterrows():

        report += f"Task: {row['task']}\n"

        report += f"  Estimated Effort: {row['estimated_effort']:.2f}
hours\n"

        report += f"  Actual Effort: {row['actual_effort']:.2f} hours\n"

        report += f"  Variance: {row['variance']:.2f} hours
({row['percentage_variance']:.2f}%)\n\n"


    return report


# Sample data from a completed project

project_data = {'task': ['Task Alpha', 'Task Beta', 'Task Gamma', 'Task
Delta', 'Task Epsilon'],

        'estimated_effort': [40, 60, 80, 30, 50],

        'actual_effort': [45, 50, 100, 25, 40]}

df_project = pd.DataFrame(project_data)
```

```
# Analyze the estimation variance

df_variance = analyze_estimation_variance(df_project.copy())

print("Estimation Variance Analysis:")

print(df_variance)



# Generate a report on significant variances

variance_report = generate_variance_report(df_variance)

print(variance_report)
```

Step-by-Step Explanation:

1. analyze_estimation_variance **Function:** Takes a DataFrame of estimated and actual effort, calculates the variance (actual - estimated), and the percentage variance.
2. generate_variance_report **Function:** Takes the variance DataFrame and a threshold percentage. It identifies tasks with a percentage variance exceeding the threshold and generates a report detailing these significant variances.
3. **Sample Data:** Creates a sample DataFrame with estimated and actual effort for tasks in a completed project.
4. **Analyze Variance:** Calls the analyze_estimation_variance function to calculate the variance.

5. **Generate Report:** Calls the generate_variance_report function to identify and report on significant estimation variances (in this case, above 20%).

Documentation:

This Python example demonstrates how to analyze the variance between estimated and actual effort for project tasks and generate a report highlighting significant discrepancies. This kind of analysis is a crucial part of a post-project review focused on estimation improvement.

My Perspective: Post-project reviews focused on estimation are invaluable opportunities for organizational learning and growth. By taking the time to honestly and systematically analyze our past performance, we can identify patterns, uncover hidden factors, and refine our estimation processes to become more accurate and reliable in the future. Don't let the lessons learned during a project fade away – actively seek them out through structured PPRs and use that hindsight to build a brighter future for your project estimations.

8.7 Identifying and Addressing Estimation Biases Systematically - Recognizing Our Blind Spots

As we strive for greater accuracy in our estimations, it's crucial to acknowledge a fundamental aspect of human cognition: **biases**. These are systematic patterns of deviation from norm or rationality in judgment. In the context of estimation, biases can lead us to consistently under- or overestimate effort, time, or cost, often without us even being consciously aware of these "blind spots." Recognizing and addressing these biases systematically is a key step towards more reliable predictions. Think of it like calibrating a scientific instrument; we need to identify and correct any inherent flaws to ensure accurate readings.

Imagine a team that has a history of consistently underestimating the effort required for complex integration tasks. This might be due to an **optimism bias**, where they tend to focus on the best-case scenario and downplay potential challenges. Without consciously recognizing and addressing this bias, they will likely continue to create unrealistic estimates for future integration work.

Common Estimation Biases:

Understanding the common types of estimation biases is the first step in identifying them within ourselves and our teams:

- **Optimism Bias:** The tendency to be overly optimistic about the outcome of planned actions, leading to underestimation of effort and time.
- **Planning Fallacy:** A specific type of optimism bias where we underestimate the time needed to complete a future task, even when we have experience of similar tasks taking longer in the past.
- **Anchoring Bias:** The tendency to rely too heavily on the first piece of information offered (the "anchor") when making decisions,[1] even if that information is irrelevant or unreliable. For example, if an initial high-level estimate is given, subsequent

detailed estimates might be unconsciously adjusted towards that anchor.

- **Confirmation Bias:** The tendency to seek out and interpret information that confirms our pre-existing beliefs or hypotheses, while ignoring or downplaying contradictory evidence. If we initially believe a task is simple, we might focus on the easy aspects and overlook potential complexities.

- **Availability Heuristic:** The tendency to overestimate the likelihood of events that are easily recalled or vivid in our memory. A recent painful experience with a particular technology might lead to overestimating the effort for any task involving that technology.

- **Loss Aversion:** The tendency to feel the pain of a loss more strongly than the pleasure of an equivalent gain. This can sometimes lead to overly conservative estimates to avoid the perceived "loss" of exceeding the estimate.

- **Sunk Cost Fallacy:** The tendency to continue an endeavor once an investment in money, effort, or time has been made, even if abandoning the course of action would be more beneficial. In estimation, this might lead to sticking with an initial flawed estimate rather than revising it upwards.

- **Halo Effect:** A cognitive bias in which our overall impression of a person or thing influences how we feel and think about its specific characteristics. A highly regarded team member's estimates might be given more weight, even if they lack specific experience in the area being estimated.

- **Parkinson's Law:** The observation that "work expands so as to fill the time available for its completion." If a generous deadline is given, the work might take longer than necessary.
- **Student Syndrome:** The tendency to delay starting a task until just before the deadline. This can make estimates based on total available time unrealistic if the work isn't started promptly.

Systematic Strategies for Identifying and Addressing Estimation Biases:

1. **Awareness and Education:** The first step is to educate ourselves and our teams about common estimation biases and their potential impact. Recognizing these biases is crucial for actively trying to mitigate them.

2. **Data Analysis of Past Projects:** Analyzing historical project data, as discussed in previous sections, can reveal patterns of consistent under- or overestimation in specific areas, potentially indicating underlying biases. For example, consistently underestimating testing effort might point to an optimism bias regarding defect discovery.

3. **Multiple Estimation Techniques:** Using a variety of estimation techniques (e.g., Planning Poker, analogy, algorithmic models) can provide different perspectives and help to surface potential biases inherent in a single approach. If different techniques yield significantly different results, it warrants further investigation.

4. **Independent Reviews:** Having individuals or teams not directly involved in the initial estimation review the estimates can help identify potential biases that the original estimators might have overlooked. Fresh perspectives can challenge assumptions and highlight inconsistencies.

5. **Devil's Advocate:** Assigning someone the role of "devil's advocate" during estimation discussions can encourage critical thinking and the exploration of potential downsides or complexities that might have been underestimated due to optimism bias.

6. **Calibration Sessions:** Regularly comparing individual estimators' predictions with actual outcomes and discussing the reasons for any discrepancies can help calibrate their judgment and reduce systematic biases over time.

7. **Anonymous Estimation:** In some situations, allowing team members to provide estimates anonymously can reduce the influence of anchoring bias or the halo effect, leading to more independent and potentially more accurate estimates.

8. **Focus on Facts and Data:** Encourage estimators to base their predictions on historical data, objective metrics, and documented assumptions rather than relying solely on intuition or gut feelings, which are more susceptible to bias.

9. **Decomposition and Granularity:** Breaking down large tasks into smaller, more manageable components can make estimation less susceptible to optimism bias and the planning fallacy, as it forces estimators to consider the individual steps involved.

10. **Post-Project Reviews with Bias Focus:** During post-project reviews, specifically discuss potential biases that might have influenced the original estimates. Encourage the team to reflect on their thought processes and identify any patterns of biased thinking.

Code Example (Illustrative - Tracking Individual Estimation Accuracy Over Time):

Python

```python
import pandas as pd

import matplotlib.pyplot as plt



def track_estimator_accuracy(estimation_data):

    """Tracks the estimation accuracy of individual estimators over time."""

    estimators = estimation_data['estimator'].unique()

    accuracy_data = {}
```

```python
    for estimator in estimators:

        estimator_df = estimation_data[estimation_data['estimator'] ==
estimator].copy()

        estimator_df['variance'] = estimator_df['actual_effort'] -
estimator_df['estimated_effort']

        accuracy_data[estimator] = estimator_df['variance'].mean()


    accuracy_df = pd.DataFrame.from_dict(accuracy_data, orient='index',
columns=['average_variance'])

    return accuracy_df.sort_values(by='average_variance',
ascending=False)


def visualize_estimator_accuracy(accuracy_df):
    """Visualizes the average estimation variance per estimator."""
    plt.figure(figsize=(10, 6))
    colors = ['red' if v > 0 else 'green' for v in
accuracy_df['average_variance']]
    plt.bar(accuracy_df.index, accuracy_df['average_variance'],
color=colors)
    plt.xlabel('Estimator')
```

```python
plt.ylabel('Average Variance (Actual - Estimated Effort)')

plt.title('Average Estimation Accuracy per Estimator')

plt.axhline(0, color='black', linewidth=0.8)

plt.grid(axis='y', linestyle='--')

plt.tight_layout()

plt.show()


# Sample estimation tracking data

estimation_history = pd.DataFrame({

    'project': ['A', 'A', 'B', 'B', 'C', 'C'],

    'task': ['Task 1', 'Task 2', 'Task 1', 'Task 2', 'Task 1', 'Task 2'],

    'estimator': ['Alice', 'Bob', 'Alice', 'Bob', 'Alice', 'Bob'],

    'estimated_effort': [20, 30, 40, 25, 35, 45],

    'actual_effort': [25, 28, 45, 30, 30, 50]

})


# Track estimator accuracy
```

```python
estimator_accuracy = track_estimator_accuracy(estimation_history)

print("Average Estimation Variance per Estimator:")

print(estimator_accuracy)


# Visualize estimator accuracy

visualize_estimator_accuracy(estimator_accuracy)
```

Step-by-Step Explanation:

1. **track_estimator_accuracy Function:** Takes a DataFrame of estimation history, groups it by estimator, calculates the average variance (actual - estimated effort) for each estimator, and returns a sorted DataFrame.

2. **visualize_estimator_accuracy Function:** Takes the estimator accuracy DataFrame and creates a bar chart visualizing the average variance for each estimator, using different colors to indicate over- or underestimation.

3. **Sample Data:** Creates a sample DataFrame tracking the estimated and actual effort for tasks by different estimators across multiple projects.

4. **Track Accuracy:** Calls the track_estimator_accuracy function to calculate the average variance for Alice and Bob.

5. **Visualize Accuracy:** Calls the visualize_estimator_accuracy function to generate a bar chart showing the average estimation bias of each estimator.

Documentation:

This Python example demonstrates a way to track the average estimation variance of individual estimators over time. Consistently positive or negative average variances for a particular estimator might indicate a systematic bias that needs to be addressed through training or process adjustments.

My Perspective: Recognizing and addressing estimation biases is an ongoing journey of self-awareness and continuous improvement. By understanding the common pitfalls of human judgment and implementing systematic strategies to identify and mitigate these biases, we can move towards more objective and accurate estimations. It requires a willingness to confront our "blind spots" and a commitment to fostering a culture of critical thinking and data-driven decision-making within our teams. Just like a skilled craftsman constantly refines their tools, we must continuously refine our estimation processes to minimize the impact of human bias.

8.8 Adapting Techniques Based on Feedback and Experience - Continuous Improvement

We've journeyed through a wide range of estimation techniques, risk management strategies, and communication approaches. However, the landscape of software development is constantly evolving. New technologies emerge, team dynamics shift, and project complexities vary. Therefore, our approach to estimation cannot be static. **Adapting our techniques based on feedback and experience** is paramount for continuous improvement and ensuring our estimations remain relevant and accurate over time. Think of it as a gardener who constantly observes their plants, learns what works best in their specific environment, and adjusts their methods accordingly.

Imagine a team that initially relied heavily on expert judgment for estimations. Over several projects, they consistently found that estimates for tasks involving a particular new technology were significantly off. Through post-project reviews and team feedback, they realized their experts lacked deep experience in that specific area. As a result, they adapted their approach by incorporating more detailed decomposition and analogy to similar (though perhaps older technology) tasks where they had more historical data.

The Importance of Continuous Improvement in Estimation:

- **Increased Accuracy Over Time:** By learning from past successes and failures, we can refine our estimation techniques and reduce systematic biases, leading to more accurate predictions.
- **Better Alignment with Project Context:** Adapting our approach allows us to tailor our estimation methods to the specific characteristics of each project, considering factors like size, complexity, technology, and team experience.
- **Improved Stakeholder Trust:** Consistently striving for better estimation accuracy and demonstrating a willingness to learn and adapt builds greater trust with stakeholders.

- **Enhanced Team Skills:** The process of reviewing feedback and experimenting with different techniques fosters a culture of learning and improves the estimation skills of the entire team.
- **Increased Efficiency:** More accurate estimates can lead to better resource allocation, reduced rework due to unrealistic timelines, and overall improved project efficiency.

A Framework for Continuous Improvement in Estimation:

1. **Gather Feedback Systematically:** Establish channels for collecting feedback on the estimation process and accuracy. This can include:

   - **Post-Project Reviews (PPRs):** As discussed previously, PPRs are a prime opportunity to gather detailed feedback on estimation performance.
   - **Sprint Retrospectives:** For Agile projects, sprint retrospectives can include discussions about the accuracy of story point estimations and any factors that influenced them.
   - **Informal Feedback:** Encourage team members to share their observations and suggestions for improvement on an ongoing basis.
   - **Stakeholder Feedback:** Seek input from clients and other stakeholders on the perceived accuracy and reliability of the estimates they received.

2. **Analyze Feedback and Identify Trends:** Once feedback is gathered, analyze it to identify recurring themes, patterns of

inaccuracy, and areas where our current techniques might be falling short. Look for specific types of tasks or project characteristics where estimations are consistently off.

3. **Experiment with Different Techniques:** Based on the feedback and analysis, be willing to experiment with alternative estimation techniques or modifications to your existing approach. For example, if expert judgment has been unreliable for highly technical tasks, try incorporating more bottom-up estimation or analogy.

4. **Track the Impact of Changes:** When you implement changes to your estimation process, track their impact on accuracy in subsequent projects. Measure whether the new techniques or adjustments are leading to more reliable predictions.

5. **Document and Share Best Practices:** As you identify techniques and approaches that consistently yield better results in your specific context, document these as best practices and share them across the team or organization.

6. **Regularly Review and Update Guidelines:** Your estimation guidelines and processes should be living documents that are reviewed and updated periodically based on the ongoing feedback and experience gained.

7. **Provide Training and Support:** Ensure that team members have the necessary training and support to effectively use the adapted estimation techniques.

Code Example (Illustrative - Tracking and Analyzing Estimation Accuracy by Technique):

Python

```python
import pandas as pd

import matplotlib.pyplot as plt


def track_accuracy_by_technique(estimation_data):

    """Tracks the average estimation variance for different estimation techniques."""

    accuracy_data = {}

    for technique in estimation_data['estimation_technique'].unique():

        technique_df =
estimation_data[estimation_data['estimation_technique'] ==
technique].copy()

        technique_df['variance'] = technique_df['actual_effort'] -
technique_df['estimated_effort']

        accuracy_data[technique] = technique_df['variance'].mean()
```

```python
    accuracy_df = pd.DataFrame.from_dict(accuracy_data, orient='index',
columns=['average_variance'])

    return accuracy_df.sort_values(by='average_variance',
ascending=False)


def visualize_accuracy_by_technique(accuracy_df):

    """Visualizes the average estimation variance for different
techniques."""

    plt.figure(figsize=(10, 6))

    colors = ['red' if v > 0 else 'green' for v in
accuracy_df['average_variance']]

    plt.bar(accuracy_df.index, accuracy_df['average_variance'],
color=colors)

    plt.xlabel('Estimation Technique')

    plt.ylabel('Average Variance (Actual - Estimated Effort)')

    plt.title('Average Estimation Accuracy by Technique')

    plt.axhline(0, color='black', linewidth=0.8)

    plt.grid(axis='y', linestyle='--')
```

```python
    plt.tight_layout()

    plt.show()


# Sample estimation data with the technique used

estimation_history_tech = pd.DataFrame({

    'project': ['A', 'A', 'B', 'B', 'C', 'C'],

    'task': ['Task 1', 'Task 2', 'Task 1', 'Task 2', 'Task 1', 'Task 2'],

    'estimation_technique': ['Expert Judgment', 'Planning Poker', 'Analogy',
'Expert Judgment', 'Planning Poker', 'Analogy'],

    'estimated_effort': [20, 30, 40, 25, 35, 45],

    'actual_effort': [25, 28, 45, 30, 30, 50]

})


# Track accuracy by technique

accuracy_by_technique =
track_accuracy_by_technique(estimation_history_tech)

print("Average Estimation Variance by Technique:")

print(accuracy_by_technique)
```

```
# Visualize accuracy by technique

visualize_accuracy_by_technique(accuracy_by_technique)
```

Step-by-Step Explanation:

1. **track_accuracy_by_technique Function:** Takes a DataFrame of estimation history that includes the estimation technique used, groups the data by technique, calculates the average variance (actual - estimated effort) for each technique, and returns a sorted DataFrame.

2. **visualize_accuracy_by_technique Function:** Takes the accuracy-by-technique DataFrame and creates a bar chart visualizing the average variance for each technique.

3. **Sample Data:** Creates a sample DataFrame including the estimation technique used for each task.

4. **Track Accuracy:** Calls the track_accuracy_by_technique function to calculate the average variance for Expert Judgment, Planning Poker, and Analogy.

5. **Visualize Accuracy:** Calls the visualize_accuracy_by_technique function to generate a bar chart showing the average estimation bias for each technique.

Documentation:

This Python example demonstrates how to track the average estimation variance for different estimation techniques used on past projects. This analysis can help identify which techniques tend to be more accurate in your specific context, informing decisions about which techniques to favor or adapt in the future.

My Perspective: Continuous improvement is not a destination but an ongoing journey. In the realm of software estimation, this means actively seeking feedback, honestly analyzing our performance, being willing to experiment with new approaches, and codifying what we learn. By embracing this cycle of adaptation, we can move beyond simply making predictions to becoming more skilled and reliable estimators, ultimately contributing to more successful project outcomes. Just as a river carves its path by constantly adapting to the terrain, our estimation practices should evolve based on the ever-changing landscape of software development.

Chapter 9: Tools and Technologies for Estimation - Your Digital Allies

By this point, you've armed yourself with a solid understanding of various estimation techniques and the crucial skills of communication and refinement. Now, let's explore the digital landscape – the tools and technologies that can help streamline your estimation process, enhance collaboration, and provide valuable insights.

Think of these tools as your trusted allies in the quest for more accurate project planning. They can help you organize your estimates, facilitate team discussions, analyze historical data, and present your findings in a compelling way.

9.1 Overview of Different Categories of Estimation Tools - A Digital Toolkit

Throughout our exploration of software estimation, we've discussed various techniques and strategies. To effectively implement these in practice, a **digital toolkit** of estimation tools can be invaluable. These tools range from simple spreadsheets to sophisticated software packages, each offering different features and catering to various needs. Understanding the different categories of these tools will help you choose the right ones for your specific context. Think of it as a carpenter's workshop – they have a variety of tools, each designed for a specific purpose, and they select the appropriate tool for the job at hand.

Imagine trying to manage a complex project timeline with just pen and paper. It would quickly become cumbersome and prone to errors. Project management software with Gantt chart capabilities provides a much more efficient and visual way to plan and track the schedule. Similarly, dedicated estimation tools can streamline the process of applying various estimation techniques and analyzing historical data.

Why Use Estimation Tools?

- **Efficiency and Automation:** Tools can automate calculations, track data, and generate reports, saving time and effort compared to manual methods.

- **Consistency and Standardization:** Using tools can help standardize the estimation process across projects and teams, leading to more consistent results.

- **Data Management and Analysis:** Many tools provide features for storing historical project data, analyzing trends, and calibrating estimation models.

- **Collaboration and Communication:** Some tools facilitate collaboration among team members during the estimation process and provide features for sharing estimates with stakeholders.

- **Application of Complex Techniques:** Tools can make it easier to apply more complex estimation techniques like algorithmic models (e.g., COCOMO) or statistical methods (e.g., PERT analysis).

- **Visualization:** Many tools offer built-in visualization capabilities (e.g., burndown charts, risk matrices) to help communicate estimates and related information effectively.

Different Categories of Estimation Tools:

1. **Spreadsheet Software (e.g., Microsoft Excel, Google Sheets):**

   - **Description:** General-purpose tools that can be customized for basic estimation tasks.
   - **Pros:** Widely accessible, familiar interface, highly customizable for simple calculations and data tracking.
   - **Cons:** Can become unwieldy for complex projects or large datasets, limited built-in estimation techniques, manual data entry can be error-prone, limited collaboration features.
   - **Use Cases:** Small projects, basic effort or cost calculations, simple tracking of actuals against estimates.

2. **Project Management Software with Estimation Features (e.g., Jira, Asana, Trello with plugins, Microsoft Project):**

   - **Description:** Primarily designed for project planning and tracking, some offer features for effort estimation (often based on story points or time tracking) and basic reporting.
   - **Pros:** Integrated with task management and workflow, facilitates team collaboration, often includes visualization tools (e.g., Gantt charts, burndown charts).
   - **Cons:** Estimation features might be basic or require plugins, may not support a wide range of estimation techniques, focus is often more on task management than dedicated estimation.

- Use Cases: Agile projects using story points, projects where estimation is closely tied to task breakdown and scheduling.

3. **Dedicated Estimation Software (e.g., CostXpert, SEER-SEM, QSM SLIM):**

   - **Description:** Tools specifically built for software estimation, often supporting a wide range of techniques (algorithmic models, parametric estimation, analogy), historical data management, risk analysis, and reporting.
   - **Pros:** Comprehensive feature sets tailored to estimation, often include built-in models and industry data, robust data analysis and reporting capabilities, can handle complex projects.
   - **Cons:** Can be expensive, may have a steeper learning curve, might require specific expertise to use effectively, might not be as tightly integrated with task management tools.
   - **Use Cases:** Large, complex projects, projects requiring rigorous and defensible estimates, organizations that prioritize estimation accuracy and process maturity.

4. **Agile Planning and Estimation Tools (e.g., Planning Poker apps, Agile boards with estimation features):**

   - **Description:** Tools designed specifically for Agile estimation techniques like Planning Poker and story point sizing.

- **Pros:** Facilitates team collaboration in estimation, supports consensus-based estimation, often integrated with Agile project management tools.
- **Cons:** Primarily focused on story point estimation, might not support effort or cost estimation directly, limited features for historical data analysis or complex modeling.
- **Use Cases:** Agile development teams using story points for backlog estimation.

5. **Custom-Built Tools and Scripts:**

- **Description:** Organizations may develop their own tools or scripts (using languages like Python, as seen in our examples) to automate specific estimation tasks or analyses based on their unique data and processes.
- **Pros:** Highly tailored to specific needs, can leverage existing data and systems, potentially cost-effective in the long run.
- **Cons:** Requires in-house development expertise, can be time-consuming to build and maintain, might lack the features and user interface of commercial tools.
- **Use Cases:** Organizations with specific data analysis or automation requirements, integration with existing internal systems.

Choosing the Right Tools:

The best estimation tools for your needs will depend on several factors, including:

- **Project Size and Complexity:** Larger, more complex projects might benefit from dedicated estimation software.
- **Estimation Techniques Used:** Ensure the tool supports the techniques your team prefers or your organization mandates.
- **Budget:** Dedicated estimation software can be a significant investment.
- **Team Size and Collaboration Needs:** Consider tools that facilitate team involvement in the estimation process.
- **Integration with Existing Systems:** If you already use project management or other tools, consider how well the estimation tool integrates with them.
- **Data Analysis Requirements:** If you need to analyze historical data and calibrate models, look for tools with robust data management and reporting features.
- **Ease of Use and Learning Curve:** Choose tools that your team can learn and use effectively without significant training overhead.

Code Example (Illustrative - Simple Cost Calculation Script using Python):

Python

```python
def calculate_total_cost(effort_hours, hourly_rate, material_cost, contingency_percentage=0.10):

    """Calculates the total project cost with contingency."""

    labor_cost = effort_hours * hourly_rate
```

```python
    base_cost = labor_cost + material_cost

    total_cost = base_cost * (1 + contingency_percentage)

    return total_cost


# Example usage

estimated_effort = 400  # hours

average_hourly_rate = 75  # $/hour

estimated_material_cost = 5000  # $

risk_contingency = 0.15  # 15%


project_total_cost = calculate_total_cost(estimated_effort,
average_hourly_rate, estimated_material_cost, risk_contingency)


print(f"Estimated Effort: {estimated_effort} hours")

print(f"Average Hourly Rate: ${average_hourly_rate:.2f}")

print(f"Estimated Material Cost: ${estimated_material_cost:.2f}")

print(f"Contingency: {risk_contingency*100:.0f}%")

print(f"Total Estimated Project Cost: ${project_total_cost:.2f}")
```

Step-by-Step Explanation:

1. calculate_total_cost **Function:** Takes estimated effort, hourly rate, material cost, and an optional contingency percentage as input.
2. **Calculates Labor Cost:** Multiplies the effort hours by the hourly rate to get the labor cost.
3. **Calculates Base Cost:** Adds the labor cost and material cost to get the base project cost.
4. **Calculates Total Cost with Contingency:** Applies the contingency percentage to the base cost to arrive at the total estimated project cost.
5. **Example Usage:** Sets example values for effort, rate, material cost, and contingency, then calls the function to calculate and print the total estimated cost.

Documentation:

This simple Python script demonstrates a custom-built tool for basic cost calculation. Organizations can develop similar scripts for automating specific estimation calculations relevant to their projects.

My Perspective: The right digital toolkit can significantly enhance the efficiency, accuracy, and consistency of our software estimation processes. By understanding the different categories of tools available and carefully considering our specific needs and context, we can select the tools that best empower our teams to make informed and reliable predictions. Remember that the tool is a means to an end; the underlying principles of sound estimation techniques and clear communication remain paramount, regardless of the digital aid we choose.

9.2 Guidance on Selecting Appropriate Tools - Finding the Right Fit

Having explored the diverse landscape of estimation tools, the next logical step is understanding how to **select the appropriate tools** for your specific needs. Just like choosing the right tool for a carpentry task, picking the right estimation tool can significantly impact the efficiency, accuracy, and overall success of your estimation efforts. There's no one-size-fits-all solution; the "best" tool depends heavily on your unique context, project characteristics, and organizational maturity. Think of it as selecting a vehicle – a bicycle might be perfect for a short commute, but a truck is necessary for hauling heavy loads.

Imagine a small startup with a single Agile team working on a relatively straightforward web application. Investing in expensive, dedicated estimation software might be overkill. A well-configured spreadsheet or the estimation features within their existing project management tool could be sufficient. Conversely, a large enterprise managing multiple complex projects with diverse estimation needs might find dedicated software to be a worthwhile investment.

Key Factors to Consider When Selecting Estimation Tools:

1. **Organizational Maturity in Estimation:**

   ○ **Low Maturity:** Organizations just starting to formalize their estimation process might benefit from simpler, more accessible tools like spreadsheets or basic features within project management software. Focus on ease of use and getting the team comfortable with structured estimation.

   ○ **Medium Maturity:** Organizations with some established processes might look for tools that support a wider range of techniques, basic historical data tracking, and collaboration. Agile planning tools or more robust project management software could be a good fit.

   ○ **High Maturity:** Organizations with a strong commitment to accurate estimation and continuous improvement might invest in dedicated estimation software with advanced features for modeling, risk analysis, and reporting.

2. **Project Size and Complexity:**

   ○ **Small, Simple Projects:** Spreadsheets or basic project management features might suffice for managing simple effort and cost calculations.

- **Large, Complex Projects:** These often require tools that can handle detailed task breakdowns, dependencies, multiple estimation techniques, and robust risk management integration (often found in dedicated estimation software).

3. **Estimation Techniques Employed:**

- **Agile Teams (Story Points):** Agile planning tools or project management software with Planning Poker plugins are well-suited.
- **Parametric or Algorithmic Models (e.g., COCOMO):** Dedicated estimation software often has these models built-in or allows for their configuration. Custom scripts can also be developed.
- **Analogy or Expert Judgment:** While these can be facilitated by any tool, features for storing and comparing historical project data (present in dedicated software or well-structured spreadsheets) are beneficial.
- **Range-Based Estimation (PERT):** Spreadsheets can be customized, but some dedicated tools offer built-in PERT analysis capabilities.

4. **Budget Constraints:**

- **Free or Low-Cost:** Spreadsheets and basic project management features are typically free or included in existing subscriptions. Agile planning poker apps can also be inexpensive.

- Mid-Range: More robust project management software with advanced features or simpler dedicated estimation tools might involve moderate costs.
- High-End: Comprehensive dedicated estimation software can be a significant investment.

5. Integration with Existing Tools and Workflow: Consider how well the estimation tool integrates with your current project management, time tracking, and reporting systems. Seamless integration can save time and reduce data duplication.

6. Collaboration Needs: If your estimation process involves multiple team members or stakeholders, choose tools that facilitate collaboration, such as shared spreadsheets, Agile planning tools, or project management software with commenting and sharing features.

7. Reporting and Analytics Requirements: If you need to generate detailed reports on estimates vs. actuals, track estimation accuracy over time, or analyze trends in your data, look for tools with robust reporting and analytics capabilities (often found in dedicated software).

8. Ease of Use and Training Requirements: Select tools that your team can learn and use effectively without extensive training. A user-friendly interface can significantly improve adoption.

A Decision-Making Framework:

You can approach tool selection by asking the following questions:

1. **What are our primary estimation needs?** (Effort, cost, schedule, story points?)
2. **What estimation techniques do we currently use or plan to use?**
3. **What is our organizational maturity level in estimation?**
4. **What is the typical size and complexity of our projects?**
5. **What is our budget for estimation tools?**
6. **How important is collaboration in our estimation process?**
7. **What level of reporting and analytics do we require?**
8. **How well does the tool integrate with our existing systems?**
9. **How easy is the tool to learn and use for our team?**.

Code Example (Illustrative - Basic Data Structure for Tracking Estimation Tool Evaluation):

Python

```python
def evaluate_tool(tool_name, features, cost, ease_of_use, integration, reporting, fit_score):

    """Represents the evaluation of an estimation tool."""

    return {

        'tool_name': tool_name,

        'features': features,

        'cost': cost,
```

```python
        'ease_of_use': ease_of_use,

        'integration': integration,

        'reporting': reporting,

        'fit_score': fit_score  # Subjective score based on needs

    }


# Example evaluations

tool1 = evaluate_tool(

    "Spreadsheet (Google Sheets)",

    ["Basic calculations, charting", "Free", "High", "Good", "Basic", 3],

    "Free", "High", "Good", "Basic", 3

)


tool2 = evaluate_tool(

    "Jira with Planning Poker Plugin",

    ["Story point estimation, task tracking", "Included in Jira", "Medium",
"Good", "Basic Agile reports", 4],

    "Included in Jira", "Medium", "Good", "Basic Agile reports", 4
```

```python
)


tool3 = evaluate_tool(

    "Dedicated Estimation Software X",

    ["Comprehensive techniques, historical data, risk analysis, reporting",
"$$$", "Low", "Medium", "Advanced", 5],

    "$$$", "Low", "Medium", "Advanced", 5

)


tool_evaluations = [tool1, tool2, tool3]


print("Estimation Tool Evaluations:")

for tool in tool_evaluations:

    print(f"\nTool: {tool['tool_name']}")

    print(f"  Features: {', '.join(tool['features'])}")

    print(f"  Cost: {tool['cost']}")

    print(f"  Ease of Use: {tool['ease_of_use']}")

    print(f"  Integration: {tool['integration']}")
```

```
print(f"  Reporting: {tool['reporting']}")

print(f"  Fit Score (out of 5): {tool['fit_score']}")
```

Step-by-Step Explanation:

1. evaluate_tool **Function:** Creates a dictionary representing the evaluation of an estimation tool based on various criteria.
2. **Example Evaluations:** Creates example evaluations for three different categories of tools, rating them on features, cost, ease of use, integration, reporting, and a subjective "fit score" based on potential needs.
3. tool_evaluations **List:** Stores the evaluation dictionaries.
4. **Prints Evaluations:** Iterates through the list and prints the details of each tool evaluation.

Documentation:

This Python example demonstrates a simple data structure for evaluating different estimation tools based on key criteria. You can expand this structure with more specific features relevant to your organization to help in your tool selection process.

My Perspective: Selecting the right estimation tools is a strategic decision that should align with your organization's maturity, project needs, and budget. Don't be swayed by the latest trends or the most feature-rich software if it doesn't truly address your core requirements. Start with a clear understanding of your challenges and goals, and then explore the available options, perhaps even conducting pilot tests with a few promising candidates. The goal is to find tools that empower your team to estimate effectively and contribute to more successful project outcomes, without adding unnecessary complexity or cost.

9.3 Examples of Popular Tools and Their Key Features - A Glimpse into the Market

Now that we understand the different categories of estimation tools, let's take a closer look at some popular examples within each category and highlight their key features. This will provide a practical understanding of what's available and help you envision how these tools might fit into your workflow. Keep in mind that the software market is dynamic, and new tools and features are constantly emerging.

1. Spreadsheet Software (e.g., Microsoft Excel, Google Sheets):

- **Key Features:**

    - **Formula Creation:** Allows users to define custom formulas for calculations (e.g., effort based on task breakdown, cost based on resource rates).
    - **Data Organization:** Provides a structured way to organize tasks, estimates, actuals, and variances in rows and columns.
    - **Charting and Visualization:** Enables the creation of basic charts (e.g., bar charts comparing estimated vs. actual effort, trend lines for project progress).

- o **Collaboration (Cloud-based versions):** Google Sheets allows for real-time collaboration among team members.
- o **Customizability:** Highly flexible for tailoring to specific project needs and data tracking requirements.
- **Illustrative Implementation (Python - Simulating Excel-like calculations):**

- **Python**

```python
import pandas as pd


# Sample data

data = {'task': ['Planning', 'Design', 'Development', 'Testing', 'Deployment'],

    'estimated_hours': [40, 80, 160, 60, 20],

    'hourly_rate': [75, 85, 90, 80, 100]}

df = pd.DataFrame(data)


# Calculate estimated cost

df['estimated_cost'] = df['estimated_hours'] * df['hourly_rate']
```

```python
# Add actual hours (example)

df['actual_hours'] = [45, 90, 180, 70, 25]


# Calculate actual cost

df['actual_cost'] = df['actual_hours'] * df['hourly_rate']


# Calculate variance in hours and cost

df['hours_variance'] = df['actual_hours'] - df['estimated_hours']

df['cost_variance'] = df['actual_cost'] - df['estimated_cost']


print(df)
```

- **Documentation:** This Python code simulates basic spreadsheet functionality by creating a DataFrame to store task information, calculating estimated and actual costs, and determining the variance. This illustrates how spreadsheets can be used for simple estimation and tracking.

2. Project Management Software with Estimation Features (e.g., Jira, Asana, Trello with plugins, Microsoft Project):[6]

- **Key Features (vary by tool and plugins):**

  - **Task Breakdown and Management:** Allows for breaking down projects into smaller tasks and assigning estimates (often in story points or hours).
  - **Agile Planning Tools (Jira, Trello plugins):** Support for Planning Poker, backlog estimation, and velocity tracking.
  - **Gantt Charts and Timelines (Microsoft Project, some Asana integrations):** Visual representation of project schedules and dependencies.
  - **Resource Management (Microsoft Project, some Jira plugins):** Allocation of resources and tracking of their availability.
  - **Progress Tracking and Reporting:** Burndown charts, velocity charts, and basic reports on estimated vs. actual progress.
  - **Collaboration:** Features for team communication and task assignment.
- **Note:** Directly demonstrating the features of these tools through code is not feasible as they are primarily GUI-based applications. However, their APIs can sometimes be used for data extraction and analysis.

3. Dedicated Estimation Software (e.g., CostXpert, SEER-SEM, QSM SLIM):

- **Key Features (vary by tool):**

- **Comprehensive Estimation Techniques:** Support for algorithmic models (COCOMO, Function Point Analysis), parametric estimation, analogy-based estimation, and more.
- **Historical Data Management:** Robust databases for storing and analyzing past project data to calibrate estimation models.
- **Risk Analysis and Contingency Planning:** Features for identifying, assessing, and incorporating risks into estimates.
- **Resource Modeling:** Detailed modeling of resource costs, availability, and productivity.
- **Scenario Planning:** Ability to create and compare different estimation scenarios based on varying assumptions.
- **Advanced Reporting and Analytics:** Customizable reports, variance analysis, and trend identification.
- **Industry-Specific Data:** Some tools include built-in industry benchmarks and cost data.

- **Note:** These are commercial tools, and direct code interaction is typically not the primary way users interact with them. They often have their own proprietary data formats and APIs for integration.

4. Agile Planning and Estimation Tools (e.g., Planning Poker apps like "PlanIT Poker," features within Agile boards):

- **Key Features:**

  - **Virtual Planning Poker:** Facilitates remote team estimation using digital card decks.
  - **Consensus Building:** Supports rounds of estimation and discussion to reach agreement.
  - **Integration with Agile Boards:** Often integrates directly with Jira, Azure DevOps, and other Agile project management tools.
  - **History Tracking:** Some tools track estimation history for learning and calibration.
  - **Customizable Card Decks:** Allows for different estimation scales (e.g., Fibonacci, T-shirt sizes).
- **Note:** These tools are primarily interactive web or mobile applications, making direct code examples less relevant.

5. Custom-Built Tools and Scripts:

- **Key Features:**

  - **Tailored to Specific Needs:** Addresses unique organizational requirements and data structures.
  - **Integration with Internal Systems:** Can seamlessly integrate with existing databases, APIs, and workflows.
  - **Automation of Repetitive Tasks:** Automates specific calculations, data analysis, and reporting.

- ○ **Cost-Effective (potentially):** Can be more cost-effective in the long run for organizations with specific, recurring needs.

- **Illustrative Implementation (Python - Analyzing estimation accuracy from a CSV file):**
- **Python**

```
import pandas as pd

import matplotlib.pyplot as plt


# Assuming a CSV file named 'estimation_data.csv' with columns:

# 'project', 'task', 'estimated_effort', 'actual_effort'

try:

    df = pd.read_csv('estimation_data.csv')

    df['variance'] = df['actual_effort'] - df['estimated_effort']
```

```python
df['percentage_variance'] = (df['variance'] / df['estimated_effort']) * 100


print("Estimation Accuracy Analysis:")

print(df[['project', 'task', 'estimated_effort', 'actual_effort', 'variance', 'percentage_variance']])


# Visualize percentage variance

plt.figure(figsize=(12, 6))

plt.bar(df['task'], df['percentage_variance'], color=['red' if v > 20 else 'green' if v < -20 else 'blue' for v in df['percentage_variance']])

plt.xlabel('Task')

plt.ylabel('Percentage Variance (%)')

plt.title('Estimation Accuracy per Task')

plt.axhline(20, color='red', linestyle='--')

plt.axhline(-20, color='green', linestyle='--')

plt.grid(axis='y', linestyle='--')

plt.tight_layout()
```

```
plt.show()
```

```
except FileNotFoundError:
```

```
    print("Error: 'estimation_data.csv' not found. Please create this file
with the appropriate data.")
```

```
except Exception as e:
```

```
    print(f"An error occurred: {e}")
```

- **Documentation:** This Python script reads estimation data from a CSV file, calculates the variance and percentage variance, and visualizes the accuracy of estimates. This demonstrates how custom scripts can be used for analyzing estimation performance.

My Perspective: The market offers a wide array of estimation tools, each with its strengths and weaknesses.[12] The key is to identify your specific needs, consider your organizational context, and explore the options that align best with your requirements and budget. Don't feel pressured to adopt the most complex or expensive tool; sometimes, a well-structured spreadsheet or the built-in features of your project management software can be a great starting point. As your estimation maturity grows, you can then explore more specialized tools to further enhance your accuracy and efficiency. The goal is to leverage technology to support sound estimation principles, not to replace them entirely.

www.ingramcontent.com/pod-product-compliance
Lightning Source LLC
LaVergne TN
LVHW080111070326
832902LV00015B/2521